THE FIRST CAMPAIGN

GLOBALIZATION, THE WEB, AND THE
RACE FOR THE WHITE HOUSE

GARRETT M. GRAFF

FARRAR, STRAUS AND GIROUX

NEW YORK

Farrar, Straus and Giroux
19 Union Square West, New York 10003

Copyright © 2007 by Garrett M. Graff
All rights reserved
Distributed in Canada by Douglas & McIntyre Ltd.
Printed in the United States of America
First edition, 2007

Library of Congress Cataloging-in-Publication Data
Graff, Garrett M., 1981–
    The first campaign : globalization, the Web, and the race for the White House /
Garrett M. Graff.
        p.   cm.
    ISBN-13: 978-0-374-15503-2 (hardcover : alk. paper)
    ISBN-10: 0-374-15503-8 (hardcover : alk. paper)
    1. Presidents—United States—Election—2008.   2. Political campaigns—
United States.   3. Internet in political campaigns—United States.   4. Elections—
United States—Computer network resources.   5. Democratic Party (U.S.)
6. United States—Politics and government—2001–   I. Title.

JK5262008 .G73 2007
324.973'0931—dc22

                                                                        2007035966

Designed by Debbie Glasserman

www.fsgbooks.com

1   3   5   7   9   10   8   6   4   2

To Mom and Dad, who against long odds taught me to love words

CONTENTS

THE FIRST CAMPAIGN

INTRODUCTION: A PERIOD OF CONSEQUENCES

The era of procrastination, of half-measures, of soothing and baffling
expedients, of delays, is coming to its close. In its place we are entering a
period of consequences.
—WINSTON CHURCHILL, NOVEMBER 12, 1936

It's nearly impossible to nail down the day a political
campaign begins. Most consultants and pundits will say that it begins
the day after the last election, but sometimes—especially with presidential campaigns—campaigns can have a time line even longer than
that. It is now the conventional wisdom that the 2008 campaign—
which is only now entering its major phase—will be the longest in
modern American history. But when did it actually start? Did it start
in February 2000 when Hillary Clinton announced that she was running for the New York Senate seat being vacated by Daniel P. Moyni-
han? Or did it start a month later, the moment when John McCain,
drubbed by George W. Bush in South Carolina, dropped out of the
race and began to prepare to fight another day? Did the real beginning
come when John Edwards took a trip to New Hampshire after the
2004 election, or when Evan Bayh hired a staffer to work in Iowa, or

when Barack Obama plopped down on Oprah Winfrey's couch and said that he was open to running in 2008?

Historians someday will determine the starting point of the 2008 campaign based largely on who wins and winds up president. For the moment, though, November 30, 2006, is as good a starting point as any—for that day offered telling evidence of what had changed in American politics and what had not. On that day, some twenty-three months before Election Day, with the weather overcast with temperatures in the twenties in Iowa and overcast with temperatures in the sixties in Washington, MSNBC threw a party at the Smithsonian Castle in the capital to launch its "Decision 2008" coverage; the political insider newsletter the *Hotline* and the University of Virginia convened a panel of potential campaign managers representing potential 2008 candidates at D.C.'s Ronald Reagan Building; and, in Mount Pleasant, Iowa, Governor Tom Vilsack announced he'd seek the presidency, becoming the first official candidate. So came together the three legs of a modern campaign: the press at the Smithsonian, the pundits at *Hotline*'s conference, and, almost an afterthought these days, the candidates themselves, represented by Vilsack in Iowa.

During an interview at stately Terrace Hill, the Iowa governor's mansion, just west of downtown Des Moines, Vilsack had told a *Washington Post* reporter that as an underdog candidate he couldn't afford to wait. "I don't have the luxury that some folks have," he said. "If I'm going to do this, I'm going to have to do it and do it hard from the git-go."[1] So while Hillary Clinton still played coy, and Rudolph Giuliani launched an exploratory committee, Vilsack strode with his family into the college gymnasium in Mount Pleasant, his hometown. Inside was a crowd of some seven hundred supporters and the local high school band, which was playing its version of "The Final Countdown" by Europe, which begins, "We're leaving together but still it's farewell." It was meant to express Vilsack's departure from the Iowa governorship for national politics, but it was, perhaps, not the most optimistic song one could have chosen.

After quieting the crowd chanting "Go, Tom, Go," Vilsack followed a pattern of announcement established by many previous candidates: He declared that he'd seek the presidency in 2008, told his personal story—how he had been born in an orphanage and adopted by a family that struggled with alcoholism and prescription drug addiction—and then described his vision for the future of the country. His campaign theme, he declared, would be "the courage to create change." America, he said, was struggling. It needed bold leadership, a readiness to change, and the courage to attack the massive problems looming ahead. He was running, he explained, "to replace the anxiety of today with the hope of tomorrow and to guarantee every American their birthright: opportunity." The crowd, with many holding signs emblazoned with a Great War–vintage V, applauded.

His speech completed, Vilsack headed to the airport, where he boarded a plane that would take him to five states in five days to repeat the speech for the crowds and the cameras. It was an approach so conventional as to defy his campaign's message of change. Only a few weeks later, admitting that he couldn't make headway in a crowded field of prodigious fund-raisers, he would drop out—months before most of the other candidates had even entered the race.

Back in Washington that same November day, representatives of a dozen different phantom campaigns—from Mitt Romney's not-yet-existing campaign to John McCain's not-yet-existing campaign to John Edwards's more-or-less-existing campaign—talked shop before an audience of several hundred people about the nascent race. The various consultants, pollsters, would-be strategists, and senior advisers were just the tip of the billion-dollar industry that was to be the 2008 presidential campaign. Add to the dozen different campaigns represented onstage those not-yet-existing campaigns that weren't present, and there were a good score of candidates out there, circling, waiting, testing. Fred Thompson's name was barely on the radar at that point, Michael Bloomberg's interest in the presidency was just a rumor, and Barack Obama's race-changing decision to enter was still two months down the road.

The energy onstage was infectious nonetheless. As keynote speaker James Carville, aka the "Ragin' Cajun," strode across the stage, warming up the crowd for the debates and discussions to come, he explained that the 2008 race promised to be one of the most exciting—perhaps the most exciting—presidential campaigns in nearly a century. What a campaign it would be!

Carville was right: The campaign would be like none in recent memory, for both parties' nominations were wide-open. Soon there were five larger-than-life icons of American politics circling the race, including John McCain and four known by first name only: Hillary, Al, Barack, and Rudy. For only the second time since 1920, when Republican Warren Harding battled Democrat James Cox, there was no president or vice president running for reelection (and the other time, in 1952, there was Dwight Eisenhower, a five-star general who had just won World War II). For the first time since 1940, there was no obvious Republican front-runner, like Reagan in 1980, Bob Dole in 1996, and George W. Bush in 2000. After a number of dreary campaigns run by political lifers—Walter Mondale's in 1984, Michael Dukakis's in 1988, George Bush's in 1992, Bob Dole's in 1996—there was suddenly an outsize collection of talent and worldly achievement in the presidential arena; even the "second-tier" candidates like Bill Richardson, Chris Dodd, and Sam Brownback had résumés to envy.

And yet the panel of campaign strategists in Washington was no less conventional than Vilsack's speech in an Iowa gym. For the strategists, to all appearances, were preparing to run campaigns much like the ones they had run in the past, and the large and open field had obscured a much more important fact: that since George W. Bush was elected in 2000, the world had changed. While the 2008 race, strictly speaking, would be the third of the new century, it would be the first campaign of a new age—an age in which the transformations brought by globalization and technology have changed America's place in the world, and so (whether the candidates realize it or not) have changed both the substance and the manner of presidential politics to a degree not seen in more than a century.

When the Supreme Court settled *Bush v. Gore* in 2001, it was a very different world. The terrorist attacks on the World Trade Center and the Pentagon were in the planning stage, Saddam Hussein and the Taliban were in power, blogs and podcasts barely existed, cell phones were a novelty, BlackBerrys were barely a year old, and the iPod was only an idea on a drawing board at Apple. Google was in its infancy, and MySpace, Facebook, and YouTube were years away. Since then—and while Bush and John Kerry traded ripostes about their Vietnam service in 2004—the world had changed; in the formulation of the *New York Times* columnist Thomas L. Friedman, it had gotten flat.

Over the past eight years, Americans could sense the change at every turn—every time they picked up a plastic good with the "Made in China" label and every time they dialed an 800 number for customer service and found themselves talking to someone in Bangalore. Industries and businesses that were once local are now international. Companies are no longer tied to a specific town or block—or even to a specific nation. We see it in Greensburg, Indiana, where just a few years ago foreign-made cars often were in danger of being vandalized in a city made up of GM, Ford, and Chrysler. Now it cheered the announcement that Honda would build a new plant there, and three hundred red-shirt-clad residents formed themselves into a human "H" logo. We see it in the images beamed back by "citizen journalists" in the wake of the 2004 South Asian tsunami long before news crews or rescue workers can reach them. We see it in every Google search by a seventy-year-old and every thirteen-year-old's MySpace page or Facebook profile, and in the thirty-three billion text messages that Chinese citizens sent to celebrate the New Year in 2007, the year of the pig.

What's more, we see it, more and more of us, in the world of electronic communication epitomized by the World Wide Web. In 2000, much of the world still used the slow (and noisy) dial-up connections. By the beginning of 2007, nearly 90 percent of Americans were using a broadband connection to access the internet, up from just over 50 percent a year earlier, and more than one of every three Americans was using the Web wirelessly. According to research by the Pew Internet and American Life Project, by mid-2007, only about 15 percent of Americans remained solidly off-line, while 30 percent were at the other extreme, using the Web to its fullest by texting, e-mailing, posting, networking, and tagging. Today there are more new-economy "creative" workers in the country than there are traditional blue-collar workers.[2] A blog like the left-leaning DailyKos.com has more "inbound links," that is, more sites linking to it and talking about it, than the *Chicago Tribune*, and the right-leaning blog Instapundit.com has more inbound links than *Sports Illustrated*.

Alas, we are only just beginning to see the effects of these changes on presidential politics. In important ways, the 2008 election will seem like the previous ones. America's stance toward Iraq, Iran, and North Korea will certainly be issues. Images of terrorism's horrors will fill our video screens. Homeland security will be debated. Hot-button wedge issues like gay marriage, flag burning, and abortion will no doubt rear their ugly heads at one point or another. Every one of these issues, though, pales in importance to the question raised by globalization: What role will America play in a globalized world? In the same way, the question of how the candidates align themselves on the usual issues pales in comparison to the question of what their vision of America's role in a globalized world is and how they will commit the time, resources, and leadership of their campaigns to confronting the challenges of the new, wired global economy.

It happens that the election comes along precisely when the question is getting urgent, when the hour is getting late. The 2004 election focused on events of the past—the intelligence involved in the Iraq invasion and the candidates' conduct during the Vietnam War—to the exclusion of a debate about the events of the future. The threads of politics, technology, and globalization have intertwined to reshape our lives and our future. The challenge for the candidates in 2008 will be to recognize the changes globalization has wrought and relate them to the political realm. They must help the nation tackle the seemingly disparate but actually very interconnected issues of technology, health care, trade, energy, and the environment and unite them into a governing philosophy.

This next election, this next president, and this next decade may be our last chance to make changes and address these looming challenges before they begin to become truly painful. The long-term national and economic security of the United States requires that in 2008 voters, the press, and the candidates themselves look beyond merely the short-term national security threats posed by Iraq and Al Qaeda to examine the full picture of the world today

Tom Vilsack, from his perch in the American heartland, knew just how much the world had changed and how the nation's leadership had ducked the challenge. "Let us stop the endless talk. Let's have a campaign of serious thought about serious problems that our nation faces," he told the crowd on the day of his announcement. "Let us have the courage to create the change that builds a twenty-first-century American economy."

The concerns and questions he raised that day will far outlast his campaign, for they are—or ought to be—the questions concerned citizens of all stripes are asking. When will Washington realize and address the changes that have reshaped the lives of every American since the 2000 election? How much longer can the United States thrive while its leaders fail to confront the challenges of the future? Who will lead the way?

Clearly, we cannot afford for our candidates to run the last campaign all over again. Which candidate will have the confidence—in his or her leadership and in America's leading role in the world—to run the first campaign of the new age?

2008 IS A "first campaign" in another way. The very technology that has transformed the global economy has transformed the campaign process as well, so that the race will be run as much on the World Wide Web as in union halls and town squares and on television.

Of course, there have been presidential campaigns in which candidates broke new ground with technology—such as the campaign of 2000, when John McCain and Bill Bradley found new money flowing to them online. And there have been campaigns in which new technology has broken candidates—such as 1960, when Richard Nixon's candidacy went sharply downhill after a series of televised debates with John Kennedy. But it appears that 2008 will be the first presidential campaign *defined* by technology, the first one in which technology is both the medium and the message. As candidates talk about innovation, the challenge facing America from the rise of India and China, and how technology is intricately linked to crises like arresting soaring health-care costs, they will be trying to raise money online, respond to YouTube attack ads, and send text messages to sites like Twitter.com. Add to these new media the breakthroughs and advances in "microtargeting"—the tools and databases pioneered by the Bush campaign in 2004 that allow a candidate to address individual voters on their most important issues—and we are in the midst of a presidential campaign that's transformed and driven by technology at every level.

In a sense, the reach and specificity of the Web have restored a "personal" or "individual" quality to the presidential campaign that went missing in the age of television. Connecting with individual voters had once been the heart of presidential politics, for the only way to reach voters was to go out and meet them. This is the story related by historian Zachary Karabell in *The Last Campaign*, which follows the 1948 campaign, the last campaign of the pretelevision age. That year, Democratic incumbent Harry Truman's whistle-stop tour traveled more than twenty thousand miles back and forth across the country, making thirty-one thousand stops at campaign events large and small. Meanwhile, Democrat Thomas Dewey and a then-fringe Dixiecrat candidate Strom Thurmond sought to unseat Truman, the plainspoken president who had ushered in the nuclear age, by visiting hundreds of towns and speaking to thousands of people from the back of a train, shaking hands, giving speeches, holding babies—and hearing from ordinary citizens about their hopes and fears. "For the last time in this century, an entire spectrum of ideologies were represented in the presidential election. And not simply represented but debated and discussed in the mainstream media," Karabell wrote decades later. "Year by year, presidential politics becomes more packaged, easier to understand, parceled into digestible bites of data that are prescreened, tested, and handed to us, the voters, with sexy graphics and bold-faced text. How different it all was in 1948, how incomprehensible by today's standards—an election with heated debate and substantive issues, candidates who disagreed passionately about the issues, a citizenry that took interest because elections mattered and were interesting."[3]

Just four years after Truman's narrow 1948 victory, Dwight D. Eisenhower, who had led Allied troops to victory in World War II, ran the first television ads—including an animated short by the Walt Disney Company in which cartoon characters crowed "I like Ike" and a series of "conversations" in which Eisenhower answered canned questions read off cue cards by ordinary people rounded up outside Radio City Music Hall in New York. "It's sad what an old soldier has come to," he said at the time, as his handlers put him through a marathon taping of forty TV spots in a single day. Eisenhower won, defeating Adlai Stevenson, and by 1954 ten thousand Americans a day were buying their first television set. By the time of Eisenhower's reelection campaign in 1956, 75 percent of households had the big glowing box in their living rooms. American politics would never be the same.[4]

In the 1960 campaign, television actually defined the candidates for the public. When John F. Kennedy and Richard M. Nixon faced off in the first-ever televised presidential debates, sixty-five million to seventy million people tuned in. As the story goes, Kennedy's big smile and quick wit played better onscreen than did Nixon's hooded, suspicious bearing; while people who merely listened to the debates on the radio thought the two candidates equally strong, those who viewed them on TV went for Kennedy. Three million people later reported that they had voted for JFK based solely on their impression of the televised debates—a stunning number in an election where his margin was only 112,000 votes nationwide. As Theodore White wrote in his campaign classic *The Making of the President 1960*, "It was the picture image that had done it—and in 1960 television had won the nation away from sound to images, and that was that."[5]

In the four decades that followed, presidential campaigning was done largely on TV: through broadcast debates and prepackaged nominating conventions, sound bites on the evening news, and ever more aggressive campaign advertising. In 2000, some $200 million went to funding television ads for George W. Bush and Al Gore, about 80 percent of the campaigns' total expenditures. By 2004, when Bush faced John Kerry, the number had tripled. At the same time, though, over the past eight years the changes wrought by the Web, the BlackBerry, the camera phone, and the like—changes that give ordinary people access to more information (and more kinds of information) than ever before in history—are being brought into politics.

And as it happens, this new technology is a defining feature in the generation of American citizens just now coming of age, a generation that all the candidates are desperate to reach and persuade, and one that has joined the voting population since the 2000 election. This generation—the largest generation since the baby boomers—is more technologically savvy and more civic-minded than the one before it. This is my own generation—I was born in 1981—and I see evidence of these qualities everywhere.

In 2006, applications for Teach for America—which recruits college graduates to teach in impoverished rural and urban districts—were triple what they were in 2000. That same year the Peace Corps took 7,810 volunteers, its highest number in thirty years. In joining those groups, those people made a commitment to a world wider than their own, and yet it was a world that through technology they've been connected to as no generation before them. Whereas for previous generations foreign pen pals had meant exotic postage stamps and blue "Par Avion" stickers, today foreign views are as accessible as those of a next-door neighbor. As the Israeli-Lebanese conflict heated up in the summer of 2006, I had lunch with a friend from college who was born in Lebanon in the mid-1980s and then immigrated to the United States. She related how she was following the conflict not by reading the foreign dispatches by correspondents in *The New York Times* or *The Washington Post*, but by reading blogs written by ordinary citizens in Beirut, Damascus, and Jerusalem. She felt the information was better and the opinions more "true" than anything she could find in the press.

The people in this tech-savvy new generation—more diverse, more educated, and more interconnected than any before it—yearn for relevant leadership, for political figures who can help bring American society all the way into the twenty-first century. They expect politics to talk to them, because in today's culture everything else does. From iPods to video on demand, technology is tailored to win the attention of individual "consumers." The United States circa 2008 is a country in which people are invited to "vote" for practically everything. In the fifth-season finale of Fox TV's *American Idol* talent show, more people voted for singer Taylor Hicks (the winner) than have ever voted for a presidential candidate in any U.S. election.

In the era of television, which reaches a great many people with a single message, national politics came to be about appealing to broad interest groups with simple positions on lowest-common-denominator policy issues. Now, as the media and media choices change, so politics must change too. Indeed, it is changing already—whether or not the candidates recognize it. The technological advances and the cultural changes that are globalizing the world are reshaping the ways we interact with our elected officials and candidates—and them with us. The candidates have profiles on Facebook.com, the social-networking website targeted at college students. A Facebook group for Barack Obama swelled to a quarter million people in less than a month, and when Hillary Clinton went onto Yahoo! Answers to solicit ideas about solving health care in the United States, thirty-seven thousand people responded. They answer questions in YouTube debates. The candidates have been producing podcasts of full-length speeches that people can download for free from Apple's iTunes Store. With the exception of some major events covered by C-SPAN, not since 1948 have people been able to hear a speech in full by a presidential candidate in more or less real time—and now they can watch the video online too.

Whether candidates can or will step out of their packaged-for-TV personae and embrace the discussions, debates, and pointed questions that take place online is an open question. Will candidates and parties be able to give up the control they've traditionally had of messaging and media? Even Barack Obama, the youngest of the 2008 presidential candidate crop, came of age in the 1970s and 1980s during the industrial economy and the television age. But with the devolution of power in the digital age back toward individuals, to a certain extent it won't matter whether the candidates "get" the technology—it will happen to them regardless. Trent Lott had little understanding of blogs before they forced him from his job as majority leader of the U.S. Senate, and Virginia senator George Allen had little understanding of the cultural phenomenon called YouTube when it cost him his 2006 reelection bid.

Ready or not, technology is here.

WE ARE LIVING in a time in which not even glaciers are moving at a glacial rate of change: Both the Helheim and Jakobshavn glaciers in Greenland are moving at speeds exceeding eight miles a year, or about an inch a minute—fast enough that you can see them move.

So it is with the issues that concern Americans as the 2008 presidential campaign begins in earnest. The war on terror, the challenges to American economic preeminence, the gap between rich and poor, the high price and low quality of American education, the bewildering variety of health care, the looming energy crisis, and the threats of climate change—all of these issues are changing faster than politics as usual can accommodate, for it is the way of Washington to assume that real social change takes place slowly, an assumption that becomes a self-fulfilling prophecy.

Marjorie Williams, the *Vanity Fair* political correspondent whose life was cut short by cancer in 2005, wrote that the failures that really matter in Washington happen so slowly that no one gets blamed for them. And such is where we find ourselves: with creeping crises in education, health care, energy, immigration, and basic day-to-day economics that aren't the fault of any one person, one party, or even one branch of government. Once identified, though, those crises are all of ours to meet and fix, but the leadership to address these creeping crises over the next decade will be the responsibility, first and foremost, of the next president, whoever that may be.

As is often the case in modern America, today's sense of unease was captured by television on *The West Wing*, that seven-year-long celebration of what politics and national discourse could have been. Left behind in Indiana by the presidential motorcade, Deputy Chief of Staff Josh Lyman and Communications Director Toby Ziegler strike up a conversation with a man at a hotel bar. He waxes about the challenges of modern life and paying for his daughter's college education, and says, "I never imagined at $55,000 a year, I'd have trouble making ends meet. And my wife brings in another 25. My son's in public school. It's no good. I mean there's thirty-seven kids in the class, no art and music, no advanced placement." He turns to Toby. "It should be a little easier. Just a little easier. 'Cause in that difference is . . . everything." The man's soliloquy of unease was palpable and poignant, and what made it so was that two senior members of the White House staff had to get accidentally left behind by the motorcade and isolated by a lack of BlackBerrys and cell phones before they would take a moment to actually listen to an ordinary American. In life today as on television, our leaders get so caught up in the "grid" that they often don't see how real life is changing for the real people they represent.

Despite all the changes, large and small, that have brought about a fundamentally different world of information, knowledge, and economic interdependence, our politicians are talking about the issues in the old language of trade and protectionism, gripes about "Benedict Arnold CEOs," and empty promises for change. The opportunity to hold the world at bay, or even to debate about it at length, has come and gone, but our discourse hasn't changed yet.

TO SEE AND UNDERSTAND this new landscape of the first campaign, in later chapters I consider four issues for the future and five technological battlegrounds that inspire political participation. After a tour of technology and its impact on politics, how it has evolved and at the dawn of this century brought people back into the political process once dominated by expensive television ads, I look at the four most critical areas for policy leaders to address in the twenty-first century: investments in technical infrastructure to speed economic development; education and workforce reforms that inspire innovation; health-care reforms that allow American companies and workers to compete in a world of open markets; and the interrelated trio of energy, the environment, and national security that perhaps more than anything will determine the nation's success in the twenty-first century.

Then to help explain the new playing field for this first technology-driven presidential campaign, I look at the five most powerful tools of the new era in politics: cell phones, YouTube, social-networking sites like MySpace and Facebook, blogs, and online fund-raising. The combination of these five battlegrounds and the empowerment they provide to individuals to hold their leaders accountable means that the 2008 election will be conducted on a playing field where the party establishment will have the least power of any U.S. election in history.

But first, I tell the story of how we got to this point. In doing so, I focus on the Democratic Party, from its decline in the 1970s and 1980s to its rebirth under Clinton to its long-overdue retrofit for the information age since the year 2000, as the changes wrought by technology in the wider world began to make themselves felt in the electoral process.

After nearly two years of reporting across the country and around the world and well over a hundred interviews with academics, business leaders, tech pioneers, and people from the political realm, including the 2008 candidates themselves, I believe that the Democrats are the party most prepared to lead America all the way into the new century. Over the century just past, it was often the Democratic Party that stood for the big ideas and challenged Americans to be great in times of strife—and rallied people around the need for government intervention to solve big problems. Franklin Delano Roosevelt challenged the nation through the lean days of the Great Depression and the dark days of World War II. John Kennedy challenged America to reach for the stars and thus beat the Russians. Lyndon Johnson promised a nation torn by civil rights struggles that it would get better, but that first it might get worse. Democrats comprised the party that won the Second World War, created Social Security, and passed the Civil Rights Act.

Republicans, too, have offered leadership at critical moments—whether building the interstate highway system, establishing the Environmental Protection Agency, or presiding over the breakup of the Soviet empire—and they could lead us also if the right presidential candidate emerged. A thoughtful, moderate Republican could implement the programs necessary and rally business and community leaders to address the issue of American competitiveness. Michael Bloomberg, Rudolph Giuliani, or even Arnold Schwarzenegger could rise to the occasion (although the Governor is prohibited by the Constitution from holding presidential office). Mitt Romney, as a venture capitalist and former governor of tech-heavy Massachusetts, understands in a key way the new playing field the United States faces in 2008. However, so far, the national Republican Party, partly because of its small-government, low-tax ideology and partly because of its single-minded focus on the Iraq war, homeland security, and Islamist terrorism, has abdicated leadership on the core twenty-first-century issues that I look at in this book.

Today, the GOP could follow its legacy of leadership and confront the new world if it chose to, but there are four key reasons—two structural and two philosophical—why it will be difficult for the solutions of the twenty-first century to come from the national Republican Party as it stands now. First, as I explore later, the answer to this problem involves expanding the role of government—not necessarily expanding government per se but at least doing more with the government we have. We have seen historically that certain problems are too large, too complex, or simply too important to be left up to the free market and the public goodwill of corporations. Globalization is one of them. Ironically for everyone involved, opening up the world markets to trade and leveling the playing field for countries around the globe has ended up creating problems that the open market alone can't solve. Second, Republican candidates face a major self-created obstacle to solving these crises: The answers to these problems lie in science, with which the GOP has, to say the least, recently had an uncomfortable relationship. Take nearly any major issue—global warming, energy, stem cells, or even evolution—and the GOP has been on the wrong side of science. Third, if the GOP maintains its current ideological base, moving the nation into an ideas economy will be a death sentence. If the Republican Party doesn't radically alter its approach on key base issues, solving the issue of American competitiveness will be akin to committing political suicide. It is no coincidence that everywhere the new high-tech economy is exploding—Austin, Boston, Raleigh, San Francisco, Seattle, Portland, Atlanta, Denver, and even northern Virginia—is trending heavily Democratic. The fourth challenge for Republicans, of course, is a historical one. Because of their distrust of government, Republicans don't like rallying people around governmental solutions. The heart of the challenge in front of us is that it will be difficult—it will require sacrifice by the American people and it will require asking something of them.

While these four challenges in 2008 for Republicans will make running in the first campaign difficult at best, they also raise the stakes enormously for the Democratic candidates. If the Democratic Party doesn't win and the new Republican president follows his party's recent history by ignoring the looming crises of the twenty-first century, America will push confronting these changes farther off into the future. America will be that much weaker and its future that much more unsure. America's future is far from secure right now, but the fact lost in debate today is that our insecure future stems more from changing economics than from terrorism or the war in Iraq. One thing is clear: We don't have much time.

Today the challenge of American competitiveness in a global economy cuts across all issues—it is a health-care crisis, a revenue crisis, an education crisis, an energy crisis, a transportation crisis, and, not least of all, a national security crisis. Unfortunately, our nation's leaders have so far paid only lip service to the blizzard of reports, warnings, and anxieties bubbling up across the country.

This is the fundamental choice of the 2008 election: Our presidential candidates can run the last campaign all over again, as has been the tendency for countless cycles, and continue to push farther into the future the moment we confront our rising problems. Or they can stand up and say that the world is different today and thus our politics must be different too.

At each critical moment in the nation's past, from the greens of Lexington and Concord to the launching of Sputnik to the rubble of 9/11, American leaders have risen to the occasion. In this critical 2008 election, when we must choose whether America will lead in the twenty-first century as it did in the twentieth, will our leaders and their ideas be up to the challenge?

PART I

THE
LAST
CAMPAIGN

THE RISE OF THE ANXIOUS CLASS

You have to be global in this business to survive.

—JACK WELCH

For every end, there is a beginning. In 1980, the Democratic Party saw the end of fifty years of the proud liberal New Deal–type politics that had defined it since the days of FDR. At the same time, thousands of miles away, a decorated army veteran was laying the groundwork for a movement that would years later reenergize the party and breathe new life into what had become a stale and voiceless opposition.

For liberal firebrand Ted Kennedy, vanquished by Chappaquiddick from his final attempt at the nation's highest office once held by his brother, the end of his presidential ambitions came August 12, 1980, in Madison Square Garden. There he took the stage of the Democratic convention in New York City and delivered one of the most memorable convention speeches in a generation, and in it made a promise to his party and to the nation.

"As Democrats we recognize that each generation of Americans has a rendezvous with a different reality. The answers of one generation become the questions of the next generation." His booming voice, thick with its trademark accent, filled the hall. "We are the party—We are the party of the New Freedom, the New Deal, and the New Frontier. We have always been the party of hope. So this year let us offer new hope, new hope to an America uncertain about the present, but unsurpassed in its potential for the future."

Later, after quoting Tennyson and rising to a crescendo, Kennedy proclaimed, "For me, a few hours ago, this campaign came to an end. For all those whose cares have been our concern, the work goes on, the cause endures, the hope still lives, and the dream shall never die."

Kennedy's speech marked an end to the aspirations of liberal Democrats, who wouldn't see one of their own nominated for president for decades.

However, the same year, 1980, in retrospect marked a beginning too, a beginning whose importance we can only now begin to understand. Far away from the crowds, television lights, and confetti of Madison Square Garden, in a dingy working-class bar in Colorado City, David Hughes was talking politics. What made him different, though, was that for the first time he was doing it online.

Dave Hughes is not exactly the typical computer geek: Now closing in on eighty and bearing wispy facial hair, Hughes almost always wears a Stetson. A Colorado native, he grew up in a rock-ribbed Republican family and, having just missed World War II, he showed up at West Point in 1946. A star student, he graduated June 6, 1950, just twenty days before the North Koreans crossed the border into South Korea. Hughes returned safely from the Korean War with a chest full of medals and stayed in the military. Eventually, in 1965, as Vietnam was heating up, he became part of a team of soldiers studying the future of combat. It was there that he began to put together the pieces of the changing technological landscape. "What I picked up was that miniaturization of technology was coming. We invented the Stinger missile that any mujahideen kid could put on his shoulder and bring down a Russian jet in Afghanistan. We and the Germans invented the shaped charge, which becomes the RPG that any damn fool can fire," he says. As he explains it, the miniaturization of technology was a tool for political radicals—violent or otherwise.

Technology allowed individuals to go behind and around the strict century-old political party structure just as individual radical militants could outwit the mechanized corps of a powerful army. A decade later, as he was leaving the military, Hughes made his home in Colorado City, later purchasing the city's first Kaypro computer and throwing himself into local economic development. Using a then-groundbreaking acoustic modem in 1977, he signed onto the nation's first national commercial online bulletin board service, The Source, to pick the brains of other commercial and economic development people across the country. Three years later, as Kennedy conceded defeat in New York and as Jimmy Carter lost the general election to Ronald Reagan, Hughes set up his own online bulletin board service with a section devoted to local politics. He named it Roger's Bar, after the real-life local Democratic Union bar where regulars debated local, state, and national politics. It is widely credited as the first such online political endeavor on the then very nascent internet.

From the earliest days, the promise was clear: "This is going to diminish the influence of special interest groups. The dominant economic interests have influenced media, but BBSs bypass the press and don't stand to lose advertising dollars. With BBSs, special interest groups cannot control where people get their information," Hughes told a computer publication in 1992.[1]

"Two can argue or fight. It takes three to politics. Each side tries to convince the third," Hughes says. "We got consensus that way, through dialogue—what screwed it up was . . . we aggregated our dialogue to news anchors. They do the dialoguing for us." The internet opened the first chance for people to debate and discuss in the television age. "The heart and soul is people being able to go back and forth, challenging the facts that they throw out—because the public had a hell of a time challenging anything that came out of the television."

Roger's Bar was a big success, or at least as big a success as something could be when it existed on a technology platform—the internet—that only a relative handful of people had ever heard of. Hughes went down to the actual namesake pub and convinced the staff to install a telephone jack in one of their booths so that patrons of the bar could log on to his online bulletin board to talk politics using Hughes's laptop and an acoustic modem—this long before most people had a laptop, let alone even understood what a modem did.

With the internet, people don't need to collect a paycheck from a major media conglomerate in order to share their opinions. They don't need to worry about offending corporate advertisers. And people on the local level who care about a particular issue can connect with others across the country to share thoughts, opinions, and ideas—just as Hughes first did with economic development thirty years ago. During one local argument over a proposed zoning ordinance, Hughes, helped by debate on his bulletin board, managed to get 175 people to show up at the planning board meeting and contest the new rules. The board, surprised by the passion and the turnout, relented. Hughes immediately understood the power the internet could bring to bear on politics, especially given the speed at which dialogue and debate happened online. "Washington is a great soggy log floating down the Potomac with a bunch of ants who think they're steering." Hughes guffaws. "This is a grassroots nation. Anything that's worth a damn in this country starts on the grassroots level. In a future-shock, accelerated-change society, by the time it gets to Washington, it's already obsolete."

WASHINGTON, AT LEAST the Democratic parts of it, certainly seemed obsolete by the 1980s. During the middle of the twentieth century, a period of liberal ascendancy and institution building stretching from 1932 to 1968, Democrats built a strong social network that helped lift the country out of the Great Depression, win World War II, educate a generation with the GI Bill, spread civil rights, and put a man on the moon. Presidents Roosevelt, Truman, Kennedy, and Johnson were strong internationalists, big thinkers, and great institution builders. They opened up global trade, founded institutions like the World Bank and NATO, established the Bretton Woods financial system that stabilized the world economic markets, and rebuilt Europe with the Marshall Plan. At home, they got America working during the Depression, established Social Security and Medicare, offered up a New Deal, a Fair Deal, the New Frontier, and a Great Society. Through this period, only a single GOP candidate won the presidency, and he—General Eisenhower—was considered for the Democratic nomination as well. No small government conservative, Ike built the interstate highway system and founded the Department of Health, Education and Welfare.[2]

The social revolution of the 1960s, with its civil rights successes and LBJ's Great Society, should have been the crowning achievement of liberalism, but instead the party began to see the first cracks that would lead it into a lengthy identity crisis. As a new wing of the GOP, born from the ashes of Barry Goldwater's 1964 presidential campaign, laid the groundwork for future supremacy, the Democrats' ruling coalition, too comfortable with power, began to break down.

Nationally, Democrats began to be seen as too beholden to their constituencies—a term best captured by Theodore Lowi as "interest group liberalism" in his seminal 1969 work, *The End of Liberalism*. By 1972 and George McGovern's loss, though, the party had begun to slip badly. Carter won in 1976 by positioning himself as a Georgia peanut farmer running against the Democratic Party establishment, but four years later the 1980 disaster of a campaign in which Senator Ted Kennedy challenged the weak incumbent president saw Carter lose, as well as the GOP capture the Senate for the first time since 1952. The Democrats, meanwhile, began grasping for a message as the party sank into a decade-long morass of special interests and "liberal fundamentalism." Lacking a unifying message, the Democrats lost any hope of their presidential candidates seizing the nation's highest office.

Meanwhile, Republican leaders had thought long and hard about their party's weaknesses, and beginning in the 1960s the GOP underwent its own silent transformation as power switched hands from a moderate bastion to a conservative, faith-based elite that established a plan for a new era. Ray Bliss took over the RNC after Senator Barry Goldwater's 1964 defeat, and his planning would lead to Richard Nixon's victory in 1968 and, arguably, everything that came after it. He put together a new model, financed through a powerful small-dollar direct mail program, that emphasized technology, donor outreach, and a united conservative message for state organizations. RNC chair Bill Brock picked up the mantle after Watergate and helped assemble a message and return his party quickly to power.

The GOP was swimming with ideas. Bliss led the Republican Co-ordinating Council, which included everyone from former President Eisenhower to freshman congressman George H. W. Bush. Its 1966 book, *Choice for America*, helped define the landscape that the party would run on in the next two decades. Brock created five advisory councils that spanned the policy gamut and would help give Ronald Reagan a blueprint for leadership when he took office in 1981.

Money started to pour in. During Brock's four-year tenure, the party's income jumped from $8.9 million raised from 300,000 donors in 1975 to $77 million from 1.2 million donors in the last year of the Carter administration. By the first few years of the Reagan adminis-tration, the RNC had built a powerhouse machine of 1.8 million donors that fueled an annual budget of $97 million, two and a half times the Democrats' paltry $39 million. When Brock left office in 1980, the RNC's national headquarters had a staff of 350, more than four times what the anemic Democratic Party had.[3]

More impressive, perhaps, than the official party machinery was the shadow organization that the Republicans had assembled to re-cruit, train, and develop conservative leaders, the idea factories that would fuel those leaders' policies, and the network of media outlets and pundits who would promote both the leaders and the ideas.

The first stop for Republican thinkers was the more than a dozen journals published by conservative think tanks and organizations—four put out by the American Enterprise Institute alone—the most fa-mous of which was Irving Kristol's *Public Interest*. Writing in 1986, *The New Republic*'s Robert Kuttner outlined the arc of a young new party leader. "A graduate student could submit a manuscript to Irving Kristol, be certified as the latest neo-conservative find, have the arti-cle distilled on *The Wall Street Journal*'s editorial page, be quoted in the Mobil Corporation's op-ed ads, appear before sympathetic con-gressmen, do a stint in a think-tank, and later go to work for the Rea-gan administration."[4]

It has been well documented now that the conservatives' impres-sive network of think tanks, training seminars, research organizations, and media outlets—one completely without peer on the left—began in the 1970s when six wealthy businessmen and families—Harry Bradley in Milwaukee, Joseph Coors in Denver, David and Charles Koch in Wichita, John Olin in New York, the Richardsons in North Carolina, and, perhaps most notorious of all, Richard Mellon Scaife in Pittsburgh—began to invest what ended up being hundreds of millions dollars, perhaps well over a billion, in such efforts. David Brock, himself once a part of the conservative machine before he "reformed," labeled it the "Right Wing Noise Machine," and there's no doubting that through vehicles like the American Enterprise Institute, Rush Limbaugh, and Judicial Watch, the right has managed to build an infrastructure that can dominate, direct, and shape the public debate.

To get an idea of just how rigorous a network the conservative wing of the Republican Party created while the Democrats were asleep at the wheel, look at what Scaife alone was able to build during the 1970s: He gave $3 million to the Law & Economics Center at Emory, $4 million to help found and launch the Heritage Foundation, $2 million to boost conservative media outlets like the *American Spectator* ($900,000) and "watchdog" group Accuracy in Media ($150,000). He even paid $500,000 to underwrite a television series on Pennsylvania's WQLN starring Milton Friedman.[5] Scaife's money was a drop in the bucket nationally—at the time businesses spent nearly half a billion annually on "advocacy advertising"—but it represented critical investments in a generation of conservative leaders and thinkers that would shape policy well into the twenty-first century.

The GOP's groups all sounded innocuous and civic-minded: Heritage Foundation, Cato Institute, Pacific Legal Foundation, Institute for Justice, Washington Legal Foundation, National Legal and Policy Center, Landmark Foundation, Rutherford Institute, Free Congress Foundation, and Moral Majority, among others.

The Heritage Foundation's 1,077-page book *Mandate for Leadership: Policy Management in a Conservative Administration* became the bible of the newly elected Reagan administration in 1981 when the president presented each cabinet member with a copy of the book at their first meeting. Covering every topic from taxes to crime to national defense, the book had a huge influence in the 1980s. By the end of the Reagan years, nearly two-thirds of its two thousand recommendations had been implemented.

As Jon F. Hale wrote, coming out of the 1980s "the Republicans were perceived as the party of ideas, the party with a sense of mission, an agenda, and policy alternatives ready to implement under the Reagan administration."[6]

It wasn't that people within the Democratic Party didn't notice what was going on in the GOP—it was that no one acted. Writing after the disaster of the 1984 elections in their influential work *Right Turn: The Decline of the Democrats and the Future of American Politics*, political scientists Joel Rogers and Thomas Ferguson outlined the millions the right was pouring into organizing and concluded, "To reverse the right turn of America and the Democrats, some set of investors would essentially have to replicate the work of the center, and particularly the right, over the last fifteen years or so, pouring millions of dollars and person-hours into political organizing at all levels."[7] From the time Rogers and Ferguson wrote their call to arms, it took nearly twenty years before the Democrats prepared an answer.

As the GOP united, the Democrats splintered. Cracks appeared as the national party, long comfortable in its ascendancy, began to break down from a national coalition into individual interest groups—women, blacks, gays and lesbians, and labor unions chief among them. Over the coming years, the debate in the party would become more focused on which issues, individual groups, and constituencies would get the most attention.

After the disaster of 1980, new party leader Charles Manatt arrived with a mission to regain the party's footing. Manatt was a powerful California attorney who had chaired the state party and watched the national rise of Governor Ronald Reagan. In the wake of the Democrats' disastrous campaign in 1980, the party turned to Manatt to lead it in the era of now President Ronald Reagan. Manatt, a lifelong Democratic operative, was horrified by what he found when he arrived in Washington.

The Democratic Party didn't even have its own permanent headquarters. The party was leasing cramped office space from the airline pilots' union on Massachusetts Avenue a few blocks from Dupont Circle. Manatt explains that party regulars told him that the only party headquarters required was the White House. "We were told not to have a space without the White House, but arriving in 1981, I wasn't sure when we'd win the presidency again," Manatt says. "The job that came upon our merry band of Democrats that was fighting our way back was modernization, computerization, media, etc." He set about securing a new permanent office for the party and looked to the model set by his counterpart, RNC chair Bill Brock, who was stepping down after an incredibly successful four-year run in the shadow of President Jimmy Carter.

More and more, Republicans were the only ones showing up at a public debate with a message and a plan. They had their bumper sticker slogan: *Lower taxes. Strong defense. Less government.* Six words in total. Democrats had nothing of the sort. Most party leaders would be hard-pressed to explain their party's ideology in ten times that.

By 1984, the party was well off the tracks. Its platform that year was forty-five thousand words long—50 percent longer than the 1980 platform and a testament to just how badly the party lacked direction. (The GOP's platform, by comparison, was just twenty-seven thousand words.) Splintering the party's backing and underscoring voters' worst fears that the party was nothing more than a unique collection of narrow special interests, the DNC officially recognized no fewer than seven different caucuses: Asians, blacks, business leaders, gays, Hispanics, liberals, and women.[8] "Groups such as these—and others with narrower agendas—fight word-by-word battles over platform items small enough to be labeled splinters instead of planks," Timothy Clark wrote in the nonpartisan *National Journal*.[9]

Mondale's 1984 campaign by almost any objective measure was another disaster for the Democratic Party. A prenomination poll found that voters believed Mondale was more beholden than Ronald Reagan to special interests.[10] In the end, he was defeated in one of the largest landslides in U.S. history—famously winning only the District of Columbia and his home state of Minnesota, and that by only some four thousand votes. Reagan won more than 60 percent of the vote in every southern and border state except Tennessee. Democratic candidates across the country found themselves tagged as "Mondale liberals," and moderate Democratic figures like James Hunt and incumbent Senator Walter "Dee" Huddleston were crushed at the ballot box. Afterward, Senator Lawton Chiles told Fred Barnes in *The New Republic*, "Most of us had been running away from the Democratic Party for years. But we were beginning to see you couldn't enjoy the luxury of that anymore."[11]

Each election cycle proved a challenge for the Democrats to raise money and not sink further into debt. George McGovern—the first Democratic presidential candidate not chosen by the party elites—had once upon a time built a grassroots fund-raising apparatus, but it was quickly abandoned by the party establishment. Alabaman direct mail expert Morris Dees had engineered for the South Dakota senator a massive direct mail base of small donors. Nearly six hundred thousand people contributed, and ten thousand eventually became "sustainers," donating $10 a month for the duration of the campaign. The effort netted a surprisingly large $4.85 million with just $650,000 in mailing expenses.[12] Whereas Goldwater's massive conservative direct mail list had become the centerpiece of the Republicans' fund-raising efforts, the new chair of the DNC after McGovern's campaign, a conservative former FBI agent named Robert Strauss, refused to adopt the McGovern list because of its left-wing activist bent. With that single decision, the Democratic Party began a generational shift further and further away from the Democrats' traditional blue-collar base to a party dominated by a handful of wealthy elite donors based in New York and Hollywood.

Senator Paul Tsongas laid out the landscape similarly during a speech in the 1980s to the liberal Americans for Democracy Action:

> If we are to mobilize a new generation to move forward with liberal leadership, we must understand that the average young American is just that—part of a new generation. A generation that never experienced the abuses and injustices that molded us. A generation that takes for granted the social equities that we had to fight for. In short, they have never known that anger that fed the liberal cause. For example, they have not grown up reading about hungry poor people; they have grown up reading about abuses in the food stamp program. They have not grown up reading about the U.S. military adventurism in Vietnam; they have grown up reading about Soviet

military adventurism in Afghanistan. They have not grown up reading about the abuse of factory workers by management; they have grown up reading about union rules that place security over productivity. They have not grown up reading about the ever expanding American economic pie; they have grown up reading about America's balance of payments problem and the demise of the auto industry's capacity to compete internationally. This is a different generation. And if we do not speak to this generation in its terms, liberalism will decline. And if we do not meet these needs, liberalism should decline.[13]

It was time to remake and overhaul the party if it wanted to survive.

The effort that would return the Democrats to power was launched by "neoliberals" on February 28, 1985, when a group of party rebels announced the mission of the Democratic Leadership Council during a press conference on Capitol Hill. "We are going to try to move the party—both in substance and perception—back into the mainstream of American political life," neoliberal leader Sam Nunn said at that first press conference. The DLC argued that the party's traditional politics of innovation had been replaced by programmatic rigidity, the traditional politics of inclusion superseded by ideological litmus tests. A new centrist wing was needed to bridge the divide with the regular voter.[14] The arrival of the neoliberals on the scene—in effect, if not in ideology—would prove not unlike the Jacobin period of the French Revolution. They did mark a transformative political and power upheaval within the party but were merely the midpoint in a process that would reshape and refocus the party. In a way, the rise of the neoliberals marked less the beginning of the end and more the end of the beginning. The wheels of unrest continued to spin and seeds of the greater rebellion continued to germinate, even as the party establishment handed over its reins to another faction.

The baby boomers, that new generation of post–World War II voters, were having families, and their experience with government was not as positive as that of their Depression-era parents, who had been helped into the middle class by the Democratic Party. Twenty years ago, Robert Kuttner wrote, "Today a 35-year-old voter of moderate means contemplating the effect of government on his or her own life doesn't see a GI Bill or an FHA loan or government-guaranteed health insurance, or policies that help him cope with the realities of juggling family and work in the imperfectly liberated 1980s. His experience with public schools, if he thinks of it as a government service, is remote, as is his anticipation of receiving Medicare or Social Security. His daily experience with the motor vehicle bureau is frustrating. The main evidence he sees of affirmative government is his tax bill."[15]

Political scientist Ralph Whitehead identified the middle-class voters of the 1980s as "new collar," explaining, "Voters tend to see the Republican Party as a force with a hard heart and a tough mind. They see the Democratic Party as a force with a soft heart and a tender mind. What voters would like, ideally, is a party with a soft heart and a tough mind. Unable to find one, they settled uneasily for the party with the tough heart and tough mind, in large part because they saw Reagan as an individual who could soften some of the hardness in that heart."[16]

Just like the voting population, a new crowd of politicians was coming of age in the party. These neoliberals—like Gary Hart, Bill Bradley, Joe Biden, Paul Tsongas, Chris Dodd, Dick Gephardt, Leon Panetta, Tim Wirth, Jerry Brown, and Bruce Babbitt—were born in the 1930s and 1940s and became the first national leaders in fifty years to lack a memory of the Great Depression and to have, if anything, only a faint hint of the glory days of FDR. The New Deal, to them, existed only in the history books. Instead their early memories were of JFK and his New Frontier; capitalists all, they were firmly for a market economy.

The Democratic Party's failings were quite clear to Gary Hart when he began to consider a presidential race for 1988: It lacked ideas. So Hart did something different—instead of founding a political action committee, he set up an institute. The Center for a New Democracy was established in early 1985 with a budget of $500,000 and an initial staff of seven. Just how basic a departure this was from the conventional wisdom was outlined in a cartoon by *Boston Globe* political cartoonist Dan Wasserman. He showed Hart talking with a voter and saying, "America needs new ideas." The voter says, "Could you name one?" Hart: "I just did." While meaning to mock Hart's approach, it was instead a damning indictment of a failed party apparatus.[17] A

Hart 1988 campaign poster promised, "The easy path is the beaten path. But the beaten path seldom leads to the future."

Hart never got the chance to put his ideas on a national stage as he was forced from the race by his dalliance with Donna Rice, and the party settled on a lackluster Massachusetts governor—a thoughtful politician but a disaster for the party. "Michael Dukakis embodied the National Public Radio wing of his party. He was stratospherically high-minded, a man of preternatural calm and utter rationality, a man who seemed to believe that emotions were a form of human frailty badly in need of legislative reform," Joe Klein recalls.[18]

After the election, a now landmark DLC publication titled *The Politics of Evasion* stated, "The Democratic Party's 1988 presidential defeat demonstrated that the party's problems would not disappear, as many had hoped, once Ronald Reagan left the White House . . . Democrats must now come face to face with reality: too many Americans have come to see the party as inattentive to their economic interests, indifferent if not hostile to their moral sentiments and ineffective in defense of their national security."

The new wing in the party that had emerged after 1988, led by officials like Bill Clinton and Al Gore, believed that fixing past mistakes wasn't enough. The party was in danger of extinction if it didn't capture some relevance. The DLC's organizing efforts markedly increased, as its budget shot up from $400,000 a year to $2 million. By 1991, the DLC's annual convention was the largest ever: More than a thousand office holders and party leaders flocked to Cleveland to build a new party. Since there were no rival idea groups with sufficient power or funding, the DLC managed to dominate the party's intellectual conversation, arguing against a straw man "traditional liberal" Democrat who never argued back.

Announcing his candidacy in October 1991, Bill Clinton sounded like a New Democrat: "The change I seek and the change we must all seek, isn't liberal or conservative. It's different and it's both." He called on the party to "reinvent government," broadening opportunities while also raising a call for greater responsibility by citizens. With Clinton, the DLC was firmly in control: Thirty-seven of the party's fifty-one specific planks were right out of the DLC's New Choice Draft.[19]

The Clinton years were glory days for the neoliberals and the DLC, which had launched itself in 1985 as an insurgent group and had now become the living embodiment of the establishment. Helped along by a booming economy, Clinton racked up year after year of successes: The budget deficit shrank and disappeared, reform drastically cut the nation's welfare rolls, millions of new jobs appeared, interest rates fell as inflation became a thing of the past. If it wasn't for the president's foibles and the GOP scandal machine, it would have been a great decade. But the focus on the Clintons and their personal affairs, as well as the loss of Congress after the 1994 election, blocked the party from developing its policy and economic success through the decade into a broader message of unity and that long-promised "bridge to the twenty-first century."

Defeated on his one big initiative to reform health care, Bill Clinton settled for what his adviser Dick Morris called "bite-sized" politics. Clinton spent his second term engaging on issues like school uniforms, as if what was wrong in the American education system could be fixed with more navy blazers, gray wool slacks, and knee-length skirts.

One might have considered the Democrats' efforts during the 1990s as a form of political benign neglect, except there was little benign about the neglect. Beyond the walls of politics, the world was changing faster than it ever had before, and increasingly politics wasn't keeping pace and didn't seem relevant or able to address what was happening.

ALTHOUGH YOUNGSTOWN, OHIO, was the birthplace of the Good Humor ice cream company and Arby's roast beef sandwiches, the city, equidistant from Cleveland and Pittsburgh, exists in the American memory as the emotional center of the Rust Belt. East of the Center Street Bridge, the giant buildings of the Campbell Works had stood proudly since the earliest years of the twentieth century. They had survived the Great Depression and thrived through two world wars. Wars are generally good for the steel industry. With strong union backing, they had prospered in the Ozzie and Harriet postwar years. But they couldn't survive globalization.

The workers at Youngstown Sheet and Tube became the first to learn the new economic rules that would govern the 1980s through these early years of the twenty-first century.[20] Youngstown Sheet and Tube manufactured much of the country's steel piping and tubing, and for decades it had prided itself on its local ownership until in 1969 it had been subsumed by the conglomerate Lykes Corporation, which by 1978 would be number 144 on the *Fortune* 500 list. The company, though, just like the industry as a whole, was on the decline, and by the mid-1970s Lykes figured it couldn't support the losses anymore with such a bleak future ahead. On September 19, 1977, it announced, without warning, that the plant would be closed and some forty-one hundred workers permanently laid off. No second chances, no negotiation, and no compensation—just a pink slip. By March 1978, nearly every worker was gone and the plant's rusting buildings were quickly shuttered.

In the years that followed, industry giants like U.S. Steel, Bethlehem Steel, and Alan Wood would close more plants, laying off tens of thousands of workers. The result was catastrophic. Real estate prices in the Youngstown area cratered. Families were devastated. "I've been employed here 13 years," Sheet and Tube steelworker Guy Fusco told the Associated Press, "and now I don't know what to do." The company's lobbyist, William D. Calhoun, made few apologies and laid out the new economic playing field: "It is the judgment of the company that it is better to bite the bullet and try to protect the jobs of the 17,000 workers nationwide who will stay with the company." Two years later, with nearly forty thousand jobs in Youngstown evaporated and the once-proud steel town in tatters, a former steelworker wrote to the local paper, "Will the last one leaving Youngstown please turn out the lights?"[21] The Rust Belt had begun to rust.

For more than forty years after World War II, the U.S. economy had hummed along: Suburbs rose from pastureland; televisions, dishwashers, white picket fences, and large automobiles from Detroit were commonplace; the middle class exploded. All of that prosperity and economic security ran smack into the turmoil of the 1970s—the collapse of the postwar monetary system, increased foreign competition, and globalization, a word that first appeared in Merriam-Webster's dictionary during World War II but came into popular usage

only in the last quarter of the century. By the early 1980s, the layoff—
what had once been regarded a sign of utter failure on the part of a
company's leadership—now became a regular part of corporate "re-
structuring" and an accepted business practice. Jack Welch, who became one of the country's most celebrated corporate leaders, laid off
one out of four workers at GM in 1980 and 1985, 115,000 people in
total, and earned himself the nickname "Neutron Jack"—just like a
neutron bomb, he left buildings intact even as he destroyed the people inside them.[22] Never before had so many Americans been dis-
carded from their employment. The Bureau of Labor Statistics began
to count "worker displacement" in 1984, and by 2004 it had counted
more than thirty million such workers—a statistic artificially low by
probably a factor of two since it doesn't include the also popular tactics of forced "early retirement" or buyouts. "Layoffs became the
measure of our national retreat from the dignity that had been gradually bestowed on American workers over the previous ninety years,"
explains Louis Uchitelle, who covered the economic shifts of the
1990s for *The New York Times*.[23]

Asian manufacturing and the ascendancy of Japan had ended a
generation of shared wealth and prosperity between workers and corporate leaders. Whereas the World War II generation would spend
almost all of its life with a single company—secure with pensions,
stock from a profit-sharing plan, and an endless string of retiree pic-
nics, as well as the added cushion of Social Security—their children
found themselves facing a world with a different employee-employer
relationship. Out of eight hundred senior executives in three hundred
major corporations studied in 1952, three-quarters had been with
their company for more than twenty years.[24] Through this joint period
of economic prosperity, as companies grew wealthy and workers established themselves as middle class, benefits had grown in tandem.
Whereas in 1950 only 10 percent of union contracts provided for pensions and only 30 percent included social insurance like health coverage, five years later, 45 percent provided pensions and 70 percent
covered life, accident, and health insurance.[25] The postwar period
that stretched to 1970 saw an expansion of economic wealth unparalleled in human history. The global GNP grew tenfold, from $300 bil-

lion to $3 trillion, and even adjusting for inflation, incomes tripled as trade quadrupled.[26]

Then in the 1980s the ground under the feet of American workers began to shift. The once distant world of Japan, China, and the rest of Asia had begun to feel much closer. A hungry Japan began to produce better goods, flooding U.S. markets with products at a third less than the domestic production cost. The swath of American manufacturing might in the Midwest, with the thundering steel plants of Pennsylvania on one end and Detroit's automotive powerhouse on the other, became the Rust Belt. In the crowning moment of a decade when the American people had watched once invincible companies like Chrysler brought low by Japanese imports, Mitsubishi paid $846 million—in cash—for 51 percent of Rockefeller Center. With the Japanese economy on the rise and on a buying spree, the wry announcer on David Letterman's show welcomed viewers to "New York, a subsidiary of Mitsubishi."[27] Forty years after Mitsubishi's fighter planes had attacked Pearl Harbor, Theodore White warned of "The Danger from Japan" in *The New York Times Magazine*, this time meaning economic, not military. And even as President Reagan was building up the massive military advantage that would eventually bring the Soviet Union to its knees and the Cold War to an end, the nation's new corporate titan, Lee Iacocca, told the nation, "I'm no Communist, folks, but it's not Russia that's laying waste to my business and to most of the rest of the business in this country. It's Japan, our friend. While we stack the missiles in the front yard, all aimed at our enemy, our friend is taking over the backyard."[28]

No one needed to tell any worker in manufacturing during the last twenty years that the economic world was shifting. The workers and their employers were already anxious. They could see that the world had changed. As an example of just how different the world of the 1980s was, in 1987, the Portland, Oregon–based Hyster Company, which made forklift trucks, complained to the government that Japanese firms were dumping their forklifts on the U.S market and pricing them below what those same companies were charging for their product in Japan. The Commerce Department promptly responded by imposing duties on forklifts, but Hyster never pointed out that it actually had more foreign parts in its forklifts than the Japanese ones. The government's more considered report later concluded, "Strictly speaking, there was no such thing as a U.S. forklift or a foreign forklift for that matter."[29]

Although Bill Clinton won the election in 1992 with a minority of the popular vote, it was clear that the voters delivered a powerful mandate for a new economic vision to replace that of the Bush and Reagan years. Combined with the 19 percent of the vote that went to archprotectionist Ross Perot, three out of five Americans had rejected the economic policies of the previous administration. As I explore later in the book, the social contract was in such tatters by Clinton's inauguration that national health care seemed a likely and achievable possibility.

The man who would become Clinton's labor secretary, Robert Reich, had begun to try to make sense of the new world. "Each nation's primary assets will be its citizens' skills and insights. Each nation's primary political task will be to cope with the centrifugal forces of the global economy which tear at the ties binding citizens together—bestowing ever greater wealth on the most skilled and insightful, while consigning the less skilled to a declining standard of living. As the borders become ever more meaningless in economic terms, those citizens best positioned to thrive in the world market are tempted to slip the bonds of national allegiance, and by so doing disengage themselves from their less favored fellows," Reich wrote in *The Work of Nations*, the book that would become a bible of sorts for Clinton's economic policy.[30]

Reich was among the first to realize that this new challenge to American competitiveness was different from those of previous eras. The transformation of corporations from local businesses to multinational conglomerates—conglomerates like the Lykes Corporation that had shuttered the Campbell Works in Youngstown—meant that their national ties were weaker than before and that it didn't make sense to protect one's "own" companies above all others. In terms of economic help to the United States, Reich realized, it might make more sense to help Mitsubishi set up a new operation in Ohio than to help GM expand its operations in Malaysia. "There is no longer any reason for the United States—or any other nation—to protect, subsidize, or otherwise support its corporations above all others," he argued. "Politicians have failed to understand that a nation's real technological assets are the capacities of its citizens to solve the complex problems of the future—which depend, in turn, on their experience in solving today's and yesterday's."[31] It's more important, in the new world, to invest in your own citizens than in your own companies. The new global corporate winner-take-all worldview was encapsulated by Gilbert Williamson, the president of NCR Corp.: "I was asked the other day about United States competitiveness and I replied that I don't think about it at all. We at NCR think of ourselves as a globally competitive company that happens to be headquartered in the United States."[32]

As Clinton's time in office rolled on, his administration gradually came to the position that layoffs weren't necessarily bad. The devil was in the transition. By his last term, Clinton was arguing that "layoffs were acceptable, a civilized form of behavior, as long as the companies doing the layoffs observed the amenities and as long as there was support for the victims, through retraining and education, so they could qualify for the next job," Uchitelle pointed out.[33]

Reich coined the phrase "the Anxious Class" to describe the millions of workers who understood that their continued paychecks were contingent on the vagaries of a now global economy. Even as the economy soared through the 1990s, creating untold amounts of wealth for those lucky enough to have bought Microsoft or Dell stock early, the underlying tension in the country never improved. Ross Perot hit a nerve during the NAFTA debate when he warned of a "giant sucking sound" of jobs heading to Mexico and overseas. The reality was much more complicated, as the free-trade agreement meant hundreds of thousands of new jobs created at the same time as hundreds of thousands of jobs were lost. It was often hard to tell whether the United States was winning or losing in the global economy, and so politicians found themselves playing to voters' fears. *The New York Times* in a seven-part series on the economic state of the country called the national state "the most acute job insecurity since the Great Depression."[34] Upon leaving office, Robert Rubin, the banker who served as Clinton's treasury secretary, penned a lengthy memoir titled *In an Uncertain World*. Whereas a generation before, such a title might have come from the defense secretary or the secretary of state, by the end of the 1990s the uncertain world—the national unease—existed not on the stage of world diplomacy or national defense but in the economy. Nothing improved in the first years of the new millennium. Even before 9/11 robbed Americans of their innocence, too many Americans seemed to have lost the sense of economic security that is critical for a successful middle class.

At the same time that the old industrial economic model was collapsing, a new technology-driven one was rising. Whole new companies with names like Apple, Cisco, and Intel were rising from the dust of the industrial conglomerates, selling products that most people couldn't understand. RAM, CPU, CD-ROM, and megabytes seemed to be a foreign language. Companies like UPS and FedEx earned billions flying the new goods around the world, ensuring that the global economy could hum just like a computer CPU. The new economy was increasingly borderless. Thanks to computers, modems, and the expansion of the World Wide Web, work started to flow overseas faster than ever, and companies liked what they saw when they examined the costs and benefits of moving routine labor to cheaper markets overseas.

In 1991, then obscure Satyam became the first Indian company to establish a 64-KB satellite connection with the United States. In Moline, Illinois, John Deere had hired Satyam as part of an outsourcing pilot project—but before the company would agree to send its work to India it had to be convinced that such an arrangement was feasible. Satyam opened an office nearby that it dubbed "Little India" and staffed with Indian workers scheduled according to Indian local time—night in the United States was the Indian day in the Satyam Illinois office. For six months the fifty workers kept the odd hours and never met in person with their counterparts across town at John Deere. Convinced by the success of the experiment and confident they could live with the outsourcing, John Deere agreed and the Satyam operations shifted back across the world. Satyam and John Deere were hardly alone in their experiment and arrangements during the 1990s.

Very little of this new world was trickling over into party politics, which every year seemed to be focusing more and more on the television, as power—especially on the Democratic side—coalesced more and more with the professional political image consultants.

Nearly a century after Theodore Roosevelt had helped lead the national transformation from an agrarian economy to an industrial one, Bill Clinton finally understood that another transformation was taking place: The industrial age was giving way to an economy based on ideas and information. He had seen the writing on the wall as early as the planning for the 1992 campaign, and his 1997 inauguration was actually the first such event webcast online, but it wasn't until 1998 that he fully grasped the significance. Clinton had taken office exactly a decade after *Time* magazine had proclaimed the personal computer the "machine of the year," a time when the entire internet numbered only 130 sites. He spent much of his presidency championing the changes that the computer would bring to the nation, but until Election Night 1998 he'd never actually used one or been on the internet himself. That night, he stood eating sausage pizza over the shoulder of political director Craig Smith and watched Smith track election returns in races across the country—sometimes even getting information before the television networks reported it. As he watched upstart Chuck Schumer defeat Senator Al D'Amato and the Republican-led Congress lose five seats, Clinton also for the first time witnessed the power of computers to deliver information in real time.[35] There would be no turning back, Clinton realized.

The following year, Clinton told an interviewer that Theodore Roosevelt's presidency "was a similar point in the history of America, where we were transforming ourselves [then from] an agricultural to an industrial society, now from an industrial to an information-technology-based society." The idea of this change and how the nation's leaders must respond consumed him. "At some points in history," he told Democratic adviser Andrei Cherny, "we go through change and no one can stop it." Clinton understood that he stood at one such crossroads. The change was under way, the wheels turning, the bytes already on their way. As Cherny later remarked, Clinton "knows that Teddy Roosevelt could no more have gotten people back to the farms than we can get people off computers."[36]

These new challenges required a new language, and Clinton, one of the most talented communicators of his age, tried to move the Democrats from their industrial age rhetoric. He spoke of "opportunity, responsibility, and community" and tried his "Third Way" to transcend the increasingly stale approach of both parties. "He instinctively understood the falseness of the choices being presented to the American people. He saw that government spending and regulation could, if properly designed, serve as vital ingredients and not inhibitors of economic growth, and how markets and fiscal discipline could help promote social issues," Cherny explained. "[He] tapped into the pragmatic, nonideological attitude of the majority of Americans."[37]

Around the country, political pioneers were beginning to understand the power that the technology sweeping the private sector could bring to the public sector. Three of them in particular would, over the course of their careers, reshape the way that politics and public debate happen in the United States. In Colorado, there was Dave Hughes; in Texas, Karl Rove; and in California, Joe Trippi.

Democratic strategist Bob Beckel recalls hearing Trippi talking about how the internet would change politics during a panel discussion after the 1984 campaign. Beckel turned to Trippi and said, "Joe, I don't have any idea what you're talking about." The internet, in that era, barely existed, and Beckel's response was hardly unique. Trippi, who has alternated his nearly three-decade-long string of presidential campaigns with years of technology work in Silicon Valley, has spent most of the last twenty years in politics telling people, "You don't get it." It was and is one of his favorite phrases—always delivered with equal amounts of anger at everyone else's naïveté and wonder at his own omniscience.

Trippi, who came of age in the Mondale '84 campaign, is the type of gritty, colorful, no-holds-barred political organizer who barely seems to exist anymore. In college, he and his father didn't speak for five years after Trippi's antiapartheid campaign caused trouble for his father's flower shop, and in Iowa while working for Mondale, a possibly apocryphal story has him driving into a ditch so he could corner one farmer while the farmer and his tractor pulled Trippi's car out. In that campaign, he helped Mondale beat Alan Cranston in a straw poll by decorating his buses filled with Mondale supporters with Cranston paraphernalia and then pulling them up to the Cranston check-in booth to receive their tickets. Politics was his lifeblood and from it he drew the necessary energy—even though every morning it seemed a struggle for him to survive until nightfall. Years later, on the Dean campaign, the manic cult figure would fuel himself with an endless supply of Diet Pepsis and cherry Skoal—his diabetes be damned.

Attending San Jose State in the 1970s, Trippi had early on gotten a seat at the computer—watching friends navigate the primitive forerunner to the internet, ARPAnet, and purchasing a computer to assist with Tom Bradley's 1981 California gubernatorial campaign. The $15,000 behemoth, perhaps the first computer ever used in political organizing, was the size of an oversized washing machine and held a mere 1.5 megabytes of memory—not even enough to hold a single MP3 today—but it proved a transformative tool for the campaign. Trippi explains, though, that he didn't fully understand the power of the internet to unite people across networks until he watched a virtual funeral unfold on the unofficial bulletin board that tracked the stock of a tech company during the 1990s. One of the lead posters, a day trader named David Haines, known online as HAINESDA, died suddenly of a heart attack, and the board saw an outpouring of emotion. "This was not a bunch of individual people sitting in front of a television alone, watching a sad program, reaching on cue for the Kleenex brand tissue. This was a rich, fully realized community, a world of real people interacting with each other . . . and crying on each other's shoulders when they lost someone they cared about, someone most of us had never met," he recalls.[38]

Trippi and Hughes weren't alone on the left in recognizing the political impact computers could bring, but they and their enlightened counterparts were certainly the exceptions to the rule. Another early adopter on the other side of the political spectrum was a little-known Austin consultant named Karl Rove, who specialized in the dark art of direct mail. Rove first purchased an HP mainframe that was the size of a desk and cost a quarter of a million dollars. And the laser printers that went with it? A bargain at only $100,000. However, as a direct mail guru, Rove instantly understood the potential: He could print personalized fund-raising letters by the boxful. Soon he was buying more computers and eventually had so many doing so many things that HP assigned him one technician full-time. (Before that, working as Rove was in Austin, Texas, he had to rely on a tiny computer repair shop on Guadalupe Street run by a guy named Michael Dell.) Before fax machines, Rove conducted business over Quip machines—a cross between a fax and a telegraph machine—and he used the first modems, however slow, to get a jump start on his competitors. It might take all night to upload a voter mailing list, but it was faster than the mail, and politics is often a game of inches. Rove learned that in technology, the inches make a difference. And, in terms of his own firm, technology helped him expand business while trimming the staff—he went from $8 million a year in business with twenty-two employees to $22 million with a staff of just eighteen. Most critically for the Republican efforts two decades later, he understood that data in aggregate form over several cycles was vital. "The cost of computer power is small, and you can over time build files that have lots of information about people's past preferences, and prejudices, and living patterns," he told one biographer. "I mean you are sitting there with a little laptop that has more computing power on your lap than the Manhattan Project had in all of its far-flung apparatus. Suddenly, you have a sense of power. You can find things, move things, manipulate things, the way the computer allows people to do it. It gives you a sense of your relevance and your power and your influence, and diminishes that of all big things, whether it's a big company, a big union, or big government."[39]

Jerry Brown thought the new technology might just help him bypass the Democratic Party's normal power structure and slip into the White House. As the establishment "neoliberal" candidates like Paul Tsongas, Dick Gephardt, and Jay Rockefeller dropped by the wayside, and Bill Clinton, a little-known charismatic Arkansas governor dogged by scandals and rumors, emerged from the pack, Clinton found Brown, a former California governor, nipping at his heels. In March 1992, Brown turned to the internet, going on CompuServe and the GEnie network, a short-lived venture by General Electric, to revive his flagging presidential campaign. "What is to be decided is whether this country shall be governed by the people or manipulated by an increasingly separated and out-of-touch elite," Brown told the GEnie town hall meeting. In that campaign, Brown became the first presidential candidate to receive e-mail from supporters—he even wrote back on occasion.

In a back room in an Orlando flower shop, Michael Moses ran Jerry Brown's information campaign. With a printer, computer, and fax machine, Moses collected thousands of names of people who called the campaign's famous 800 number and corresponded with people who had sent e-mail or left messages on bulletin boards. Calling his small office a "100-square-foot global village," Moses boasted, "This is warfare until November 7. What we've done is commandeered the theories of Aldous Huxley, Marshall McLuhan, and George Orwell and plugged them into the theories of the MIT media lab." It was, as is often the case with tech pioneers talking about their work, hyperbolic to the extreme—but it also was the beginning of a sea change on the presidential level that would take more than a decade to begin to bear real fruit.

Two years later, in 1994, the internet grew beyond bulletin boards into the World Wide Web, and Dianne Feinstein, a candidate for U.S. Senate in tech-heavy California, created the first candidate website. It, and the hundreds that would come after in the 1990s, was little more than an online brochure—with basic information about the candidate, perhaps some issue stances, and maybe a form to print out and mail in with a contribution. On the right, the Heritage Foundation's online town hall began linking together hundreds of conservative activists—a community still growing strong today.

The power of a single individual to drive the national debate got its first real test in January 1998 when a gossip website called the *Drudge Report* first broke allegations of President Clinton's affair with Monica Lewinsky. In his block type reminiscent of an old wire service teletype machine, Matt Drudge published a "World Exclusive" with the screaming headline, "Newsweek Kills Story on White House Intern: 23-year-old, Sex Relationship with President." The item was short, but it rocked the nation: "At the last minute, at 6 p.m. on Saturday evening, NEWSWEEK magazine killed a story that was destined to shake official Washington to its foundation: A White House intern carried on a sexual affair with the President of the United States!" CNN heralded the transformation of the news world: "Welcome to journalism in the Internet Age: an age when a 30-year-old former CBS gift-shop clerk like Drudge, armed with a computer and a modem, can wield nearly as much power as a network executive producer or the editor of *The New York Times*."[40] For better and for worse, Drudge's pioneering site grew to attract millions of visits a day and helped drive the Lewinsky affair and the Clinton impeachment story throughout the year.

As talk of impeachment continued through the fall, Silicon Valley entrepreneurs Joan Blades and Wes Boyd had had enough. In September, they launched a petition online encouraging Congress to "censure President Clinton and move on to pressing issues facing the nation." Their press release explained they were a " 'flash campaign,' possible only through the organizing capabilities of the Internet. Using email and the web, we can focus a broad and deep consensus in the American public into action." Thousands signed up, and the entrepreneurial couple, whose old company had created the decade's popular "flying toasters" screen saver program, took the campaign up a notch, creating a political action committee to raise and donate money. Their PAC, with an initial donation of $12,000 from Boyd and Blades themselves, launched just days before the November election, would over coming elections be one of the nation's most powerful and richest progressive funding forces.

That same fall of 1998, at the ballot box too, the world was changing. The revolutionary use of the Web in the 2000 presidential campaign had seen its genesis two years earlier, when consultants and staffers who, as Trippi might say, "got it," tested out approaches and tactics on the midterm congressional elections. Will Robinson was a lifetime Democratic operative who also happened to be, in technology parlance, an early adopter—an early comer to the power of the internet. In the 1980s, he fooled around with a Kaypro with its 256-KB boot-up disk, was one of the first members of AOL, and was even member 317996413 in CompuServe's short-lived experiment with easily forgettable online handles. Now in his forties and still working in politics, Robinson explains that he spends most of his days "channeling new technology to old people."

Like many of the top staff of Bill Bradley's campaign, Robinson—after stints with Mondale in 1984 and Dukakis in 1988, and with Ron Brown at the DNC—largely sat out the Clinton-Gore years, toiling away in the field, where he amassed five GOP congressional upsets in 1996 and 1998.

In 1998, more than one-third of House campaigns had websites, but they were little more than the "brochureware" pioneered by Dianne Feinstein. Robinson, along with his wife, Lynn Reed, had an idea for something more. In his race with Brian Baird, a clinical psychologist running for Congress in Washington State, Robinson created the first website tied to a television ad. The site, www.missedvotes.com, tracked all of the votes that opponent Don Benton had missed while a state legislator. Benton's campaign quickly turned around and launched the website www.flipflop98.org, which cataloged alleged inconsistencies in Baird's statements. Looking at the Wisconsin congressional race of state assemblywoman Tammy Baldwin, Robinson saw even more potential for the Web with one of the few populations then heavily wired: students.

Wisconsin's Second District was home to moderate Republican Jo Musser as well as seven universities and colleges—including the behemoth University of Wisconsin and its forty-one thousand students. With gerrymandered voting precincts splitting campus, the campaign created a Web page where students could enter their dorm location and get not only where to vote but also a map and a photo of the polling place taken with a giant digital camera. "It was like, 'Wow, we took this photo and put it on the internet.' 'Wow, did anyone get radiation burns from it?'" Robinson recalls. It was, he admits, "the Paleolithic era of internet campaigning."

While statewide turnout was 45 percent, Baldwin's Dane County saw 55 percent turnout, and some of the polling places frequented by UW students even ran out of ballots. Baldwin won by 13,600 votes, becoming the first Madison politician since 1973 to win on the basis of the student vote. Baldwin's victory, termed a "youthquake" by a local newspaper, made her the first openly gay nonincumbent ever elected to Congress and taught Robinson that the Web could make the difference in a race. In nearby Minnesota, independent Jesse Ventura's innovative use of the Web to build youth support also helped catapult him over two establishment party candidates into the governor's mansion.

A year later with Bill Bradley, Robinson and Reed were pouring the campaign's resources into the Web. The site consisted of hundreds of photos, and as the campaign began to understand how critical online fund-raising could be, it pushed the FEC to recognize credit card donations online. Although allowing donations to be submitted online, the FEC had not permitted those donations to count toward the federal matching funds so vital to candidates.

Lynn Reed sent a plea for the FEC to change its policy. By the time the FEC issued its verdict, Bradley had already raised $169,000 online. Gore, whose campaign didn't accept online credit card donations but instead asked donors to print out a form and mail it in, had raised only $17,000. The 2000 race also saw the first rumbles of MoveOn.org, which raised more than $358,000 online for five Democratic congressional candidates in 2000.

Campaigns also began to realize that a website was a great venue to present a more complete picture of the candidate. George W. Bush posted baby pictures. Elizabeth Dole's Senate race posted things like her favorite Bible stories and ice cream, vanilla Swiss almond.

Steve Forbes invited four hundred online supporters to pay $10 and join him virtually at a $1,000-a-plate gala at the Waldorf-Astoria—they could watch by slow-streaming video and send messages to the live event. The same event was then broadcast online, where eighteen hundred people watched it—more than the number who were actually at the event. Gore's youth-targeted GoreNet fundraising effort, asking for donations of $35, had great success online. Bradley used his e-mail list to notify supporters near his appearances and build crowds.

Truly transformative change in politics always comes as the result of forces from outside. Christmas 1999 was a key moment in the economic revolution of the internet, when millions of Americans went online and made their first purchases with a credit card on sites like Amazon.com and eBay.com. An Ernst & Young survey found that 26 percent of internet users made a purchase online during the holidays, and overall online shopping went from $3.1 billion in the last two months of 1998 to $11 billion in November and December 1999—a figure larger than the entire online shopping revenue of 1998. Many more families also got online for the first time with Christmas presents of new computers, modems, and internet access through portals like America Online.

And so it was that by the end of January, when McCain and Bradley were surging against the party's anointed front-runners, George W. Bush and Al Gore, the two rebels found a population ready to donate. In the ten days after his upset in the New Hampshire primary, McCain raised $2.2 million online—money that just one cycle before might not have arrived in time to help an upstart insurgent take on a powerful front-runner. With snail mail, the time from when a person mailed a check to a campaign to when the money was available to use often was more than ten days. Gary Hart's burgeoning campaign in 1984 had run out of money and he'd been forced out of the race because the mail couldn't arrive fast enough. Tens of thousands of dollars poured into Hart's offices around the country in the wake of his stunning victory over former Vice President Walter Mondale in New Hampshire, but it arrived too late to overcome the superior financing of Mondale's juggernaut. "For people to do that they had to know who I was, find my address, get a stamp, write the check, which I then had to deposit. Can you imagine how much more there would have been if all they had to do was go to a Gary Hart web site?" John Emerson, Hart's California campaign manager, lamented to the *Los Angeles Times* in 2000.[41]

By the time the Super Tuesday primaries rolled around, McCain had raised more than $10 million, about 40 percent of it on the internet, and built himself a war chest almost equal to Bush's. Of course, the internet benefited the front-runners too: When Gore's New Hampshire staff picked up after the primary and landed in Minnesota to organize for the primary there, they met a force of one thousand activists who had signed up online to work for Gore.

Politics would never be the same again—but neither would the U.S. economy.

GOOGLE AND PEOPLE-POWERED POLITICS

At the surface level, very little changed between the presidential elections of 2000 and 2004. For starters, John Kerry bested Al Gore by more than eight million votes—a number larger than the population of thirty-nine states—receiving more votes than any presidential candidate in American history except, of course, for George W. Bush, who bested his 2000 total by 11,500,000 votes. Bush improved in forty-eight states, even boosting his total in the very blue state of New Jersey by three hundred thousand votes. That said, Bush also won by the lowest percentage of any incumbent president ever; his 2.45 percent margin of victory snuck in well below Woodrow Wilson's poor showing in 1916, when he won by 3.2 percent.

Looking at the electoral map, New Hampshire and its four electoral votes, which had gone to Bush in 2000, went to Kerry, and two states—Iowa and New Mexico, with a combined twelve electoral votes—that had previously gone to Gore went to Bush. That was it. No other states changed hands between 2000 and 2004. In the red and blue maps that the television networks had begun to use to represent the country, the nation looked basically the same. But that's not the whole story.

Beyond those numbers, two enormous and related transformations were taking place, one within the world of politics and one outside, in the lives of ordinary voters across the country. Technology was giving rise to a new way of interacting with the world, participating in politics, and following the news.

Since at least the assassination of Abraham Lincoln or perhaps the sinking of the USS *Maine* and at moments like the Kennedy assassination, America had felt tragedy as a nation, but September 11, 2001, was, along with the explosion of the *Challenger* space shuttle, one of the first times it had seen tragedy. Three cameras, all run, ironically enough, by foreigners—French filmmaker Jules Naudet, German Wolfgang Staehle, and Czech Pavel Hlava—recorded American Airlines Flight 11 crossing over Manhattan and crashing into the World Trade Center at 8:46 a.m. that morning. The scene was live on CNN within three minutes and much of the country was watching by 9:03 a.m. when United Flight 175 followed. The 102 minutes between the first crash and the collapse of the twin towers riveted the country and became the defining national tragedy—a moment of lost innocence—for a generation, as the assassination of JFK had been for their parents. As David Friend wrote in *Watching the World Change: The Stories Behind the Images of 9/11*, whereas everyone asks where someone was when he or she heard about JFK's shooting, after 9/11 everyone asked where someone was when he or she saw the 9/11 attacks occur. "This was terror as sadistic global reality show," he says.

After a decade of peace and unparalleled prosperity in the United States, a period that had given rise to the quiet, issueless election of 2000, 9/11 was a cold plunge into globalization. Americans suddenly were hungry to learn about the world and those who had attacked us—the attacks had been massive, here at home, and also live in color on every television screen from the multistory jumbotrons in Times Square to those in homes and college dorms.

For many people, the Web became the primary source of news, and many of those people turned first to Google. In 2000, the little-known search engine had achieved the milestone of becoming the first billion–Web page index in the world. By 2001, though, it was increasingly the home page of the world. While news sites like CNN.com and NYTimes.com overloaded and crashed from the heavy onset of traffic on 9/11, people were left to turn to Google's search engine for more information. News-related searches like "Osama bin Laden," "Afghanistan," and, following rumors that he had forseen the 9/11 attacks, "Nostradamus," soared by a factor of more than sixty in the weeks after the terrorist attacks. The next year, driven in part by the demand of 9/11, the company launched its "Google News" feature, an editorless news site that through complicated algorithms put together a home page of the world's top stories.[1]

Tamim Ansary, an Afghan author who had lived in the United States for thirty-five years, found himself moved to write an e-mail that became widely followed in the attack's aftermath as the focus turned to American action in Afghanistan. "I've been hearing a lot of talk about 'bombing Afghanistan back to the Stone Age,'" he wrote in an impassioned eight-hundred-word e-mail sent to a small group of friends and colleagues. Ansary's e-mail, detailing the recent past of the already rubble-strewn Afghanistan under the Taliban and the looming confrontation with Islam, was forwarded hundreds of times and became the subject of much discussion. The power of an ordinary eloquent individual to write to friends and, in doing so, influence a nation's thoughts on war, Islam, and the country's path was new. It never could have happened during the Cuban missile crisis, the Iranian hostage crisis, or in the wake of the fall of the Berlin Wall.

We experienced September 11 and the days after together—we watched it on television, read the updated news online, and e-mailed our friends and family with news and thoughts of love. The cell networks overloaded and crashed in the hours after the attack, blocking telephone calls, but the lower-bandwidth BlackBerry network stayed up, which helped transform communications over the next year as businesses and government rapidly deployed BlackBerrys to key staff—congressmen and top staff were handed them within days of 9/11—and thereby helped to speed the pervasiveness of e-mail, instant communication, and the "always on" world where home and the office have no distinction.

All around us, the online transformation that in 2000 had surprised John McCain and Bill Bradley—the one forecast decades earlier by visionaries like Karl Rove, Joe Trippi, and Dave Hughes—was finally arriving, maturing, and growing in directions no one had foreseen.

In the years after the 2000 election, regular citizens found themselves suddenly empowered to buy their own plane tickets, rent cars, and research hotels through websites like Expedia or Orbitz—they didn't need to go through travel agents anymore. They could find people with similar interests through sites like Friendster.com, which launched in 2002. They could purchase almost any book in existence and get it delivered overnight from Amazon, and the online auction site eBay was proving that one man's junk is indeed another's treasure. The site's first item in 1995, posted by founder Pierre Omidyar, was a broken laser pointer that he had meant just to post as a test item, but to his astonishment it actually sold for $14.83. When Omidyar contacted the winning bidder to clarify that the laser pointer was broken, the buyer simply explained, "I'm a collector of broken laser pointers." At the start of 2000, eBay had 7.7 million registered users; by 2004 there were 95 million, including more than 45 million regularly active buyers and sellers. Daily listings had grown tenfold, from 375,000 a day in 2000 to 3 million a day by the beginning of 2004. Almost half a million people made a living buying and selling on the site.

An entire generation, myself included, had now grown up on computers. We started on now ancient-seeming Apple IIEs, playing "The Oregon Trail" and "Where in the World Is Carmen Sandiego?" in elementary school and then signed up for our first e-mail addresses in middle or high school. Now that same generation turned to Craigslist.org, the online community marketplace that had sprung up in 1995 in San Francisco, to help sell sofas, find roommates, and find jobs or dates. Craigslist.org, a onetime side project of founder Craig Newmark that quickly became one of the most popular sites on the Web, began to expand aggressively in 2000—beginning with Boston, then New York; Washington, D.C.; Portland; Seattle; Atlanta; and eventually hundreds more.

Google continued its online ascent, launching services like Froogle (2002) and Gmail and a Desktop Search (both 2004), and grew its search index to more than six billion items by 2004, the year it went public on the Nasdaq. As Google grew, one of the companies it snapped up was a program called Blogger.com, which allowed people easily to post their thoughts and observations to the Web. Blogger was one of the key drivers, along with sites and programs like LiveJournal and Movable Type, of a new trend. The new medium of online journaling called blogging was ready to go mainstream.

The first online journal, started by a student at Swarthmore College, had begun in 1994, and the term "blog," shorthand for "Web log," was coined in 1999. By 2001, blogs—especially political blogs—had begun to take off. Online commentaries by pioneers like conservative Andrew Sullivan's AndrewSullivan.com and Taegan Goddard's Political Wire, as well as Glenn Reynolds's Instapundit on the right and Jerome Armstrong's MyDD.com on the left began to attract wide audiences. In 2002, Markos Moulitsas Zúniga, a friend of Armstrong's, began DailyKos, which by the 2004 election would grow into the internet's most popular political blog, earning page views larger than mainstream newspaper sites—sometimes as many as a million a day during peak events. In his first post, shortly after lunchtime on Sunday, May 22, 2002, Kos outlined what would be his guiding principles: "I am progressive. I am liberal. I make no apologies. I believe government has an obligation to create an even playing field for all of this country's citizens and immigrants alike. I am not a socialist. I do not seek enforced equality. However, there has to be equality of opportunity, and the private sector, left to its own devices, will never achieve this goal." The online conversation that Dave Hughes had started twenty years before at Roger's Bar was growing.

The fall of 2002 also saw blogs for the first time drive a national debate. Up until this point, talking about news online basically meant one of two things: a mainstream news organization's website, like CNN.com, or the *Drudge Report*, the muckraking news and gossip site that had helped drive the Clinton impeachment saga. Now, though, ordinary people were stepping into the space.

On December 5, 2002, Mississippi senator Trent Lott, then the

Senate majority leader, rose at a ceremony honoring the one hundredth birthday of his South Carolina colleague Strom Thurmond. Out of all the mainstream press in attendance, only ABC News's Marc Ambinder noted what came next: Lott said, apparently in reference to supporting Thurmond's 1948 segregationist presidential bid, "I want to say this about my state: When Strom Thurmond ran for president, we voted for him. We're proud of it. And if the rest of the country had followed our lead, we wouldn't have had all these problems over all these years, either." The press might not have noticed, but bloggers certainly did. "It's safe to assume that, before he flushed his reputation down the toilet, Trent Lott had absolutely no idea what a blog was," *Wired* magazine wrote in December.

Bloggers like Joshua Micah Marshall at TalkingPointsMemo.com and Andrew Sullivan picked up on the remark and the terrible inference Lott had so casually thrown into the birthday remarks. The online hubbub kept attention on the matter through four different apologies Lott offered, all to no avail—by Christmas Lott was out as majority leader. The *New York Post* called Lott "the internet's first scalp." It surely wouldn't be the last.

The nation's war footing after 9/11 and its run-up to the Iraq war, coupled especially with the ineffective or altogether lacking response from the Democratic Party, helped radicalize the blogosphere and sites like MyDD and DailyKos. After the 1998 impeachment saga, subsequent online campaigns on issues like campaign finance reform had helped push MoveOn.org's membership to over half a million, but the looming Iraq war helped it truly take off—by the invasion, membership was over a million and by the 2004 election more than 2.5 million people were on the group's e-mail rolls. The MoveOn.org PAC took out full-page newspaper ads opposing the war, ran expensive television campaigns, and rallied support online. MyDD bloggers Matt Stoller and Chris Bowers note that the progressive blogosphere grew some twentyfold between the run-up to the war and 2005, eventually including some three to four million daily readers.[2]

In this new world, where anyone could join the national conversation and where ordinary people sitting at home in front of their blogs could help take down the Senate majority leader, presidential politics—conducted largely on the television by a small crowd of consultants and professional staff—had begun to seem an anachronism.

TEXAS GOVERNOR George W. Bush's 2000 campaign of "compassionate conservatism" had papered over his ideological differences with Gore; many going to the polls in 2000 during a lengthy period of unbroken peace and prosperity saw little difference between the two major party candidates. It seemed almost that America was headed for a postpolitical world—the "end of history" that had been forecast a decade earlier with the fall of the Berlin Wall and the collapse of communism; the 170-year-old two-party system was giving way to a middle-of-the-road national consensus. The world beyond our borders had seemed to settle on a free market, with democratic principles as its chosen manner of governance. Given that sense, it was especially jarring that the 2000 election, beginning with the Florida recount and the *Bush v. Gore* Supreme Court decision, kicked off the period of most intense partisanship and division in modern American history, both at home and overseas.

Looking ahead, though, it was clear that the 2002 and 2004 elections would be close—the nation was closely divided politically—and so both parties set out to expand their base and get the parties moving. To do so, the parties turned to two very different minds. The Democrats, just as they had brought in Charles Manatt two decades earlier to rebuild the party after the crushing 1980 election, turned to a new face. After eight different chairs in the eight years under Clinton, Terry McAuliffe, who had served most recently as the chair of the 2000 Los Angeles party convention, entered the fray.

McAuliffe, a fast-talking Irish ball of energy with an ego as large as his multimillionaire's checkbook, had been a party booster and fundraiser for nearly his entire career and had become fast friends with the Clintons during their White House years. Tenacious and unrelenting, McAuliffe had once wrestled an alligator to collect a check. In fact, he even stopped at one Democratic fund-raiser on the way home from the hospital with his wife, Dorothy, and newborn baby, Peter. "I felt bad for Dorothy, but it was a million bucks for the Democratic Party," he explained.[3]

What he found when he became chair of the party in February 2001 shocked him. Just as Chuck Manatt twenty years earlier had been disgusted by the shell of the party he had discovered when he took over as chair, McAuliffe found that he had inherited a Democratic Party that seemed to be a national organization in name only. "I'd always known that the DNC headquarters was in bad shape, I just didn't know how bad," he said. Mice roamed freely; sky-high phone bills based on unused lines installed years ago as well as mix-ups had the Democratic Party paying random phone bills for Americans all across the country. Ten-year-old computers and outdated technology were the norm throughout the understaffed yet cramped organization. The Democrats were so far behind and so disorganized when it came to technology that—to this day—the party doesn't own www.Democrats.com. (That key Web address belongs to a group headed by Bob Fertik, a long-time party and women's rights activist, who describe themselves as "aggressive progressives.") McAuliffe found that even after the huge election in 2000, the DNC had a database of only seventy thousand e-mail addresses—representing roughly one out of every 729 Gore voters from the previous election. The national party had no voter files to help contact potential supporters, and when he dove into the state party lists he found that there were twenty-seven million wrong addresses and phone numbers—meaning that in the 2000 election, won by some five hundred votes in Florida and one vote on the Supreme Court, the Democrats had failed to contact twenty-seven million potential supporters. In highly contested and razor-close Florida, the Democratic Party had more than 1.1 million incorrect files. McAuliffe fumed. "Don't you think we could have found 537 votes if we had corrected that information earlier and contacted 1.1 million more people?" he asks today.[4]

The fund-raising picture was hardly better. President Clinton had excelled at the high-dollar backslapping schmoozefests that landed big checks, but once again ordinary small-dollar voters had been ignored. McAuliffe explains that in 1979, the party had raised $1.6 million through direct mail at a cost of $850,000, or about 53 cents on the dollar. In 1999, it raised $17 million at a cost of $8 million—47 cents on the dollar, still far too expensive and yielding too little. "We had been spoiled for eight years. We had a Democratic President and he was such a master communicator, we could overcome whatever problems we had with direct mail or e-mail lists. We hardly noticed the cracks in our party because Clinton could work his magic and fire everyone up," McAuliffe recalls.[5] Once he figured out exactly how bad things were, he set out on a national fund-raising drive that would provide a new party headquarters, new technology, and new resources across the board. As one donor told *The New York Times*, "When you look at Terry's presentation, you kind of go, 'How can it be that we have two main parties in this country, and one is functioning in the twenty-first century and the other is functioning in the Stone Age?' "[6] McAuliffe, being so close to the Clintons, was too polite to lay the blame for the party's atrophy at the feet of its leader for the previous eight years, but that's the only possible explanation.

The Republicans, meanwhile, had a clearer path and were starting from a stronger position, even though they hadn't controlled the White House for the past eight years. Since Bush took office in 2001, his team had been developing a comprehensive plan for reelection. They had lost the popular vote in 2000, and if the game stayed the same, they knew they'd likely lose the 2004 election, even though they had the White House. The Republicans needed more voters. As Ken Mehlman, who managed the 2004 Bush/Cheney presidential bid and later in 2005 became chair of the Republican Party, explains, "One of the most important things was that we needed a plan to try to expand the electorate and particularly expand our part of the electorate. There was a four-year plan to accomplish that, which included lots of different things. Fundamentally, it included two big things. One, to use the 2001 and 2002 elections to test out all kinds of different political tactics and make sure that we were being most effective in 2004." The tactics building for 2004 would include the whole range of tools at the Republicans' fingertips, Mehlman says. "It was turnout, it was television advertising, it was where we bought, how we bought, it was all those things. It was the effectiveness of voter contact, and the different programs to do that."[7]

Mehlman said that the GOP spent more than $50 million in 2002 in coordinated expenditures with an eye toward Bush's reelection bid two years later.

Ultimately, what we were doing when we spent that money was using it as a way of testing our tactics—testing and researching. The
thing I got out of this process that was most important was that we
now live in a world where the old ways of communicating—the traditional buying ads on three channels, doing some robo calls, and
doing some paid mail as a voter contact program—are insufficient.
What we learned and what we concluded was that we needed, from
a paid media perspective, a plan that was very multifaceted—that
reached people not just on the networks but increasingly on cable,
increasingly on radio, increasingly in different venues—and that our
mail and our phones needed to be supplemented by a huge volunteer effort. The thing we got out of it was that the contact that is
both personal and from a credible source is most effective. That
informed where you bought television, where you earned media,
where you booked people, how you built your ground organization,
and how you reached new voters.[8]

The television landscape was shifting and the GOP knew it was at
a disadvantage—Democrats watched more TV than Republicans, so
more of the GOP ad dollar was being wasted. They realized that by
better targeting their dollars, they could better reach the narrow segment of the population they were actually interested in. As early as
1998, Republican operatives had tried to get Nielsen to measure partisan ID but found that the cost was excessive. In 2001, though, Will
Feltus, who headed the team that bought Bush's television media,
crossed paths with Scarborough Research, which he discovered had
been tracking party ID, along with hundreds of other characteristics
like health club memberships, movie viewing, insurance coverage,
purchases, and spending habits. Scarborough was the Holy Grail Feltus had long been seeking—and he immediately set about putting it
to work for the RNC, transforming the way campaigns bought ad
time.

Cross-referencing the data allowed the party to figure out, for instance, which cars trended to which demographics. Jaguar, Land
Rover, and Porsche owners all trended toward Republicans; the last
were 59 percent GOP. Subaru, Hyundai, and Volvo were bought by

Democrats, the last by more than 12 percentage points. They also correlated TV viewing with party. Not surprisingly, *Fox News Sunday* was the most partisan of all news shows, with nearly all its viewers Republicans, whereas CBS's news programming all tended to appeal most to Democrats. The cable channels Speedvision, which covers NASCAR, the Outdoor Channel, and the History Channel were solidly GOP bastions, whereas Bravo, Lifetime, Court TV, Nickelodeon, and TNT skewed Democratic. *The West Wing*? No surprise, Democratic. *JAG* and *NCIS*? Again, no surprise, Republican.[9] Also not surprising, gun ownership and religion (both what faith and how observant) were the two most powerful predictors of partisan ID.

The GOP approached its efforts with awe-inspiring methodicalness. It ran tests during the 2002 cycle in the Texas Senate race and in a Colorado congressional race that were so focused that the GOP knew the roads Republicans drove as they commuted to work, which allowed the party to target its billboards only where they would do the most good.

"Kerry ran a traditional campaign in 2004 if you look at what they said, where they advertised, and what they built. We ran an untraditional campaign. Our ads often started out on the Web, we used the new media effectively, we used consumer data to identify new voters, we split two states because of our improved performance among minorities—African Americans in Ohio and Hispanics in New Mexico," Mehlman told me. "We built a 1.4-million volunteer database so that teachers knocked on the doors of teachers to talk about education. That's far more effective than any television ad."

With the new data, the campaign shuffled its resources. Whereas the 2000 campaign had spent 95 percent of the media budget on broadcast TV ads, the 2004 efforts spent only 70 percent on that medium. National cable buys soared from nothing in 2000 to more than $20 million in 2004, and ads on religious, talk, and country music stations jumped from a tiny share to nearly $12 million. Thanks to its technological and infrastructure advantage, the GOP knew where its voters were and it could talk to them. From 2001 to 2004, the RNC, where much of the planning was based, outspent the DNC by $122 million.[10]

The information let the GOP reach the specific people it needed to reach and leave the others aside. The Democrats, on the other hand, in 2004 focused their ad dollars on blanketing the targeted swing states, even ignoring opportunities to reach key voter blocs that might have made a difference. The Democratic Party never ran a single national cable ad. It never bought an ad on younger liberal-skewing MTV. It never bought an ad on *The Daily Show with Jon Stewart*. The GOP's national buys helped move numbers even where it seemed unlikely—Bush had a brief boomlet in Hawaii thanks to the cable advertising that disrupted Democrats' plans and forced Kerry's campaign to siphon resources to a state once thought a sure win. The Democrats, of course, had no similar residual gains since the thirty-seven states not considered battlegrounds were almost ignored when it came to ads.

AS THE 2002 ELECTION closed in with the Iraq war looming, it appeared that the Republicans had a stronger team in place and that President Bush might not suffer the normal presidential embarrassment of losing seats in Congress at the midterm—as President Clinton and the Democrats had lost both the Senate and the House in the Republicans' "Contract with America"–led revolution in 1994. One key reason for the weak showing by the Democrats, though, was a lack of fire in the belly. Writing in *The New Yorker* after the election, Joe Klein fumed about the congressional campaign. The Democrats had run a national campaign on "three tiny and mostly bogus themes: scaring senior citizens about the imminent privatization of Social Security; pandering to senior citizens by proposing an expensive and ill-considered prescription drug plan; and blaming George W. Bush—in vague terms, without offering an alternative—for the economic downturn."[11] The nascent progressive blogging community was just as angry at the party for ignoring the war in Iraq and pushing aside monumental issues in favor of, well, nothing.

In fact, in many circles, 2002 would come to be known as the Seinfeld election—it was about nothing. Neither party had figured out how to win with a twenty-first-century grand plan or how to debate the big issues; thus, neither side bothered. The GOP cruised to a rare midterm electoral success. Writing in *The Washington Post*, David Von Drehle and Dan Balz observed, "Strategists in both parties think and talk about the need to roll out big ideas and make bold new moves to break this deadlock—but for now it's just talk."[12]

As Democratic pollster Stanley Greenberg told the *Post*, the parties were "so evenly matched at the moment that all the incentives are to be careful." It wasn't that there weren't big ideas out there to debate, but Clinton's programmatic successes and the recent political fascination with invented electoral subgroups like "soccer moms" and "NASCAR dads" had narrowed the political worldview. "We have tactical elections, we don't have big elections, because there's every prospect that you can win by thinking small," Greenberg said. "There's a temptation to find one small group that gets you a couple of extra percentage points, rather than thinking grander."[13]

It took the unexpected death of a U.S. senator just days before the election to revive the Democratic Party. On October 25, the twin-engine turboprop carrying Senator Paul Wellstone crashed in a snowstorm near Eveleth, Minnesota. The crash killed the populist senator, first elected in 1990, as well as his wife, daughter, three staff, and two pilots. At the sometimes raucous funeral, speaker after speaker recalled Wellstone's proud tradition of holding the powerful accountable and fighting for the "little guy." Paul Wellstone, the message seemed to be, would not have stood silent, as the national party was, at such a critical point in our country's future. "Let's win this election for Paul," the activists said. The incident, although it drew criticism from Republicans and might have cost the Democrats the Minnesota senate race, reminded activists around the country that the Democratic Party had an important voice and message to share.

Three months later, with the Democratic Party, especially the party establishment, embarrassed and silenced at the ballot box and rushing to support President Bush on the imminent war in Iraq, Howard Dean took to the stage in Washington and invoked the fallen Wellstone. Dean's message was simple and, for thousands of activists who felt voiceless, compelling: Let Democrats be Democrats. "We don't need two Republican parties," he intoned. We need ideas. We need leadership. We need opposition.

When it was Dean's turn to address the Democratic National

Committee's winter meeting in Washington on February 21, 2003, the party loyalists had already listened to their supposed leaders drone on and on. The little-known governor from Vermont, fresh off a red-eye flight, roused the audience with a speech sketched out half an hour earlier and never once practiced.

"What I want to know is why in the world the Democratic Party leadership is supporting the President's unilateral attack on Iraq." The crowd burst into cheers. "What I want to know is why are Democratic Party leaders supporting tax cuts. The question is not how big the tax cut should be, the question should be can we afford a tax cut at all with the largest deficit in the history of this country." More cheers. "What I want to know is why we're fighting in Congress about the Patient's Bill of Rights when the Democratic Party ought to be standing up for health care for every single American man, woman, and child in this country." The crowd was on its feet, cheering, stomping, and applauding. "What I want to know is why our folks are voting for the President's No Child Left Behind bill that leaves every child behind, every teacher behind, every school board behind, and every property tax payer behind." And then it was time for the big finish: "I'm Howard Dean and I'm here to represent the Democratic wing of the Democratic Party."

That last line belonged to Wellstone, but it would come to define Dean's campaign more than anything. Amid a lackluster and uninspiring field, the party's troops—especially online supporters on sites like DailyKos and MyDD—rallied to Howard Dean. Excited by the hope he embodied and the energy he brought to the race, and finally finding a place to direct their anger over Iraq, the party faithful saw Howard Dean as their last best chance to wrest control of the party from a timid leadership and restore the liberal greatness last known during the rise of the New Deal.

THE DEAN CAMPAIGN is one part of this story that I had the opportunity to witness firsthand. I grew up in Montpelier, the Vermont state capital, and a few years after Dean—"Dr. Dean," to those around him, on account of his training as a physician—took office in 1991, I began an internship at the governor's press office as part of a community-based learning program at Montpelier High School. When I was hired on as a part-time press assistant after my freshman year, I was young enough that the governor's legal counsel had to make sure I could legally work for them without violating child labor laws. Over the next four years, I spent every afternoon I could and several summers collating news clippings, writing press releases, and sending out Dr. Dean's weekly public appearance schedule. Among ourselves, the small staff often discussed with varying levels of seriousness whether the boss might run for president one day.

I left Vermont for college, and as I entered my senior year in 2002, it suddenly appeared that the once faraway idea of a presidential run by Dean was becoming a reality. I interviewed for a job with the nascent campaign and got a glimpse of the barely controlled chaos of a presidential run in its early stages. The Dean for America headquarters was sandwiched into a tiny suite of offices above the Vermont Pub and Brewery in downtown Burlington, which, despite its stature as Vermont's largest city, would never be confused with a metropolis.

Ten days after I graduated from college in 2003, I set up a folding table from Staples at the Dean headquarters. It would be my desk for the next nine months. The campaign had already outgrown the office above the pub and had moved to an office park closer to the governor's home in South Burlington. Although I had been hired as a communications staffer, there was no room in the two cramped offices that held the press team, so I set up my "desk" in a vacant space in the internet bullpen, sandwiched between (on the right) the campaign's bloggers—Zephyr Teachout and Matt Gross—and (on the left) the Web team, led by one Nicco Mele, a loud Italian from Queens. A few feet away was the office of Joe Trippi, who was already Dean's second campaign manager. It was no mistake that the Web team was the part of the campaign closest to his office—he thought it was integral to the whole campaign. Although at heart quite friendly, Trippi was generally gruff and had an explosive temper; he once screamed at a volunteer, "Do you have a fucking political bone in your body?" The phrase would become one of the campaign staff's frequent refrains.

Two decades after he bought his first computer to work on Tom Bradley's California race, Trippi was still fascinated by computers and their power to connect, share, and build community. On the World

Wide Web, a shadow campaign for Dean was emerging, complete with websites, blogs, video sites, and bulletin boards—which were still popular in some parts nearly a quarter century after Dave Hughes founded the Roger's Bar BBS in Colorado. The campaign had already had some success raising money online from antiwar activists around the country, but with only a few million in the bank, the campaign was still being run on a shoestring.

When I joined the campaign, we were already working around the clock to prepare for Dr. Dean's official announcement of his candidacy on June 23 when his son was arrested as part of a group of teenagers attempting to steal liquor from a Burlington country club. The Vermont press corps descended as the candidate canceled his travel schedule and raced home from the campaign trail.

That weekend, Dean went from a local hero to a national figure. Two days of media attention, much of it unfavorable, culminated with a prescheduled hour-long interview with Tim Russert on *Meet the Press*. Dean seemed to stumble a few times on the show, including one screwup when he didn't know how many soldiers were in the U.S. military. The Washington establishment—what then–ABC News political director Mark Halperin had labeled the "Gang of 500" to describe the group of reporters, consultants, political operatives, and elected leaders who made "conventional wisdom" conventional— quickly labeled the interview a disaster. He had failed their test and was labeled not presidential timber.

But the Democratic Party's grassroots activists, Dean's would-be rebel army, saw it differently—and the difference showed that, thanks to the internet, things were finally changing in Democratic politics. That Sunday, nearly $100,000 came in over the internet. The money trickling in online throughout the spring had added significantly to Dean's bottom line, but numbers like that were incredible, even more so for a Sunday in late June the year before an election.

On Monday, June 23, when Dean officially announced, another $200,000 rolled in. The Web team and the finance team, most of whom had been solid members of the establishment before joining Dean's nascent effort, watched stunned as the money kept coming. As the end of the fiscal quarter approached, the amounts kept increasing: $300,000 each on Tuesday, Wednesday, and Thursday, and

$500,000 on Friday. Trippi sat down on Sunday and realized that, over the last eight days, twenty-one thousand people had given money on-line, for a total of $2.1 million—exceeding the amount once budgeted for the entire campaign.

Recognizing a fund-raising moment without precedent, Trippi sought to capitalize on it, using a technique associated with charity fund drives rather than political campaigns: He posted the campaign's fund-raising numbers on the Dean for America website and asked for help in reaching a new quarter goal of $6.5 million. Finance staffer Larry Biddle came up with the idea of posting a cartoonish baseball bat on the home page that would "fill in" as people donated, like those oversized cardboard thermometers that show the progress in hospital charity drives. The moment was without precedent in presidential politics—campaigns generally guarded their fund-raising numbers like the recipe for Pepsi. When the governor saw the number posted on the website while he was out on the trail, he immediately called Trippi to report that the website had been hacked. It hadn't—it was just a new way of doing politics.

That Monday, June 30, the spigot just opened. Every half hour Nicco posted updates and let the bat fill in a little more. The Gang of 500 watched stunned. Newsweek's Howard Fineman told Chris Matthews on MSNBC's Hardball, "In newsrooms around the country, I'm told, people have the Dean screen up on their computers and they're watching the totals go up like a telethon."

On that final day of June, the land under the American political system shifted. By the time the clock struck midnight and Nicco posted the final update to the bat, more than seventy-three thousand people had contributed $7.6 million to Howard Dean in the second quarter, with an average contribution of just $112.

The party status quo could hardly have been upset more if William Wallace and his Scottish army had charged across the moors to the doors of the DNC in southeast Washington to tar and feather Terry McAuliffe.

DEAN FIRST GAINED ATTENTION outside Vermont for his opposition to the Iraq war, and for much of the campaign he would be dismissed as the antiwar candidate, but his campaign was about much more than that. Beyond the war, he had sensed two important feelings among the electorate. First, especially among the activists who had gone online, there was a sense that the Democratic Party had reneged on its role as an opposition party. It offered nothing to contrast with the Republican agenda. Second, he sensed that people were still anxious about their lives—they felt the country was rolling along without a clear path. Dean offered a sort of twenty-first-century populism. He understood that the things that bothered Americans were not the details of Bush's tax plan or the environmental rollbacks—what they were most troubled by were their own lives, the shrinking two-income family. Two Harvard professors had, in their separate works, nailed down the growing unease across the country. In *Bowling Alone*, Robert Putnam sketched out how the very idea of American community—of a communal society—was splintering; fewer Americans were participating in civic life, interacting with their neighbors, helping out in the schools. Most basically, Americans were giving up on being citizens and instead retreating to isolated climate-controlled living rooms with big-screen TVs. Elizabeth Warren explained some of the pressures facing the modern family: "Today a fully employed male earns $41,670 per year. After adjusting for inflation, that is nearly $800 less than his counterpart of a generation ago. The only real increase in wages for a family has been the second paycheck added by a working mother . . . Today's families have budgeted to the limits of their new two-paycheck status." Her bottom line: "Now a pink slip, a bad diagnosis, or a disappearing spouse can catapult a family from solidly middle class to newly poor in a few months."[14]

This message—the pressures of living the American dream—stood in stark contrast to the message coming out of the White House under George W. Bush. Our challenge at the campaign headquarters in Burlington was to dramatize this as effectively as possible—and by any means necessary.

On July 28, Vice President Dick Cheney stopped briefly in Columbia, South Carolina, raising $300,000 from 150 people during a thirty-minute luncheon stop at the house of Gayle Averyt, the chairman emeritus of Colonial Life Insurance Co. The stop was routine— just another part of a massive and successful fund-raising apparatus that allowed the Bush campaign to build a war chest worth more than $260 million. Joe Trippi decided that Columbia was an opportunity to highlight the differences in fund-raising approaches between Dean and Cheney—literally the differences between the people and the powerful—and sent out an e-mail laying out a challenge to match Cheney's $300,000 in big-donor money with small-dollar contributions over the internet. "Let's show George W. Bush and Dick Cheney that we will not let our government be sold to the highest bidder. Let's show that the grassroots are stronger than the special interests," he wrote in his characteristically fiery language—which more often than not belonged to one of the staff bloggers.

By 2004 the Bush-Cheney machine had perfected a system developed for the 2000 campaign: The vast majority of the money was raised by a handful of 246 "Pioneers" who pledged to raise $100,000. For the '04 race, the campaign added a new "Ranger" category worth $200,000. More than 220 people met that goal, while another 323 became "merely" Pioneers. Of course, the perks of achieving the special status far exceeded the prestigious title and the opportunity to purchase a special set of silver "Lone Star of Texas" cuff links (Rangers could buy a pricier belt buckle). An AP investigation found that of the 246 Pioneers from the 2000 campaign, a third of them or their spouses ended up with governmental appointments ranging from cabinet posts to ambassadorships to positions on boards and commissions. Texas rancher and Senator M. Teel Bivins, who was a Pioneer in 2000 and a Ranger in 2004, was blunt about the trade-off. "You wouldn't have direct access if you had spent two years of your life working hard to get this guy elected president, raising hundreds of thousands of dollars?" he told the BBC in 2001 while he awaited his Senate confirmation hearing after being nominated as ambassador to Sweden. "You dance with them what brung ya."

How could we compete with that? As money began to pour in in response to Trippi's challenge, I came up with the idea of grabbing the governor a $3 turkey sandwich from the seedy little store on the first floor of the campaign building where most of us bought our meals—thereby showing the difference between a campaign run by rich people and one run by regular people. We photographed Dr. Dean munching on his sandwich while blogging at one of the office computers that afternoon—his virtual $3-a-plate grassroots fund-raising effort contrasting with the vice president's in-and-out lunch—and the photo went right on the blog. It would prove to be one of the iconic images of the different campaign.

The three-day-long drive highlighted that the end of June wasn't just a fluke: 9,621 donors gave $508,640.31 with an average contribution of $52.87—or, as we liked to point out, $1,947.13 less than the cost of attending Cheney's exclusive fund-raiser in South Carolina. Time and again over the coming months, we'd whip out the "bat" and the money would start to come in. In the normally quiet days of August, the campaign chartered an aging jet—a shiny late-model jet was still too pricey—and Dean set off on a national tour dubbed the "Sleepless Summer Tour." As Dean, the prodigal candidate, descended on capacity rallies that attracted ten thousand or more people, the Web team sat back in Burlington watching the donations flow in. It was the first time in a generation that the Democrats had managed to build a people-powered campaign-funding operation.

For the final stop in Manhattan's Bryant Park, we all decamped to the city, setting up shop under a tree and working feverishly to update the bat in those final hours as the campaign reached its million-dollar goal. Dean took the stage, his shirt sleeves rolled up, and waved a red baseball bat. Here, in easy walking distance to the Upper East Side salons where the checks that paid for Democratic campaigns were written and to the Park Avenue apartment where he had been reared, Howard Dean returned to remake the party's image. The message was clear. The reign of the big donors was over. The era of small-dollar fund-raising had begun. The internet—and the economic transformations of the internet age—would save the party from the money race.

To understand just what a burst of enthusiasm this change brought to the Democratic Party, one need to look at only the donations under $200. The total of these small donations to Democratic presidential candidates rose elevenfold—from $11 million in 2000 to $127 million in 2004. Republicans saw a much smaller increase, not even double, from $43 million to $78 million. This brought some much-needed parity to the party system too—the DNC, which is usually beaten at least two to one by the RNC, raised 80 percent of the GOP's $392.4 million in 2004.[15]

Internet fund-raising also served as evidence of another major change: Ordinary people were hungry to get involved in party politics again. This had been clear since March, when, at a Dean event in Manhattan just two weeks after his rollicking speech to the DNC winter meeting, a crowd showed up that surprised everyone, even Joe Trippi, the original true believer in people-powered politics.

Outside the Essex Lounge on Manhattan's Lower East Side, the crowd kept building as the clock neared 7 p.m. No one had seen this coming. A then-obscure online networking site, Meetup.com, had organized a gathering for Dean, who was then little known outside Vermont. Meetup.com, which was primarily used by people to organize small groups around shared interests like pets, knitting, or—in the case of the site's largest group—witchcraft, had recently added presidential meetups. Most of the big-name candidates fared poorly, but this Vermont governor who was against the war in Iraq started to take off. When Trippi first discovered the site, John Kerry had 310 people nationally in his Meetup group, Edwards 141, and Dick Gephardt was in the low double digits. Dean, meanwhile, had 432. After battling the staff for a few days, Trippi got the Web team to post a link to Meetup on the campaign home page. The Meetup numbers kept growing, and a few weeks later the Meetup number actually crept past the witches to become the largest group in the country. Trippi persuaded the campaign's scheduler to schedule a drop-by at the Essex Lounge.

Meetup groups would meet at the same time on the same night around the country—in the case of Dean for America, the groups gathered at 7 p.m. on the first Wednesday of the month. They tended to be smaller than a dozen people and usually met in coffee shops or the back rooms of bars. But once the campaign announced that Dean would attend the New York meetup, it surged to more than a score, then fifty, then more than one hundred people. By 7 p.m., the line was snaking around the block. The candidate pulled up to discover that eight hundred people had braved the evening to hear him speak. "When I got out of the car and saw hundreds of people lined up outside the Essex Lounge, and walked inside to find hundreds more, I felt in a direct, powerful way, the awesome force of the Internet," Dean later wrote on the campaign blog.

Columbia student Brian Schaitkin described the feeling inside the bar to a reporter as "electric." "There was the feeling that 'Hey, we are capable of building a movement that can successfully compete with traditional campaign tactics on any level,'" Schaitkin said.

By the end of the campaign, more than 180,000 people had signed up for some 2,000 presidential meetups around the country. On the first Wednesday of the month, all across the country, people would gather for a Dean meetup. They'd write letters to voters in Iowa and New Hampshire; they'd help organize in their neighborhoods; they'd shower elected officials with letters asking them to endorse Dean. Groups, like cells growing, split again and again as they got too large for their venue. Ordinary citizens stepped up to lead their meetup since the national campaign's organization could never hope to staff so many events. In the Burlington headquarters, a young Middlebury College graduate, Michael Silberman, coordinated and ushered along the growing numbers of meetups, leading a team working almost around the clock to provide the letter-writing supplies, campaign stickers, and resources that the groups demanded. Conference calls between the campaign and the meetup hosts would stretch late into the night, yet despite the long hours, Silberman and his team never fully got their arms around the meetups—the phenomenon was growing too fast in too many places ever to be controlled by a central campaign. It was a new model for politics: people not waiting for leadership but instead taking the initiative for change and organizing themselves.

IN ITS OWN SMALL WAY, the meetup at the Essex Lounge was the answer to the party's long-standing problem of reaching people at the grass roots. But at the same time, it was an expression of a profound change that had taken place outside of politics, as people used the internet not only to communicate and shop but also to find affinity groups—to join together with people of like mind.

As more and more people turned to the internet for purchasing goods and services, researching medical issues, reading news, and browsing blogs, the medium's reach and ability to influence politics grew more powerful. The ease of fund-raising and online organizing

helped transform races up and down the ticket. Beyond Dean's incredible success online in 2003, during a special election in Kentucky
in early 2004, Democratic candidate Ben Chandler was highlighted
on dozens of blogs and found himself showered with money as if from
a magic wand. He won against long odds, granting the Democrats one
of their few bright spots in the otherwise dreary election cycle. As
Dean's rallying cry said, Democratic activists wanted their party back
and they wanted their country back.

Nearly twenty years after political observers began noting the Republican rise and the network of think tanks, media outlets, and
foundations that helped power the GOP's national ascendancy, a
Democratic activist named Rob Stein sat down and organized a
PowerPoint titled "The Conservative Message Machine Money Ma-
trix," which challenged the Democrats to organize their own network
of think tanks and outlets. Stein showed his work to various forward-
thinking big-dollar Democratic donors, and they began to assemble a
network of institutions to support the party's message.

A number of major Democratic donors stepped up and offered extensive funding to help try to jump-start change in the party. Steve
Rosenthal ended up running one of the largest voter registration projects ever for the left-leaning Americans Coming Together. "Part of it
came from my frustration overall with the Democratic Party for not
having done this work for so long . . . frustration that the state parties
and the Democratic Party overall had failed in a lot of ways to build
the infrastructure that really was needed to begin to engage voters
again," he explained.

Rosenthal's efforts yielded abundant fruit—one of the few bright
spots in the national election for Democrats. Spending $135 million
on get-out-the-vote efforts, ACT registered 450,000 primarily Democratic voters. More than that, though, it demonstrated to a wide swath
of the party just how broken the Democrats' infrastructure had become. "There's nothing I would love to see more than the Democratic
Party really rebuild its organization, build the state parties, make them
into a real force of neighbors talking to neighbors. That is the most effective type of communications in politics," Rosenthal remarked just
after the 2004 election. "I think there's a real opportunity out there
right now to really build and engage and develop organizations that

talk to people and get them involved in politics again . . . Donors came forward in big numbers this year because they believed that the direction the country was headed in was the wrong direction. There's an enormous opportunity to build on that in the coming years."[16]

One of the key lessons ACT learned, though, was that the party's activists were hungry to get involved. In Pennsylvania, for instance, ACT had planned to hire twelve thousand paid workers for Election Day. It ended up with more than seventeen thousand people who volunteered for get-out-the-vote efforts. The grassroots Democrats were hungry to win, but the party had long forgotten to ask them.[17] When the dust began to settle from the 2004 election cycle, the entire obsolete landscape of American politics would have been remade.

HOWARD DEAN RAN AWAY with the Democratic primary campaign for the rest of 2003. By December, the nation's two largest and most powerful unions had endorsed him, and Al Gore himself stood before crowds in Harlem and Iowa to intone his devotion to Dean.

In the end, Dean didn't win the nomination, but the enthusiasm and passion that he had begun to generate would shake the foundations of the party. As Dean's pollster, Paul Maslin, said with pride, "Howard Dean gave this party its voice back. Some people might say he gave it its soul back. He showed people the way to become Democrats again, and how to speak out."[18]

Maslin recalls a story from early July 2003, a few days after Dean for America blew the other campaigns away with its second-quarter fund-raising numbers. He called campaign manager Joe Trippi, and said, "Joe, you know what this is, don't you? This isn't Jimmy Carter or George McGovern or Jerry Brown or Ross Perot or any of the analogies people are making. You know who this is?" Invoking the founder of the Democratic Party, Trippi said, "Yeah, I know exactly who. It's Andrew Jackson." Maslin continues, "If we'd pulled this off, you'd have the equivalent of that moment when Andrew Jackson becomes president and the people just break down the fence at the White House and say, 'This is our place.'"

THE DEMOCRATS REBOOT

Bob Shrum—the powerful Democratic consultant who wrote Ted Kennedy's 1980 "The Dream Will Never Die" convention speech and the man whom *The Atlantic Monthly* in 2004 dubbed "Kerry's consigliere"—divides the 2004 election into two separate primaries: "There was the 2003 campaign, which Howard Dean won, which was 'Who dislikes Bush the most or who can express, most fervently, opposition to Bush?' Then there was the 2004 campaign, which was 'Who do I think might beat Bush and who do I think should be president?' "[1] On Election Day 2004, Americans decided that the Democrats had chosen the wrong guy in that second primary. Despite winning more popular votes than any previous presidential candidate in history, John Kerry lost.

The results of the 2004 election were, for Democrats, devastating. November 2 was a crushing and unexpected defeat. Despite an increasingly ominous-looking war in Iraq, despite the poor economic conditions, despite and in spite of everything, the voters had felt that John Kerry and the Democratic Party nationally had failed to deliver a compelling message. It was a strong repudiation of an opposition party that nominated as its presidential candidate a man who voted for the Bush tax cuts, voted for Bush's judicial nominees, voted to go to war in Iraq, and voted for Bush's environmental rollbacks. Now the online activists thought it was time for the Democrats to define their message and stand for something.

Sitting at his computer the next day in Burlington, Vermont, Joe Rospars, who had remained with Howard Dean's new group, Democracy for America, watched the president's victory speech as his fingers pounded away at the keyboard on his laptop. He clicked Send, and the e-mail began landing in hundreds of thousands of in-boxes around the country. It was a humbling e-mail but one that rallied the faithful beginning with its title: "What You Won't Hear on TV Today."

Rospars began by cataloging the Democratic victories: "Montana, one of the reddest states, has a new Democratic governor. First-time candidates for state legislatures from Hawaii to Connecticut beat incumbent Republicans. And a record number of us voted to change course—more Americans voted against George Bush than any sitting president in history. Today is not an ending. Regardless of the outcome yesterday, we have begun to revive our democracy. While we did not get the result we wanted in the presidential race, we laid the groundwork for a new generation of Democratic leaders." It ended with the quote from Martin Luther King Jr. that Dean had used a year before when declaring his presidential candidacy: "Our lives begin to end the day we become silent about things that matter."

Rospars could hardly have understood it at the time, but at the end of the 2004 campaign, the party's netroots, as the newly energized online activists were called, weren't ready to throw in the towel. They were just getting started.

For a month the party lay silent, licking its wounds. Angered by the outcome and the party's lackluster showing during a critical election, and hungry for solutions, progressive bloggers and discussions on sites like DailyKos and MyDD helped propel books by Thomas Frank (*What's the Matter with Kansas?*) and George Lakoff (*Don't*

Think of an Elephant) to the top of bestseller lists. Their theses were hotly debated in Democratic circles as a possible way to the future: Democrats needed to do a better job connecting with the middle of the country.

Don't Think of an Elephant, by Lakoff, a portly and grizzled Berkeley linguist, sold hundreds of thousands of copies, largely thanks to its buzz on left-leaning blogs. DailyKos's founder, Markos Moulitsas Zúniga, named it the "best book this cycle." Lakoff had first burst into political debate in 1996 when his *Moral Politics* argued that the GOP and the Democratic Party had grown out of fundamentally opposing family metaphors. Conservatives are the "strict father," who believes that an industrious work ethic, a strong moral compass, and rules that are set in stone ("Be back at 11 p.m., not a minute later") are all that are required for success in life. Liberals, on the other hand, are the "nurturing mother," someone who believes in caring for others and the pursuit of happiness, wherever that may lead. Lakoff sums up the differences as such: Arnold Schwarzenegger, who labels his opponents "girlie men," is a typical strict father conservative; Oprah Winfrey, who sits guests down for a heart-to-heart on her couch, is a typical nurturing mother liberal.

All around, on cable television, in newspaper columns and magazine articles, and online, the excuses in the wake of the 2004 loss were manifold. But many of those fingers were pointed directly at voters—"they" voted against their economic interest; "they" got scared by terrorism; "they" didn't understand our message. At a certain level, blaming the voters is a ridiculous argument even to attempt. "I've never actually seen a business model that blames consumers for not buying the product," Democratic activist Malia Luka says. "I think we might be able to take a lesson from Nike and other corporations who don't blame people for not buying their sneakers but instead figure out what's wrong with their sneaker so that people will buy it."

So what's wrong with the Democratic pair of sneakers? How'd it get to the point that the party founded by Andrew Jackson, championed by Franklin D. Roosevelt with his New Deal, and celebrated by Lyndon Johnson's Great Society has fallen to the point where the best it could manage in 2004 was yet another Massachusetts liberal who will be memorialized in *Bartlett's Famous Quotations* only for, "I actually did vote for the 87 billion dollars before I voted against it"?

In the first three national elections of the twenty-first century—2000, 2002, and 2004—Democrats turned time and again to economic populism, without realizing that times had changed and their message no longer resonated with broad swaths of the electorate. Additionally, as the Democratic Party's infrastructure atrophied, it relied increasingly on its interest groups to turn out their voters—meaning that the party didn't speak all that directly to voters. Messages were filtered through labor unions, feminist groups, environmental groups, or black leaders. There were few talking to the middle class. By 2004, ABC News exit polls indicated that the Democratic presidential vote now came from the most and least educated strata of the electorate, while Republicans could claim everything in between.

As former *Washington Post* political reporter Tom Edsall laid out, the "downscale" wing of the Democratic Party—which accounts for about 60 percent of the party's voters—consists of victims of economic competition, the unemployed and unemployable, union members, ethnic and racial minorities, the seven million Americans entangled in the criminal justice system, and those who are HIV positive or have AIDS. Meanwhile, the minority "upscale" wing, which dominates the party's debate and leadership, is completely different: They are 83 percent white, have the highest education level of any voting group, one-third have never married, 43 percent seldom or never attend religious services, four out of ten earn at least $75,000, 77 percent do not have a gun at home.[2] This latter group—the elite—has little in common with those who make up the majority of their own party—and are almost the polar opposite of the average Republican voter.

The party also has long struggled with a growing gender gap: The party now skews female by 10 percentage points. Clinton, who carried women by 16 points and lost men only by 1, fared far better than Kerry—he lost men by 11 and won women by only 3. It was not always this way. During the heydey of the Democratic ascendancy, from 1948 to 1976, the party always won the male vote, then heavily middle class and heavily organized labor. Now, among male and female voters with high school degrees or less—which pollsters often use as a proxy for working-class, blue-collar voters—Bush beat Al Gore by

17 points and then beat Kerry by 23 points. It was the college-educated whites who saved both Democratic candidates from an even larger drubbing.[3]

Karl Rove, who has made a career of stereotyping Democrats, has found his job made easier over time by the shifting focus of the party. A look at the language he uses reveals a lot of truth for the party circa 2000–2004: "desperate, out of the mainstream, willing to say or do anything to get elected, out of touch, wild-eyed, extreme, purely political, old, tired, unrepresentative of the people who elected them, sharing the sensibilities of Hollywood elites, obstructionist, out of ideas, more interested in partisan politics than in solving problems for the American people, liberal, captive to the Democrat Party's special interests, appealing to the Michael Moore, Howard Dean, MoveOn wing of the Democratic Party, loser, weak, negative."[4]

Perhaps most of all, potential Democratic voters felt betrayed and left behind. Politicians no longer addressed issues that mattered to the middle class.

Among those who felt that the Democratic Party had lost its way was a favorite of the bloggers: Andy Stern, the head of the powerful Service Employees International Union, the son of middle-class parents in West Orange, New Jersey, a graduate of the Ivy League University of Pennsylvania with a degree in urban planning, and a former state social worker. Soft-spoken, with warm but tired eyes, Stern had, as he sought to modernize and grow his union, warned of the dangers facing the Democratic Party and its traditional labor base.

Over nearly a decade, he had built SEIU into one of the most powerful forces on the left; his 1.8 million–strong, purple-clad service employees union in 2004 poured $65 million into Democratic election efforts. With that force at his back, his gentle and not-so-gentle musings carry real force. By 2004, though, he felt a bit like Don Quixote, chasing windmills across Washington in a futile quest for change; his thinking was years, if not decades, ahead of the party establishment.

On the opening day of the carefully scripted 2004 Democratic National Convention, Stern sat down with *The Washington Post*'s David Broder, its legendary political reporter, and fired another shot across the bow of the Democratic Party. It might be better for the Democrats and labor unions, Stern said, if John Kerry, the embodiment of the establishment he was battling, lost come November. "Both the party and its longtime ally, the labor movement are 'in deep crisis,' devoid of new ideas and working with archaic structures," Broder quoted Stern.

The labor union chief issued the necessary caveats—that from his perspective John Kerry would certainly be a better president than George W. Bush and that his union would do everything it could to ensure a Democratic victory—but his message was clear: The Democratic Party was fundamentally broken, rotten at a deep, core level—a "hollow party," in Stern's words—and the momentum for reform, the impetus of the revolution, would be lost if Kerry suddenly found himself in office. To see why Stern was so concerned about the effect of Kerry winning on the party's long-term investments, one needs to look no further than the Clinton years and the atrophied DNC that Terry McAuliffe had inherited in 2001.

Now, with Kerry's loss capping a disappointing election season, the party had time for real reflection and reevaluation. Beyond messaging, in the days and weeks after the November 2004 election, the party faithful decided that a more fundamental change needed to take place: They didn't want to talk about message until they settled the issue of leadership. Under Terry McAuliffe, the Democratic Party had finally paid off its $18 million debt, seen a sevenfold increase in donors from 400,000 to 2.7 million, boosted its collection of e-mails from 70,000 to 3.8 million, and taken its voter files from zero to 178 million. As McAuliffe's wife, Dorothy, jokes, "I often hear it said that my husband has been the greatest chairman in the history of the Democratic Party. And each time I hear it, my reaction is the same: 'Yes dear, I know.' "[5] But on Election Day—the only day that matters—the changes and advances weren't enough.

On DailyKos the morning after the election and even before Bush had formally been named the winner, founder Markos, a native of El Salvador and a feisty former army soldier, rallied his troops. "The McAuliffe reign has ended in disaster, with the Democratic Party in worse position electorally than when he came in as Chair in February 2001. We have lost seats in the House and Senate, and failed to cleanly take out the Worst President Ever. While McAuliffe was an artful fund-raiser, the party continued to lack the ability to develop a clear message or properly frame the political debate. And it's been killing us. Even if Kerry can pull off the victory, it's clear the Democratic Party as currently constituted is on its deathbed. It needs reforms, and it needs them now. Quite frankly, the status quo simply won't cut it." He concluded, "Howard Dean for DNC Chair."

A month later, on December 9, MoveOn.org's Eli Pariser fired off to his 1.6 million supporters an e-mail that returned to Howard Dean's rallying cry: "You have the power to take back the Democratic Party." Titled "Who will lead the Democratic Party?" Pariser wrote, "For years, the Party has been led by elite Washington insiders who are closer to corporate lobbyists than they are to the Democratic base. But we can't afford four more years of leadership by a consulting class of professional election losers. In the last year, grassroots contributors like us gave more than $300 million to the Kerry campaign and the DNC, and proved that the Party doesn't need corporate cash to be competitive." His next line read like a revolutionary's cry at the head of a mob armed with torches and pitchforks: "Now it's our Party: we bought it, we own it, and we're going to take it back."

By that point, the organization that had started out opposing Clinton's impeachment in 1998 had morphed into one of the true powerhouses of the left—thanks in no small part to its vigorous opposition to the Iraq war in sharp contrast to a party establishment that, until long after the invasion, had largely supported the president amid fears of being labeled soft on terrorism. MoveOn.org's political action arm had poured more than $11 million into the campaign, contributing to eighty-one candidates across the country. More than three hundred thousand people had contributed, mostly with donations under $100. Now Pariser and MoveOn.org wanted to exercise their newfound muscle. The online activists who had rallied to Dean's side during the early days of 2003 and 2004 now wanted him to lead them and the rest of the party. They were tired of losing.

While the party establishment singled out Tom Vilsack as a possible replacement for McAuliffe, the netroots weren't having any of it. When the blogosphere underscored that it would fight the establishment for the chairmanship, Vilsack backed down, and other establishment candidates demurred as well. The showdown dragged on. At the Democratic state party chairs' meeting in Florida, Jerome Armstrong and Matt Stoller of MyDD were thrown out for blogging the meeting, and bloggers turned their collective living room opposition research powers on possible chairs like cable mogul Leo Hindery, a longtime party funder who, when he found his path to the chairmanship blocked by bloggers, turned his jet around and flew home. Similar ignominious ends came to the chair campaigns of former congressmen Martin Frost and Tim Roemer, who were targeted by bloggers Kevin Drum, Chris Bowers, and Josh Marshall. Online groups helped organize a large Dean presence at each of the local and regional DNC events, and the grassroots-driven group that Dean had converted his presidential campaign into after his loss, Democracy for America, kept up a drumbeat too. Powered by intense pressure from the blogosphere, one by one the other establishment candidates for the DNC chairmanship dropped by the wayside, and Howard Dean, thanks to his grassroots leadership, online network, and online fund-raising prowess, emerged triumphant.

It suddenly appeared that an outsider would end up in the party's most insidery position. "The DNC chair race has exposed deep fissures within the Democratic Party. Some of these are ideological, but the real story of the race is the diffusion of power away from Washington and to new people and entities that have rushed to fill the power vacuum at the top of the party," reported Ryan Lizza, one of the best observers of the modern left, in *The New Republic*.[6]

On February 12, Howard Dean stood before thunderous applause in the main ballroom of the Washington Hilton—popularly known as the Hinckley Hilton for being the site of Reagan's attempted assassination in 1981. Dean, who won the position on a united voice vote, promised, "Today will be the beginning of the reemergence of the Democratic Party."

The next two years, even as the Democratic Party found itself without control of any branch of government, saw the party resurgent in every way as the Republicans' once-promising electoral victories seemed to melt away. In the days after the 2004 election, hubristic Republicans talked of a fundamental realignment in American politics—one where the Republicans would control for decades to come and the Democratic Party might go, as they said, "the way of the Whigs," disappearing into historical obscurity and irrelevancy. It might be a generation before Democrats regained any traction, some

Republicans boasted. However, over the next two years, the worsening situation in Iraq, a string of congressional Republican lobbying scandals led by Jack Abramoff, Randy "Duke" Cunningham, and Bob Ney, and the government's lack of response to Hurricane Katrina made the previously invincible Republican fortress appear more a house of cards. At the same time, the Democratic Party found that the energy within the party was taking place online through blogs, meetups, and groups like MoveOn.org.

In June 2006, the insidery political weekly *National Journal* asked its "Political Insiders" roundtable what impact the netroots would have on the midterms, and the resounding consensus was that it would help the Democrats. As one anonymous Republican grudgingly reported, "The one—and only—item that national Democrats can credit Howard Dean with: Galvanizing the Democrat internet efforts. The Democrats seem to have the upper hand, presently." An anonymous Democrat, meanwhile, wrote, "They have the capacity to instantly cut through and counter the Limbaughs and the Fox News' blubbering heads like the other corporate media entities should but don't have the guts to do so. Democrats are lucky they are doing what they are doing."[7]

The biggest contribution Democratic bloggers made to the 2006 campaign was fighting to expand the field of viable congressional candidates by raising money and attacking vulnerable Republican incumbents. Throughout the 2006 elections, the Democratic blogosphere received special attention from party leaders. As the *Chicago Tribune's* Naftali Bendavid reported, "Blogs had become a locus of activity for the party's frustrated left wing. They allowed combative liberals, diffused across the country, to form a bloc that could not be ignored, and they presented a challenge to those trying to move the Democratic Party to the center." Democratic Congressional Campaign Committee Chair Rahm Emanuel held regular monthly conference calls with influential bloggers to keep them in the loop on the party's increasingly promising attempt to win back the House, and DCCC staff posted on the blogs themselves. "The DCCC can focus on districts that are the most winnable," DailyKos's founder Markos explained. "We can do the others, every district, to spread the Republicans thin and to have a body there in case someone resigns. Some districts haven't seen Democrats in decades. This is where we can help them."[8] A group of bloggers, including Kos and MyDD's Chris Bowers, along with Matt Stoller of the "Swing State Project," endorsed a slate of congressional candidates on the grassroots fund-raising site ActBlue.com who had one major thing in common: They weren't expected to win. Tens of thousands of dollars in small-dollar contributions poured in and helped several of the targeted candidates win in November.

MoveOn.org, which was eight years old now and still growing strong, ran ads across the country targeting Republicans who had been caught "red-handed" taking contributions from industries seemingly at odds with their responsibilities to constituents. The millions of dollars in ads, paid for in small-dollar donations, targeted primarily at Republican incumbents in "second-tier" races, helped move several of the targeted races into top-tier pickup possibilities for Democrats, including Nancy Johnson in Connecticut, who was eventually defeated. The devastating ads opened, "Congresswoman Nancy Johnson. Seniors relied on her. Yet, Congresswoman Nancy Johnson accepted $400,000 from big drug companies and got caught red-handed voting for a law that actually prevents Medicare from negotiating lower drug prices for our seniors." Onscreen, the ad showed Johnson with one hand dyed bloodred, then photos of Tom DeLay, Dick Cheney, and Jack Abramoff all filled the screen with their hands also red. The ad's voice-over continued, "Tom DeLay, Dick Cheney, Jack Abramoff. And now Nancy Johnson. Another Republican caught red-handed." MoveOn.org ran the ads not just in an incumbent's home district but also in Washington, D.C., to ensure a psychological impact on Republican Hill staff. Just a few years earlier, the Democratic Party itself would never have dared such an in-your-face attack, but now the power in the party lay in grassroots organizations that, through small-dollar donations, could fund ads as they wanted.

Johnson's November defeat, as sweet as the victory was for MoveOn.org, paled in significance to another Connecticut race and the role there of bloggers. After years of being on the sidelines, progressive bloggers weren't content to sit by and let the party leaders make all the decisions. They were out for blood too. The first week in July 2006 saw a watershed moment for the new world involving the

Democratic primary for the U.S. Senate race in Connecticut. The week itself was largely unremarkable. After weeks of unseasonably cool weather and some torrential rain on the East Coast, it was beginning to settle into the uncomfortable heat and humidity of the middle of summer. Out west, wildfires raged. The World Cup finals were in full swing in Germany; Israeli tanks had invaded Gaza; and Mexico held a presidential election. It was also a landmark moment for old media and new media.

For one thing, it was the lowest-rated week in the history of broadcast television. Whereas a generation earlier the three broadcast giants virtually controlled the evening airwaves, by the early twenty-first century, the now four big networks—CBS, ABC, NBC, and Fox— garnered an average of only 20.8 million viewers per minute of prime time. The top-rated show of the week, Simon Cowell's *American Idol* spin-off, *America's Got Talent*, reached 12.03 million viewers, the only prime-time show to break ten million. Six out of the top ten shows reached only eight million and change. Out of a country with three hundred million people, the broadcast channels couldn't garner even 10 percent. Although the end had been coming for years—hastened along by the proliferation of cable channels, DVDs, video games, and the internet—one could make a good argument that it was this week in 2006 that marked the end of the television era. It was the first year that none of the trio that had headlined network news for a quarter century appeared at 6:30 p.m. in households around the country— Tom Brokaw, Dan Rather, and Peter Jennings were gone, replaced with Brian Williams, Katie Couric, and Charles Gibson. It was the second-lowest-rated year ever for the Academy Awards, and it was, also, the first year that cable's audience eclipsed that of the four major networks.

As the one-to-many broadcast world died slowly, the rising new world was, ironically, also marked in a television studio that same week. In Hartford, Connecticut's NBC 30 affiliate, Ned Lamont, a businessman and schoolteacher, walked into the studio and greeted Joe Lieberman, the veteran three-term U.S. senator and Al Gore's 2000 running mate for the presidency. Lieberman, always a bit dour, was visibly unhappy to be there. Lamont, whose entire public service career entailed a term on the Greenwich select board, was in the middle of an increasingly promising-looking primary challenge, threatening Lieberman's reelection as Lamont accused him of being out of touch with the people of Connecticut and for being too closely aligned with President Bush and the war in Iraq. Testy and combative throughout the debate, Lieberman seemed to hope that if he only swatted hard enough, this fly would go away.

Lamont's campaign had been powered and driven in large part by a national network of liberal bloggers, including support from MoveOn.org, upset over Lieberman's conservative views and his ongoing support for the war. Just days before the debate, dire-looking polls had forced Lieberman to announce that even if he lost the primary, he'd file as an independent in the general election. It was, historically, a stunning admission: This senior and respected senator, free of scandal and of an unimpeachable moral fiber, who had been chosen just six years prior as his party's nominee to the second-highest office in the land, was admitting that he was unsure whether his own party would nominate him to return to the job that he'd held for nearly two decades. Recognizing its importance, both MSNBC and C-SPAN broadcast the debate nationally, and although the hour-long debate itself was at best a draw—filled as it was with the vacuous promises, charges, countercharges, and veiled negative attacks that make up modern political discourse—it was a victory enough that the debate occurred at all.

A few weeks later—six years to the day after he was named Al Gore's running mate—Lieberman went down to a bitter defeat in the Democratic primary. Across the country, bloggers cheered in their living rooms. Lieberman, as an independent, would bounce back and win the three-way race in November, but the netroots had unmistakably flexed their muscles. They had held the mighty to account.

The Lieberman experience is perhaps one of the most potent examples of the new world: Politicians who have spent centuries isolated from direct accountability are now accountable for almost every word they say anywhere at any time. The digital playing field is a difficult adjustment for a system that despite its claims of honoring representative democracy doesn't particularly love actually being held responsible. For its first century and a half, the United States didn't allow senators to be elected by the people—preferring that it be left to the state legislatures—and the law still doesn't allow us to vote directly for the president—instead, technically, the president is still elected by electors chosen from each state. However, as the political machines of places like Chicago, Brooklyn, and Tammany Hall died after decades of dictating who got elected to what office, a new class of potentially even more powerful machines was coming onto the scene: computers.

EVEN THE MOST optimistic Democratic bloggers could hardly believe the news when they woke up on the morning after the November 2006 elections. Democrats had captured the House in a sweeping victory and even eked out a narrow majority in the Senate. For the first time since 1922, a political party did not lose a single seat in the House or the Senate. Not only did the Democrats win back thirty-plus seats in the body that had been held by the Republicans since 1994, but no Democratic incumbent was defeated and every retiring Democrat was replaced by another Democrat.[9] The newly installed party chair, Howard Dean, along with fiery DCCC chair Rahm Emanuel and DSCC chair Chuck Schumer, had led the party out of the political wilderness. Democrats were back.

Perhaps the most surprising aspect of waking up that morning, though, was realizing that a good argument could be made that YouTube, a website that didn't exist in 2004, had delivered the U.S. Senate to the Democrats. In two crucial Senate races, in Montana and Virginia, key Republican incumbents who had been the target of "gotcha" campaign journalism on the Web went down to defeat. The Democrats won control of the body by just a single seat.

The 2008 presidential election might have been a vastly different race were it not for the August day in 2006 when Virginia senator George Allen, considered one of the leading contenders for the Republican presidential nomination, looked straight into the camera held by S. R. Siddarth, a twenty-year-old staffer of his opponent's campaign, and uttered what was to become the most famous slur of the YouTube era. "This fellow over here with the yellow shirt, Macaca, or whatever his name is. He's with my opponent. He's following us around everywhere. And it's just great. We're going to places all over

Virginia, and he's having it on film and it's great to have you here and you show it to your opponent because he's never been there and probably will never come." Then Allen looked around at the audience, paused for a beat, and proceeded to complete his political suicide. "Let's give a welcome to Macaca, here. Welcome to America and the real world of Virginia."

Siddarth, a senior at the University of Virginia of Indian descent assigned to track Allen, had struck gold. Macaca, as America would come to learn in the following days, was the name of a long-tailed Asian monkey and an obscure racial slur. The video hit YouTube and quickly went from there to CNN and local TV news stations. Allen spent the rest of his losing campaign offering one apology or another. On Sean Hannity's radio show, for instance, he said, "I take full responsibility. I'm not offering any excuses because I said it, and no one else said it. It's a mistake. I apologize, and from the heart, I'm very, very sorry for it."

The power of the moment wasn't just the words—which connected with the latent fear among voters that Allen was a racist—but also in the video of him saying it. If Siddarth had merely had a tape recorder, the tape probably wouldn't have had the same impact and the statements certainly wouldn't have if it had just been a written summary of what Allen said.

The irony of the moment is that Allen, who went into the race with a vastly stronger operation and piles of cash, probably would have won if he'd spent the final four months of it lying on a beach not campaigning. It was only his actions on the campaign trail, captured on video and uploaded to the Web for all to see, that kept him from reelection. The loss moved Allen from the role of presidential heir apparent to presidential afterthought, landing him on the scrap heap of failed ambitions. As a popular former governor and senator, Allen would have been a formidable presidential candidate, and as the only top-tier social conservative in the race, he might easily have found himself the front-runner in terms of money, support, and organization.

Across Montana during the 2006 election, Republican Senate incumbent Conrad Burns also felt the impact of YouTube. Numerous clips showed Burns's rough edges—enough clips, in fact, that someone pulled together a "highlights" reel of the best.

His Democratic opponent, Jon Tester, assigned twenty-three-year-old staffer Kevin O'Brien to follow Burns and tape him whenever possible. Many of O'Brien's efforts made it onto the Web, including a snippet of Burns appearing to doze off during a farm bill hearing in Great Falls, which was watched more than one hundred thousand times online. Other clips showed some generally bizarre behavior: Burns claiming to have a secret plan for Iraq; Burns answering his cell phone in the middle of speaking at an event to talk to Hugo, the "nice little Guatemalan man" who was working on his house back in Virginia, and, although a tough conservative on immigration, noting with amusement that Hugo might not have a green card. It was all on tape.

Of course, YouTube's impact was felt beyond Virginia and Montana. In Missouri, a controversial ad by actor Michael J. Fox, who has Parkinson's disease, that attacked Republican senator Jim Talent for his opposition to possibly lifesaving stem cell research helped put Democrat Claire McCaskill over the top on Election Day—and the ad on YouTube garnered nearly three million views from around the country. In Florida's Thirteenth Congressional District, Tramm Hudson, a Republican primary candidate, found that his comments implying that blacks can't swim created quite a stir when the clip appeared online at the conservative blog RedState.com. Underscoring the role of too-candid moments being posted online, the Google video clip was titled "Tramm Hudson just lost." Indeed, he finished third in the primary.

Part of the power of these clips was that they were all played on local and, in some cases, national news shows, widening their reach far beyond YouTube or Google's video service, but their appearance first online helped fuel the story and drive attention. The sea change was that no network had to be convinced to run a video—online-only ads and YouTube "gotcha" moments could be posted by anyone anywhere—and with the increasing proliferation of handheld video cameras and video-capable cell phones, all politicians have to reorient themselves. Any public moment, any slip of the tongue, could bring them down.

As transformative as the 2006 congressional midterm elections were, though, in terms of technology and netroots power, the nation was now ready to enter an even larger playing field: the presidential race. This election in 2008 will be the first campaign in which YouTube can hold presidential wannabes accountable. The myriad threads of technology and politics are getting more and more intertwined with each passing month. As technology empowered individuals and the party establishment loses its stranglehold on power and message, outside of the political world some of the same technologies revolutionizing politics are busy changing the world.

2008: THE LAY OF THE LAND

There never was such a break-up. All the old buoys which have marked the channel of our lives seem to have been swept away.

—LORD ESHER, WRITING IN HIS DIARY AFTER THE FUNERAL
OF EDWARD VII ON THE EVE OF WORLD WAR I

There was a time when being president of the United States was a primarily domestically oriented job. Civil War–era Secretary of State William Henry Seward once roughly summed up American foreign policy as weak neighbors to the north, weak neighbors to the south, fish to the west, and fish to the east. It wasn't until the presidency of Theodore Roosevelt that a U.S. president even traveled overseas while in office. Roosevelt journeyed to Panama by boat to watch the construction of his beloved canal for three weeks in November 1906. By the end of the century, thanks to the majestic and jet-powered Air Force One, President Clinton visited twenty-two countries in 1994 alone, ranging from Hungary to Kuwait to the Philippines.

Even just eight years ago, foreign policy seemed to be slipping back into the distance, and the United States was comfortable electing a president remarkably aloof about the world around him. George W. Bush had traveled abroad only a handful of times before becoming president: three trips to Mexico, two to Israel, a three-day Thanksgiving visit in 1998 to Rome with one of his daughters, and a six-week-long 1975 China visit when his father was the U.S. envoy to Beijing.

Such provincialism would be a disqualification in the presidential election that is now upon us. In the past eight years, the forces of globalization and worldwide Islamic terrorism have made experience and knowledge of the larger world a prerequisite for elected officials from the president to big-city mayors to leaders of the local Chamber of Commerce. The World Wide Web reminds us at every moment just how interconnected the affairs of different peoples are. Today, we can read the front pages of the world's newspapers in our living room before work, and we understand more clearly than ever before how unrest in Africa or the Middle East can impact oil prices, how new technology can affect whether our job stays domestic or heads overseas, and how Chinese labor can make the prices at Wal-Mart lower every year.

Today, it's hardly possible for a presidential candidate to campaign without heading overseas. An Iraq visit is a command performance, as is generally Israel, and increasingly so are India and China. Massachusetts governor Mitt Romney, who saw the beginnings of globalization through his work around the world as a venture capitalist, took a weeklong tour of Japan, Korea, and China just before leaving the governorship. "When you look at what's happening right now in China, in Asia [we find] a much tougher competitor than we've ever faced before," he said in a speech just before departing. However, his position, he explained, was, "Boy, we're facing some tough competition, but Americans can compete with anybody."

The trip was, obliquely, a response to a question Romney got on one of his first journeys to Iowa in 2006 as a potential presidential contender. During one meeting, the first question from the audience was how would he make up for his lack of experience in world affairs. Romney quickly replied, "I think the answer is I gotta be seen in a lot of places . . . excuse me, not that I'll be seen—I will see a lot of places and will over the coming period of time." It was a Freudian slip of sorts, as the Boston Globe noted, since it's almost more important for

Romney to be seen visiting overseas and apparently learning about the world than it is for him actually to do it.[1]

In Beijing, Romney, wearing his trademark dark suit, white shirt, and patterned blue tie, spoke to about 110 students at the prestigious Tsinghua University, following in the footsteps of President Bush, who spoke there in 2002, and President Clinton, who spoke there in 2003. Romney told some personal anecdotes about his life at Bain Capital, quipping that the company's strong growth was almost as good as China's, and talked about U.S. foreign policy. He provided some business advice to the students from his career and answered questions about Iraq. He did, though, show that he was still learning how to navigate the world stage: Romney had to turn to the accompanying U.S. embassy staff to answer how much Chinese money is worth against the dollar, an issue that is a frequent flash point between the two nations.

The candidates and the voters understand that America's role in the world and our relationships with other nations are going to be front and center in the 2008 presidential campaign. One of John McCain's key selling points in entering the presidential race was his extensive knowledge of foreign policy, even as his trip to a Baghdad farmers' market proved one of his campaign's early stumbling blocks. Hillary Clinton, too, has made much of her visits to Iraq and her service on the Senate's Foreign Relations Committee. Barack Obama got much mileage out of his two-week tour of Africa just months before entering the presidential race, and one of his campaign's official press photos is of a thoughtful Obama standing in Moscow's Red Square, his jacket slung over his shoulder, watching and thinking about the world. We expect our leaders today more than ever to understand the fragile and unique place of the United States in the world.

The nation expects a foreign perspective from its leaders because of the dawning realization in the years since 9/11 that almost without notice, the world has gotten so intertwined economically that the "World Wide Web" describes today's economy as well as the internet system we all use. Today there are U.S. troops on the ground battling radical Islamists in Afghanistan and Iraq, and American men and women staring across the demilitarized zone on the Korean peninsula at a Communist North Korea. Thousands more are waiting for action in foreign ports like Germany and Japan. Yet the front lines of foreign policy in the twenty-first century are much more likely to be economic fault lines than ideological ones.

Through two terms, the Bush administration has struggled to figure out the right tone and approach to the global economy. Even as the economy came out of its official recession, the situation for American workers didn't appear to improve. Health-care premiums continued to climb. Jobs seemed fleeting. Debt soared and the national savings rate dropped into the negative range. The first six years of the twenty-first century were, in the words of *The New York Times*, "the first sustained period of economic growth since World War II that fails to offer a prolonged increase in real wages for most workers."[2] Whereas a family during Richard Nixon's administration had, in any given year, a one-in-fourteen chance of seeing its income drop by half, a family under George W. Bush faces odds of one in six. The nation's margin of safety is getting smaller each day. An admittedly unlikely populist, Kurt Andersen, who pens an economic column for *New York* magazine that celebrates the exploits of hedge fund managers and Wall Street investment bankers, says, "Middle-class Americans live more and more with the kind of gnawing existential uncertainty that used to be mainly a problem of the poor."[3] What Robert Reich termed the "Anxious Class" is growing larger as the world gets flatter, technology advances, and life shifts.

Yet due to the Bush administration's bungling of the war and its aftermath, most of the nation's leaders have remained focused on the worsening situation in Iraq. "Iraq has really swallowed the Bush presidency. It's the story that has blotted out the sun," explains Carl Cannon, a longtime White House reporter for *National Journal*. "To have an issue that dominates your presidency not be going well, it's tragic for all of us. There are so many other issues that just go ignored."

Of course, there are plenty of pressing reasons to focus on the war and its consequences—for they, no less than globalization, have effects far beyond the Persian Gulf. Bin Laden remains at large and Al Qaeda is still a threat. Neglect of the Middle East peace process has led to violence in the West Bank and Gaza, and in Lebanon as well. Just five years after it was routed in a brilliant and short war in Afghanistan, the Taliban is rising again. Iran is unruly at best, a loom-

ing threat at worst. Somalia, a haven for terrorists, is unstable and un-
governed, the site of war and U.S. attacks. Israel is at battle stations;
Hamas controls the Palestinian government. Saudi Arabia's state and
social compact appear ready to collapse at any moment.

And yet the war has obscured fundamental changes in the global
economy—changes that won't wait until the U.S. forces have departed from an orderly Baghdad. "I believe that fifty years from now,
when history is written, the rise of India and China will be seen as far
more important than the rise of Al Qaeda and 9/11," says Edward
Luce, the former bureau chief for the *Financial Times* in South Asia.
"These are truly epochal events that will change the face of the world,
but their rise is happening slowly. They're not happening in news
bytes. The rise is steady." He pauses for a moment and then continues. "What's that saying? The urgent drives out the merely important."

Globalization won't remain "merely important" for much longer.
Without quick and decisive action by the leaders elected in 2008,
America's title as the most powerful, most prosperous, most creative
country in the world will be under threat. The American people already know this. When the National Governors Association asked
pollster Frank Luntz to help them pitch innovation and investments
in the future to the public, he was shocked by what he found. For
starters, Americans believe that the country is on the wrong track, by
a margin of some 51 to 41 percent. The results are even more stark
when people are asked how the country is doing compared to five
years ago. While many Americans individually feel like they're better
off, by 62 to 20 percent they say the country is going off the rails.
Only one out of three people Luntz surveyed feels the country is doing better than it was in 2002. When Luntz asked whether they were
more concerned about their own future or the country's, 71 percent
said it was the future of the country that worried them. These are not
the numbers of a restful populace.

Americans also have strong opinions on the world economy. When
asked which country has the most innovative economy in the world
right now—Japan, China, or the United States—the United States
leads China 29 to 25 percent. Projecting twenty years into the future,
though, people see it as a 36–34 split for the United States and
China. As for the most powerful economy in the world, the United

States clearly leads China 51 to 20, but twenty years out people see the Asian power's rise; the 31-point lead today shrinks to only 11.

They know exactly where the fault lies: The number one reason people choose to explain why America won't have the most innovative economy in the world is their belief that other countries are more committed than the United States to education, schools, and youth. They know it's not because other countries have a lower-cost work-force—only 9 percent of people believe that's the main reason. It's about the schools and education. The numbers are even stronger for why the United States won't have the strongest, most powerful economy twenty years from now. Luntz's research shows that Americans believe the number one reason is still "other countries more committed to education/schools/youth than U.S." This is particularly troubling because two out of three Americans believe that in recent years our schools have not improved or have gotten worse—and one out of four believes schools have gotten "much worse."

They know, too, that solutions for problems on such a grand, national scale will not come magically from the open market system. In centuries past, the U.S. government recognized the massive investments and commitment of attention needed to ensure that the country's economy continues to thrive. Projects from the Erie Canal to the Panama Canal, the Brooklyn Bridge to Hoover Dam to the interstate highway system and the transcontinental railroad were all undertaken with commerce in mind. Acting on and addressing today's challenges in such a complicated political environment will require serious reconsideration of some popular long-held beliefs.

They know, in short, that the next president will need to think bigger than any president since Franklin Roosevelt—and is going to need the tax resources behind him or her. "You're going to need greater revenues than you have today in order to meet the challenges our country has," Robert Rubin told the nation's governors in February 2007, acknowledging that "the politics of that are very difficult" in a country where the rhetoric (if not the reality) skews antitax and antigovernment.

Studies and polls consistently show that people are willing to pay for gold-plated social and government services as long as they know why they're paying. In his polling, Luntz, who is considered the architect of the 1994 GOP "Contract with America," found that Americans of both parties are so concerned with the future that they'd support higher taxes to improve our prospects. In a poll, he told people that a major new campaign is under way to "revitalize America's competitiveness" that would involve better science and math education, skills training, and research and development, but also would require additional government funding—a pollster's code word for higher taxes. He found that 85 percent of those who voted for George W. Bush and 93 percent of John Kerry voters would support the effort. Here we have an issue so troubling that nine out of ten Americans are willing to pay out of their own pocket to solve it.

Why are they willing to pay more and invest in the future? No one doubts the consequences of failing to act. Nine out of ten Americans believe that if we fail to innovate, our economy and our children will be left behind in the twenty-first century.

ON SOME LEVEL, most of the politicians in Washington understand that the nation needs to make changes to compete in the twenty-first century, but understanding it and taking decisive action are two very different things.

In the summer of 2003, cabinet secretaries John Snow, Elaine Chao, and Don Evans took a two-day, six-city bus tour of Wisconsin and Minnesota. The "Jobs and Growth" tour didn't end up finding a lot of either. During a tour of a Harley-Davidson plant, the cabinet officials promised workers that the Bush tax cuts ensured that good times were ahead. The workers weren't convinced. As worker Mike Retzer complained to one journalist, "[Snow] did not address how we're controlling this free trade that's decimating our manufacturing and service jobs. Increasingly, service jobs are going overseas."[4] The questions at the Harley plant focused on the growing trade imbalance with China, and at a Green Bay roundtable, the trio of officials faced criticism on soaring health-care costs. Treasury Secretary Snow faced the wrath of an angry unemployed software programmer at the drive-through at Culver's Frozen Custard and ButterBurgers in Wausau, Wisconsin.[5] Throughout the tour, the bus caravan had been trailed by John Andrew, who had recently lost his job as a client-services manager, and he went through the Culver's drive-through almost twenty times before he caught Snow leaving the event inside.[6] When he confronted Snow through the driver's side window of his blue Honda Odyssey, the nation's top economic official offered him two words of advice: "Just wait." Things will get better. Andrew was furious. "I was stunned by the response," he said. "I'd like to see those words on a PR banner behind Snow at the podium: 'Jobs and Growth: Just Wait.' Maybe I should call Citibank, which holds my mortgage, and tell them 'Just Wait—I can't pay you this month.'" Andrew's account of the incident, posted on his website, www.jobforjohn.com, quickly became a rallying point for the victims of the new economy.

Four years later, the situation had hardly changed. Early one morning in February 2007, Arizona governor Janet Napolitano took the stage at the J. W. Marriott hotel in Washington to open the annual winter meeting of the National Governors Association. Standing with her vice chair, Minnesota governor Tim Pawlenty—whose name had been bandied about Republican circles as a possible 2008 vice presidential nominee—she began to discuss the issue on which the meeting would focus. Each year, the chair of the NGA chooses a theme, and Napolitano had chosen "Innovation America." At the press conference, where staff and corporate officials outnumbered the scattering of reporters by a ratio of about four to one, Napolitano launched into the challenges facing the states on the interrelated issues of economic development and education. "The plain fact of the matter is that the world has changed, it's changed very rapidly, and it's changing more rapidly still," she said. "I think that the American people understand that."

After Napolitano finished her introductory remarks, Pawlenty stepped up to the podium and thanked her for her leadership. "Governor Napolitano has called us to focus on innovation because the United States is under a great challenge in the world marketplace. We're not the biggest country—we're 300 million people—and increasingly we're not the low price provider of certain goods and services. We have to have a value-added proposition beyond volume and price. We have to think about value-added propositions like invention, innovation, productivity, and an increasingly skilled and efficient workforce," he said.

When Pawlenty finished summarizing the weekend's events, the media launched in with questions. Iraq promptly came up. During the twenty minutes of questions, not a single reporter asked a question about innovation, Napolitano's initiative, or any of the related issues. In fact, none of the articles about the NGA conference over the course of the weekend in *The Washington Post* or *The New York Times* even mentioned the word "innovation"; they focused instead on the governors' views of the presidential race and the rising cost of health insurance, missing the larger picture entirely.

What will it take for the challenges of globalization to take hold of our leaders the way the challenges of the war on terror did? It may take a crisis of the kind that no one would wish upon us. Unfortunately, this process that has bound the world together through bits, bytes, and bandwidth has been mostly silent—a quiet force sneaking up on us far from the front pages of the media. In most crises, there's almost always a single precipitating event that makes everyone sit up at the same time and pay attention—the launch of Sputnik, the Japanese attacking Pearl Harbor, the explosion of the battleship USS *Maine*, the firing on Fort Sumter. In America, at least, the current creeping crises—from global warming to globalized competition— have few moments that rise to the level of front-page news. In their way, the attacks of 9/11 were a warning of the effects of globalization, but one in which the United States didn't necessarily learn all the lessons it should have. The September 11 attacks were a product of the globalized, interconnected world—where money, people, and skills move freely and easily between countries and across oceans.

As the historian Walter Russell Mead explains, "Technological progress creates new challenges as well. If the strongest military force on the planet on September 11, 1901, had steamed into New York Harbor—I'm referring to the British Navy—and decided to spend the morning doing all the damage it could to New York, the British Navy in 1901 probably would have done as much damage as al-Qaeda, an NGO, was able to accomplish on September 11, 2001." In other words, a century ago, all of the firepower of the most powerful military force yet assembled in history would have struggled over several hours to do the amount of damage to America's largest city today inflicted by a score of minimally trained individuals funded by a shadowy man in a cave half a world away in a country most Americans couldn't locate on a map. And that's just the beginning. The attacks were a cold plunge into globalization, a wake-up call from a decade of post–Cold War peace and prosperity under President Clinton, when the United States seemed to be heading toward a world where our biggest concerns were shark attacks and missing blond girls.

President Bush's schedule that fateful morning, in its own way, was indicative of what the nation had come to expect of its government: He sat in a Florida elementary school classroom reading *The Pet Goat*. It was what the United States, in the days and hours before the power of globalization struck home, expected of our national leadership: very little. Since then, the nation has moved in countless ways to address the relatively narrow threat of jihadist terrorism without addressing with anywhere near the same fervor the larger, more complicated, and—as Edward Luce argues—more important issues of the rise of the world economy. The imbalance of attention cannot continue. Better airport security and border-crossing checks address only a narrow sliver of the threats of the twenty-first century—and, as I explore later, the stricter immigration policies since 9/11 actually hinder the nation's ability to compete globally. The campaign in 2008 will surely address terrorism in depth—pundits already predict it will be a "national security election"—but what about the threats to America's future that are more ephemeral? Will the candidates be able to step back from the day-to-day pressures of terrorism to see the larger framework?

"We're unlikely to have a 9/11 or a Pearl Harbor that launches this discussion," says Patrick Wilson of the Semiconductor Industry Association, and, he says, that's a big problem for the U.S. political system, which often responds only to strong stimuli. World War II was a distant thought for most Americans until Japan surprised the nation at Pearl Harbor. Years of reports and briefings on terrorism went largely ignored until Mohammed Atta boarded American Airlines Flight 11. "The reason that we're the wealthiest, most powerful nation in the history of the world is because we listened to those moments, and I don't know because of globalization and other problems whether we'll have a Sputnik moment. It's possible that this'll just be a slow ebb, but maybe there'll be a moment." As Wilson explains, the challenge for industry and workers in today's economy is that absent a headline-grabbing precipitating event, the U.S. government often moves very, very slowly. As he says, "The dynamism of the United States just isn't in its government."

Slow isn't an acceptable pace in a world connected by the internet. As much as technology is lowering costs, improving efficiency, and connecting people—empowering individuals and countries to reach new heights and present new economic challenges to the dominance of the United States—technology is also confronting the nation with new threats and challenges unthinkable even a few decades ago, as Walter Russell Mead described.

While the internet is a powerful tool for the spread of free markets and democracy, it is at the same time proving to be a dangerous re-cruiter for jihadists the world over. David Kilcullen, an Australian army officer who has spent a decade tracing the roots of the global radical Islamic upheaval now engulfing the United States and its al-lies, explains that the same technology that has made the war in Iraq the most covered in history has helped broaden the base of the insur-gency in Iraq and connect it to a larger struggle. "When you go to YouTube and look at one of these attacks on Iraq, all you see is the video," Kilcullen says. "If you go to some jihadist Web sites, you see the same video and then a button next to it that says, 'Click here and donate.' "[7] Kilcullen once figured out how many sources of informa-tion were available to a villager in Vietnam in 1966 as the U.S. war ef-fort heated up there and to an Afghan villager forty years later. The answer? Of the ten sources available to the Vietnamese villager, half were controlled by the government. In 2006, an Afghan could access information twenty-five ways—the internet counts as only one source in his list—and the government controlled only five. The balance were as open or more open to insurgents like Al Qaeda or the Taliban than the Afghan or U.S. government. Technology, after all, flattens for friend and foe alike, helping both our enemies and friends.

ASK JUST ABOUT any American today where the next foreign policy crisis will arise for the United States and you'll get a handful of answers, mostly focused around the trio of countries that President Bush painted broadly as the "axis of evil": Iraq, Iran, North Korea. Ask where the front line of conflict is, where the "hot spots" are, and you'll get answers like the mountainous regions of Afghanistan where Al Qaeda and the Taliban are regrouping. Or you might hear of Anbar province in Iraq or maybe the Gaza Strip and the West Bank in Israel. It's unlikely that you'll hear anything about the Hsinchu Industrial Park in Taiwan, potentially one of the biggest political fault lines in the modern world.

Taiwan, an island nation about the size of Connecticut and New Hampshire combined, founded the Hsinchu Industrial Park in 1980, and it now stretches to more than nineteen hundred acres. Among the 370 companies with combined revenues of some U.S.$25 billion that have offices in the park are the world's two leading semiconductor manufacturers—Taiwan Semiconductor Manufacturing Company and United Microelectronics Corporation—both of which were founded nearby at the gleaming Industrial Technology Research Institute, the largest research institution on the island. The park now encompasses offices, educational institutions, and even residential units for some hundred thousand employees and families. The two nearby universities have more than twenty thousand students, and they can relax at the nearby amusement park. Hsinchu is so critical to the world economy today that a September 1999 earthquake that led to a week-long shutdown saw worldwide production of electronics fall 7 percent below predictions, hurting profits and manufacturing for dozens of companies.[8] In addition to being near the geologic fault line that caused that 1999 earthquake, the park—ground zero for the new economy—is the center of one of the biggest political fault lines in the twenty-first century. Both the Chinese and Taiwanese armies and navies regularly hold exercises aimed at either invading or defending the island, and the U.S. Navy regularly bases ships nearby to ensure safe passage through the Taiwan Strait.

It's these potential crises and fault points that will be as critical to the president elected in 2008 as defeating Al Qaeda or stabilizing Iraq—perhaps, as the *Financial Times*'s Luce says, even more important. If nothing else, the appearance of the newly reinvented Beijing on the world stage in the middle of the presidential campaign should galvanize leaders to address how their worldview will help the United States compete in the twenty-first century.

By now the incredible rise of China has been so well documented that sometimes it seems the American media is part of the Communist propaganda machine, but the truth is simply that the country's growth is amazing. To compete in the twenty-first century, the next president must understand China and how its rise impacts the United States, which explains why so many of the 2008 candidates, like Romney, are making the journey across the Pacific. Even though China's booming economy is widespread knowledge, most Americans don't have any idea what that really means on the ground. In 2008, Beijing will launch itself on the world stage with the Summer Olympics. The celebration will be reminiscent of the 1936 Berlin Olympics where Adolf Hitler showcased the amazing revival of Nazi Germany. Long gone is the primitive third-world Chinese capital filled with bicycles and street markets. In its place is neon, CNN, luxury cars, and more than 450 of the Fortune 500 companies. Three hundred new buildings will greet Olympic visitors to Beijing in 2008, including masterpieces by Pritzker Prize–winning architects Rem Koolhaas and the Swedish team of Jacques Herzog and Pierre de Meuron, and a $700 million National Theater Building by French master Paul Andreu.[9]

The situation that the presidential candidates must face in 2008 is a China ascendant in every realm—economically, militarily, technologically, and educationally. "No country has ever before made a better run at climbing every step of economic development all at once," writes Ted C. Fishman in *China Inc.*[10] As the Chinese economy grows by leaps and bounds, the scale of the nation's power and scope is unfathomable to the United States with its "puny" three hundred million people. While official estimates put the Chinese population at 1.2 billion, intelligence agencies say it is more likely 1.5 billion—a number that if true would mean that the entire workforce of the European Union is unaccounted for in China's estimates.[11] China's economy is exploding, lifting a million people a month out of poverty and into the middle class. The construction boom in its major cities is stunning; six of the world's tallest buildings now are in China, and in 2005, Beijing alone, where one out of four cranes in the world is at work, used over half of all cement produced in the entire world. Nationally China's growth rate in 2006 topped 10 percent, its best year since 1995.

Even as it builds up its military, China understands that its role on the world stage will be determined more by its economic than its military might. Having millions of capitalists and entrepreneurs means more to a growing power these days than having millions of soldiers. Thus, when traveling abroad, China's leaders often make sure their trips focus not necessarily on diplomacy but on business. When China's prime minister, Wen Jiabao, made his first trip to India in April 2005, he didn't head right for New Dehli, the center of diplomacy, but instead traveled to Bangalore, a center of the nation's high-tech industry. At the gleaming new technology park that held Tata Consultancy Services, the nation's lead software exporter, he declared that the partnership between India, which provides software, and China, which provides hardware, would help signify the coming of the "Asian century." Almost exactly a year later, China's leader Hu Jintao visited the United States. Just like on Wen Jiabao's India trip, his first stop wasn't the White House or the New York Stock Exchange. Instead, he headed right for the center of what he saw as one of his nation's most important international relationships: Microsoft. After arriving at the Seattle airport, he met with the head of Starbucks, Howard Schultz, before touring Microsoft's Redmond campus and sitting down to dinner with tech pioneer Bill Gates. At Gates's sixty-five-thousand-square-foot mansion on Lake Washington, one hundred guests, along with the regular local elected officials, executives from Microsoft, Amazon.com, Boeing, Costco, and Weyerhaeuser, dined on smoked guinea fowl salad, Alaskan halibut, and rhubarb brown butter almond cake.[12] Jintao was far from the first world leader to stop by for a chat with Gates. "Increasingly, the Microsoft billionaire and his palatial Medina estate serve as an extension of the State Department. Sort of a White House West," noted the Seattle Post-Intelligencer.[13]

While the United States will be shocked awake in 2008 by the glittering modern city that greets athletes for the Beijing Olympics, India's transformative moments are more ephemeral. Britain experienced one in October 2006 when the Tata Group, the Indian-founded conglomerate that is becoming an increasing world presence, bought Corus, the company that had once been British Steel in a U.S.$8 billion deal. Prior to the deal, Tata was much smaller than Corus—it was ranked fifty-sixth in the world for steel production— but the rising Indian star found no shortage of global financial lenders who were ready to back the deal and gamble that the future of business lay in the East. With the combined outputs of Corus (then the ninth-largest world steel producer) and Tata, the new company produces more steel than once-proud giant U.S. Steel. The British papers were, all at once, proud, troubled, and curious—the largest foreign takeover ever by a company from Britain's former colony was a cause for joy and concern. BBC business editor Robert Peston called the acquisition "the changing of the guard on a global scale."[14] The successful Corus takeover bid, though, was only one of the deals under way at the sprawling Tata conglomerate. When it announced the bid in October 2006, it had already that month bought the Ritz-Carlton Hotel in Boston as well as a 30 percent stake in Joekels, the South African tea company, adding to its expanding drink portfolio, which includes Tetley Tea. Earlier in 2006, it had bought two major U.S. brands: Eight O'Clock Coffee and Glaceau's line of flavored waters. So far Tata's international expansion and the implications of the supersized growth of Indian firms have stayed mostly off the political radar in the United States. Don't expect that to continue, predicts Edward Luce, the former *Financial Times* South Asia bureau chief. "At some point soon, we're going to see the same thing in the U.S.," he says. "ICICI Bank will buy Citigroup or Wipro will buy IBM and then there'll be this rush to understand India. Right now, it's not urgent— it's just pressing."

Of course, the world is already so closely intertwined that seemingly localized events like the Taiwan earthquake ripple across the global markets. In his work forecasting the weather, early twentieth-century meteorologist Edward Lorenz noticed that incredibly small changes in his data eventually yielded vastly disparate outcomes. Tiny, almost unnoticeable things can set in motion massive change. His observation, now central to the idea of chaos theory, was boiled down to the famous line about how a butterfly flapping its wings in Brazil can lead to a hurricane halfway around the world.[15]

Lorenz's butterfly also describes the economically flat and inter-connected world of the twenty-first century. Huge damages can come from very unexpected places. In the United States, the Southwest is known for its stunning thunderstorms. Bolts of lightning cut across the wide-open sky during intense but often brief storms. Thus the storm that blew up one evening near Albuquerque, New Mexico, in March 2000 was hardly out of the ordinary. One bolt ignited a fire at the local Phillips Electronics semiconductor plant, but even that wasn't catastrophic. The plant staff extinguished the fire in less than ten minutes, and by the time the fire department arrived there was no fire to fight. The damage, at first glance, was minimal as well: eight trays of wafers used to make several thousand radio frequency chips used in cell phones. Phillips, properly, promptly informed its two main customers, Ericsson and Nokia, about the problem and said that production should resume quickly. It was only in the coming days that Phillips realized it had a much larger problem on its hands: The fire and rush of firefighters and plant staff had contaminated many of the clean areas necessary for chip production. What had been thought to be a week-long closure stretched to months. Nokia had acted quickly to line up a secondary source for its chips, but Ericsson had waited, thinking that the Phillips plant would soon be back online. Left with-out a supply of its new phones, Ericsson lost the global battle for the next generation of cell phones and ended up posting a $1.7 billion loss. By 2001, it had dropped out of the competition to manufacture phone handsets, handing that portion of its business over to Sony.[16]

In the new twenty-first-century economy, a single lightning bolt in Albuquerque led to a Swedish company losing the global battle over cell phones to a Finnish company and forcing it to hand the business off to a Japanese firm. Edward Lorenz and his butterfly would be proud, but the United States and its leaders need to be wary of mo-ments like this and the 1999 Taiwan earthquake that demonstrate just how much our future success is tied to the rest of the world. It's too late to stop this process—in the future technology will only bind the world more closely—but our leaders have many important choices to make in the next decade about the role of the global economy at home and abroad.

Eight years ago, at the end of a decade of relative peace and prosperity, it was possible for the world's most powerful country to elect a leader who wasn't interested in the world around him. We were, until 9/11, happy to have the president read books to children. Since then, the United States has rallied to address some of the national security threats posed by globalization—a world where we can now watch terrorists' propaganda videos on YouTube right next to the highlights of last week's *Saturday Night Live*. The United States, though, has not moved as aggressively to address the economic security threats posed by globalization. To say the pace of the U.S. government in addressing globalization has been merely "slow" is an understatement. Four years ago, John Snow told John Andrew, "Just wait," but unfortunately for the United States today, the Indians, Chinese, Irish, Australians, Finns, and Islamic terrorists aren't waiting. They're moving ahead now. Today the United States is playing and working in a high-stakes, worldwide competition, and U.S. voters expect their presidential candidates in 2008 to understand this new economy. They're impatient because, as Frank Luntz's research shows, they realize that domestic politics is now all too often tightly tied to our foreign policy.

THE COUNCIL ON COMPETITIVENESS, a group charged with examining the challenge of the rise of the Japanese, came together in the wake of the Reagan Commission on National Prosperity in 1986. Put together by Katharine Graham, the famed publisher of *The Washington Post*, and John Young, who headed the commission, the council was a unique mix of academics, labor leaders, and corporate titans. The world was mired in the Cold War, and the word "globalization" didn't even exist in popular parlance.

Twenty years later, the council—still in existence and now facing a very different world from the one it set out to address in the mid-1980s—sat down to examine how the United States was doing. Its 2006 *Competitiveness Index* found America preeminent by nearly every measure. In a country that has only 5 percent of the world's population, the United States has nearly one-third of the world's science and engineering researchers, 40 percent of the world's research and development investment, and 30 percent of all the scientific journal articles published worldwide. Yet in every single one of these categories—as well as by nearly any other metric—America's share of the science and technology pie is shrinking. "What is indisputable is that the world is changing in fundamental ways—and that the mix of policies and practices that worked so well historically may not assure the same outcomes as the future," the report concluded.[17]

Today the council is headed by Deborah Wince-Smith, and a visit to her corner office on Washington's K Street corridor makes clear how the world changes. Although her day job is as an expert on global economies, education, and trade, she's an archaeologist by training, and her office is decorated with the remnants and artifacts of past world powers—there are vases, rugs, crafts, and artwork from peoples and civilizations that once ruled the seas and empires that stretched across the known world. All of the cultures represented in her office have one similarity: At a critical point in some critical way, the civilization proved uncompetitive with its neighbors or others on the world stage. Crops failed, a war took its toll, a trading network collapsed, climate changes ravaged its prosperity, or disease struck the area. Some still exist today; some have been wiped off the earth altogether. Looking around her office is a humbling lesson in the inevitability of world change, the rise and fall of once invincible and powerful empires.

"All of these politician leaders in 2008 need to have a good vision and articulate that vision about what needs to change to drive a standard of living and prosperity that's as good and hopefully even better than what exists today. There's a real danger that this generation will be the first who's not better off than their parents," explains Bill Booher, Wince-Smith's deputy at the council, in his slow southern drawl.

"Will these candidates be appealing to our better angels or our fear factor?" Booher wonders. "Will the political better angels prevail or will candidates slip into the traditional views? What makes us sad is that in politics, negativism sells. To paint a very negative picture [of globalization] has proven to be a good way to get elected as both a Republican and a Democrat."

Booher says the council has hope that 2008 will be different—it has the potential to be the first time that globalization and competitiveness are addressed in a hopeful, meaningful way. "Two thousand eight will be the first campaign where the issues are viewed in a more positive way," he says. "This is becoming a genuine issue and it's a bipartisan one."

In the new world, what Booher calls the "dirty, dumb, and duplicative" jobs are heading overseas, and that's just fine. America's best work and its best talent have always been higher up the value chain—inventing, thinking, and creating what's new. "For two and a half centuries, we've been on an incredible opportunity path," he says, tracing his hand upward through the air like an airplane taking off. "It really does fall on our political leaders to see that it's not about fear but about continuing that opportunity path . . . The brain jobs are going to sustain America's prosperity and standard of living."

This is, in essence, the heart of a major problem for presidential candidates in the 2008 race: As the global market expands, it's easy to see the losers—the shuttered factories, abandoned parking lots, and headlines of more pink slips. It's harder to see the winners. A worker can't see the new markets opening up overseas, and few noticed the founding in a dorm room by Michael Dell of the soon-to-be computer giant Dell—which has provided jobs for seventy-eight thousand employees and brings in nearly $60 billion in revenue a year. Since new companies and new jobs are harder to see, workers tend to focus on the negative economic changes they can see. "You know who you are if you're going to lose a job. You don't know who you are if you're about to gain a job," says Pat Cleary, a longtime executive at the National Association of Manufacturers. "People can really play on those fears."

American competitiveness, trade, and the challenges of a global economy have long been potent subjects in politics. There are few easy choices and almost no easy answers. In 1988, Dick Gephardt won the Iowa caucus partly because of an ad that directly attacked the Korean government on trade policy. He stated he was "tired" of hearing American workers blamed for the economic woes when it was Korea's high taxes and tariffs on Chrysler's K-Car that drove the price from $10,000 to $48,000. If Korea wouldn't play fair, neither should the United States. He closed with the powerful line: "How many Americans are going to pay $48,000 for one of their Hyundais?"

Among Democrats especially, it's getting harder and harder to find vocal free traders anymore. Whereas one hundred Democrats voted for NAFTA in the early 1990s, by the time the Central American Free Trade Agreement rolled around in 2005, only fifteen Democrats supported it. Under pressure from labor unions in failing industries, it's easy, as Gephardt did in 1988, to revert to protectionist impulses— but it's the wrong way forward. The same is true of Democratic politicians who insist on always traveling in vehicles made by American companies—a photograph of a presidential candidate stepping out of a Nissan could be poisonous to union support. They fail to grasp that in 2008 it's more important to the U.S. economy that Toyota manufactures cars domestically than that Ford sells well in the Philippines. The politicians have allowed themselves to be cowed by Lou Dobbs's cheapening of the national discourse, but as is too often the case, politics is lagging behind reality.

Given the way that pundits like Lou Dobbs talk, it seems incredible that anyone would support trade, considering that it's sending all of our jobs overseas. But the truth is that it isn't. In fact, the National Association of Manufacturers (NAM) is a strong supporter of free trade because its members realize that protectionism only hurts their operations in the United States. NAM argues that free-trade agreements are the best thing that can happen to global trade—it's the countries like China, with which the United States doesn't have free-trade agreements in place, that cause the vast majority of our manufacturing trade deficit. In fact, protectionism in some cases costs more jobs than it protects. Domestic subsidies and tariffs have caused the price of sugar in the United States to rise 350 percent above the international average, which has driven some ten thousand jobs in midwestern candy factories overseas to where companies can buy sugar more cheaply. "There's an understandable temptation in America today . . . to think in terms of creating trade barriers. I think that'd be hugely counterproductive," former Treasury Secretary Robert Rubin says. "What we need to do is combine trade liberalization with a powerful domestic agenda . . . Too often, those who support trade liberalization don't support the domestic agenda, and those who support the domestic agenda don't support trade liberalization. We need to bring the two together."

Since the early days of this debate, though, our understanding of global trade and open markets has evolved significantly. Today, the critical point for policy makers is that it's possible for India, China, Europe, Africa, and the United States all to succeed. In fact, if the United States plays its cards right, the success of China and India—and the addition of nearly two billion new middle-class capitalists—could help power the United States to even greater heights. As Harvard professor Michael Porter stresses, the world economy is not a zero-sum game: "The success of other economies is not a failure of U.S. competitiveness—a job created there does not mean a job lost here, a new R&D lab built there does not mean one lost here, a rise in another country's exports does not necessarily mean a decline in ours. As all nations improve their productivity, wages rise and markets expand, creating the potential for rising prosperity for all." There's a very real—and achievable—scenario, though, where the United States can thrive and succeed in the global economy, if we begin to take these issues of competitiveness seriously and address them in a sustained, ongoing manner. Between now and 2020, the global middle class, which today represents around 1.3 billion people, will grow by another billion—and nine out of ten of those new consumers will come from the developing world, according to A. T. Kearney.[18] Bruce Mehlman, who served as the Bush administration's assistant commerce secretary for technology policy, explains that, according to Metcalf's Law, which states that the value of a network increases exponentially as more people connect—for instance, going from ten to one hundred users increases the value of a network by more than a factor of ten—the growing world pie is a huge benefit to the United States, one we should encourage as much as we can. "We will all be better off—as businesses, as nations, and as citizens of the world—when five billion people are online, instead of the five hundred million who have logged on so far," he says.

The choice that confronts the presidential candidates in 2008 is whether to take Mehlman's advice and recognize that the only successful future for the United States involves embracing globalization, or to continue the economic fearmongering that too often was the focus of the last campaign. The easy—and perhaps the most likely—route is certainly to continue pandering to Americans' worst fears. The harder route is to acknowledge the challenges ahead but explain that as a nation the United States can succeed and thrive in the global economy. Twenty years ago, Gary Hart's campaign posters challenged his party to recognize it needed new ideas with the slogan "The easy path is the beaten path. But the beaten path seldom leads to the future." Today, new thinking is again needed. The political debate in 2008 must blaze a new path that recognizes the realities of the economic and technological landscape today.

To see a success story of the new global economy, as well as how the complicated politics of America's role in the world played out in the last campaign, it's worth taking a look at Tony Raimondo, who represents the face of the new twenty-first-century global businessman. For more than a quarter century, he has been the head of Behlen Manufacturing in Columbus, Nebraska, a city of twenty-one thousand about ninety miles west of Omaha. Soon after he took over Behlen, which makes steel and agricultural products, he began to invest in exporting, saying, "It would be a key step to making our company stronger." His biggest market through the 1990s became China, where Behlen steel went into more than one hundred buildings. Then he realized that shipping steel overseas wasn't enough. "We weren't able to compete by exporting anymore," he says. "If you're going to get a significant market share . . . you're going to need to be inside that market." So Behlen launched a new joint venture in Beijing, manufacturing steel inside one of its most important markets.

Soon thereafter, in 2004, Raimondo's tiny venture into global trade ran smack into a wall of Democratic talking points and the toxic political landscape of globalization. When the Bush administration came under pressure to appoint its first "manufacturing czar" to address the growing challenges to the U.S. manufacturing industry, it turned to Raimondo. He went through several interviews, passed the security check, and the administration was all set to announce his appointment as assistant commerce secretary for manufacturing in March when word of the selection leaked to the Kerry campaign. John Kerry denounced the selection because of Behlen's manufacturing venture in China, saying that Raimondo was "a poster person" for policies "that have affected millions of Americans negatively." Raimonde ended up withdrawing before the announcement ever was made official.

Of course, the truth is a lot more complicated. All of the steel

Behlen manufactures in China stays in China—not an ounce is exported back to the United States—and there are, Raimondo says, many more people working at the company's Nebraska headquarters because of the additional work in China. Creating jobs in China, it turns out, can create jobs here. In fact, this is a critical point in understanding the new economic landscape in the United States: Global trade has been a huge benefit not just to international conglomerates but also to small firms—today small businesses with fewer than five hundred employees make up nearly 97 percent of all firms exporting from the United States.[19] To understand how important it is to foster innovation and entrepreneurship in the new economy, recognize first that economic growth is driven by small companies. In every year since 1991, job growth at those small firms with fewer than five hundred employees has outpaced growth of larger ones—in some years even providing all of the growth in the U.S. economy. The same is true for young new companies—those less than five years old—as opposed to older "mature" companies. Since 1980, the entire net growth of U.S. jobs has come from new companies. Mature companies have lost jobs over that period.[20]

Today Raimondo's brief foray into national politics is a distant memory and Behlen China is going gangbusters: More than two hundred tons of its steel is being used in the construction of the 2008 Olympic basketball arena and many more tons in the nearby building that will house the officials and referees. Raimondo, who continues to visit his Chinese operations each quarter, says, "I'm quite a China fan . . . They're on the move." Meanwhile, the United States, as Raimondo sees it from the middle of the country, has a tremendous challenge ahead, but the nation's leadership hasn't figured out how to address it positively and move forward. "We really need to make a decision about the competitiveness of our companies in the U.S., or our businesses are going to keep slipping away from us," he says. "I see the developing nations trying to improve the lives of their citizens and being tremendously successful for decades."

Looking ahead, he hopes that the 2008 presidential race is a bit more realistic and positive than the antitrade, antibusiness rhetoric put forward by John Kerry and John Edwards during the last campaign. And, though this may seem an odd position for a conservative businessman from Nebraska, he's hoping that someone steps in and solves the health-care problem. Behlen has seen its health-care bill soar from $2 million a year in 2000 to $6 million a year in 2006, an increase of roughly a million dollars a year—a pace his business certainly can't afford to see continue. America's success is contingent upon recognizing and confronting the future, and that requires a commitment by each candidate to lead with smart twenty-first-century policies and thoughtful debates.

"I'm hoping we're going to see a fresh face come out of this presidential campaign and one who understands that the competitiveness that we're talking about is the quality of life of our children and grandchildren. If we keep this burden on business, they're not going to have the opportunity to continue to improve their quality of life as we have for centuries," Raimondo says. "It's getting down to our kids having jobs. If we stop making things in America, there's no doubt in my mind that our quality of life will start to decline. Somewhere here we need someone who understands American competitiveness and [can] take us on a more positive course to compete in the long run globally."

The nation can't afford to see the rhetoric of the last campaign repeat itself, yet too often Raimondo's scenario still seems to be the norm. Politicians love to score cheap points by raising the outsourcing bogeyman of trade, especially in the era of Lou Dobbs and his endless fearmongering series "Exporting America." That's not helping and it's not going to make America more productive or competitive in the twenty-first century. Instead of walling off the U.S. economy, the nation should be worried that by not addressing the changing world economy, the United States could find that the best jobs go elsewhere. In 2008, the nation needs leaders who are willing to lead on this issue, not more of the same outdated protectionist rhetoric. It's no longer realistic.

Candidates must recognize the new landscape of the first campaign and have a plan for tackling the world as it actually exists today—one where terrorists, goods, and jobs can all move around the world almost effortlessly.

Both Republicans and Democrats too often have played to economic fears instead of hopes, but at the heart of facing these challenges in the coming decades are also larger party differences about ideology and beliefs. On more issues than not, the Republican Party's belief system, crystallized in the mid-1960s under Barry Goldwater, seems out of step in today's economy.

The national Republican Party since 2000 has pursued a policy that could best be described as a return to a modern version of Hobbes's state of nature. Without government, Hobbes argued, a state of nature exists—life is, in his famous phrase, "nasty, brutish, and short." Millennia ago, ancient peoples came together to form governments to protect, enrich, and prolong their lives. In return, they traded certain liberties to the state for protection. Under the Republican leadership at the dawn of the twenty-first century, everyone once again seemed on his or her own. Using the meaningless platitude of an "ownership society," the Republican Party did its best to let individuals have complete control over their own lives—plan for their own retirement, find their own health insurance, and pay for college. Those rights ceded by society centuries ago to the state were ours again to do with as we pleased.

Since the Goldwater revolution, the national GOP has been focused on reducing the size and influence of government at every chance—notwithstanding, of course, the ideologically inconsistent massive increase in spending and government size under President George W. Bush. The GOP view was perhaps must succinctly put in Reagan's 1981 inaugural address: "Government is not the solution to our problems; government is the problem." Grover Norquist, the hero of the right and godfather to much of the current GOP, has famously quipped, "I don't want to abolish government. I simply want to reduce it to the size where I can drag it into the bathroom and drown it in the bathtub." While both are great slogans and rallying cries, they are cheap shots and intellectually dishonest. Historically, national economic advancement has come only with government help. The railroads received huge government backing to crisscross the nation. A century later, Eisenhower—a Republican—understood that the interstate highway system, the largest public works project ever undertaken, was critical to commerce and the economy. And the internet would never have existed without backing from the government and the Defense Department. So it must be now: Reforms of health care and further expanding access to quality education will not come in a free market, and neither will a national broadband network or an energy policy that saves us from a future plagued by global warming.

In the next four chapters, I examine four of the most critical issues facing the United States—all of which must be addressed by the next president to ensure that the United States remains dominant in the world. Unfortunately, all four of these issues were largely ignored in the last campaign. We can't afford to see that happen again, to push this debate farther down the road. None of these problems have easy solutions. All of them require government intervention and investment. Previous models of education and health care, developed under agrarian or industrial economies, must undergo aggressive changes to be relevant in a knowledge-based economy. In some cases, it will not be easy. Achieving some positive ends down the road will require some up-front sacrifices.

The bold leadership necessary for the American people to endure sacrifice has a proud tradition in the White House. Abraham Lincoln, the father of the GOP, promised during the Civil War that the Union would be reunited, but he was honest in admitting that it would be long and difficult. It would require sacrifice and hardship, but in the end the Union, the nation, the people of the United States, would prevail. That type of leadership appears to be long gone from the Republican Party. In the last quarter century, Republican presidents have shown little inclination to ask anything of their voters—the record deficits under Reagan and George W. Bush let people think they can have it all without actually paying for it. When George H. W. Bush explained that sacrifice was needed to get us out of the recession under his administration and raised taxes, he was pilloried. Now the GOP's tendency is to do exactly the opposite—make government as easy as possible for the electorate. Far from challenging the American people in the months after 9/11, Bush pushed through the nation's first tax cuts in a time of war. He promised the country that everything would be okay if we all just went to the mall to shop.

The United States can thrive in the twenty-first century, but it's not assured and it won't be easy. Succeeding and thriving in a global age will be the result only of dedicated work at all levels of government, but most of all it will come only from honest and thoughtful leadership. The world has changed, but often politics seems stuck at least a decade behind in its rhetoric. We can see that the old models have broken down, but it's unclear whether the candidates today are up to the task—and to prove that he is ready is one reason Mitt Romney went to China. He knows that "Just wait" isn't an acceptable answer in 2008. The last campaign failed to tackle the future. This one must be different.

THE DIFFERENCES BETWEEN the last campaign and today's landscape aren't confined to issues of trade and economics. The transformed landscape of the first campaign in 2008 is also visible in the ways voters today will follow and interact with the presidential candidates as they roam the country. Whether the candidates like it or not, the whole world will be watching their campaigns, seeing how they react daily on the trail, and whether they're up to snuff and ready to face the challenges ahead. For one, the whistle-stop train tours of Harry Truman have long given way to multistate "fly-arounds" on chartered jets, but beyond that a host of new technologies allows candidates to reach more individuals with specially tailored messages and at the same time allows those individuals to see more of their candidates.

In the early 1970s, Timothy Crouse was just three years out of college when he convinced the editors of *Rolling Stone* to send him out on the presidential campaign trail with a unique mission: Cover the press instead of the candidates. The young Crouse, son of Broadway legend Russell Crouse, who wrote *The Sound of Music* among other hits, headed out into the middle of the 1972 presidential campaign between George McGovern and Richard Nixon, which became one of the most devastating blowouts in recent political history when Nixon beat McGovern by 520 electoral votes to 17. It remains the only election in the last half century when Minnesota voted for a Republican. Crouse's popular *Rolling Stone* tales from the trail became the best-selling book *The Boys on the Bus*, which related the story of the campaign through the eyes of the press and for the first time captured the pack mentality of the nearly all-male corps of correspondents who followed the candidates from place to place—including ink-stained wretches like Jules Witcover, Johnny Apple, and Robert Novak. At the time, Walter Mears, the correspondent for the Associated Press, was well on his way to establishing himself as one of the biggest names in political journalism. At the end of an event as the press corps filed its stories, the writers would clamor, "Walter! Walter! What's my lead?" The reporters understood that if they filed their stories and led with something other than that which led the AP wire story, their editors would complain. There was one story, and it was determined story by story, day by day, only by the Associated Press, the oldest and largest news-gathering organization in the world. If the AP didn't report it, it wasn't news. It was as if it had never happened.

Some thirty-five years later, it's hard to imagine such a world. Certainly the campaign plane that John Edwards used on his first official trip as a presidential candidate would have been unrecognizable to any of the "boys on the bus" from '72. As the sleek charter jet departed from New Orleans, the first stop on Edwards's four-state announcement tour, he settled back into his beige leather seat, while all around him the internet hummed. A photographer, who was shooting all digital with her Canon 5D camera, posted her work to the photo-sharing website Flickr.com. A videographer, Chuck Olsen from the site Rocketboom.com, was busy posting clips from the announcement to the video-sharing website YouTube. As the trip director, Sam Myers, who was on his eighth presidential campaign, plugged away on his Apple iBook, campaign internet strategist Matt Gross monitored what was happening online using Google searches and the blog aggregator site Memeorandum. Edwards's speech in New Orleans's Lower Ninth Ward, still devastated from the effects of Hurricane Katrina in 2005 and the disastrous federal response, had been broadcast live on the internet.

There were two reporters from the traditional mainstream media on board the Edwards plane—Michael Finnegan of the *Los Angeles Times* and *The Washington Post*'s Dan Balz, a legend in the press corps who had been with the paper since 1978. Balz typed furiously on his Dell laptop and, using his Verizon aircard, was able to post his repeatedly updated article to the paper's website. Sitting with the two of them, though, was perhaps the most unlikely political reporter in the country: former Microsoft engineer Robert Scoble, whose blog had catapulted him into the elite of the blogosphere.

Born seven years before Crouse took to the road with the "boys on the bus," Scoble had grown up about a mile from Apple's Cupertino headquarters in the heart of Silicon Valley, where his mother had worked for the computer company making Apple IIs. He learned to solder a computer motherboard at age eleven. In the 1990s, blogging pioneer Dave Winer convinced him to leave another in a string of tech jobs to work with Winer on blogs. The start-up ran out of money, and Scoble turned to Craigslist to find another job, where he promptly started blogging again, answering customer service questions. That job caught the attention of an executive at the technology beast itself: Microsoft. Scoble started in 2003 as their "technical evangelist." His blog, Scobleizer, quickly became a destination for geeks around the world, and his model of openness and honest discussion of Microsoft's flaws would come to be seen as a model for how powerful corporate blogging could be as a PR tool. When he announced in mid-2006 that he was leaving Bill Gates's world to join a video-blogging start-up, one of his colleagues lamented, "Robert did more in his three years at Microsoft to improve the corporate image than anyone I know." *The Economist* magazine dubbed him the technology behemoth's "Chief Humanizing Officer."

And so it was that Scoble ended up getting invited on the Edwards trip by Ryan Montoya, another campaign internet strategist—itself another position new to elections—to blog and provide a fresh perspective on the political ritual of the presidential announcement tour. Scoble's mainstream media credentials? Well, he remains one class short of a journalism degree at San Jose State, where he dropped out with one class to go. "I just didn't see the need to get a piece of paper seeing that I had already done 99.99 percent of the work and gotten as much value out of the process as I was going to get," he remarked.

The world Scoble entered when he started covering Edwards's campaign in New Orleans was as foreign to him as he seemed to the national press corps present. He spent hours sitting with Balz, picking the veteran's brain about politics, the process, and what campaigns were really like. He tried to photograph everything, but that became more difficult after his camera fell on the ground, so his video camera was ever-present, recording the moments big and small of the campaign's tour. His presence was a new experience for both him and the

campaign. When he began one interview with the candidate by asking, "Who are you?," Edwards, who first ran for the Senate in 1998
when the internet was just taking off and bloggers were an unknown
quantity, looked momentarily confused, blinked several times, and
rubbed his temple before replying, "I'm John Edwards."

Getting such a ringside view of a presidential campaign changed
Scoble's attitudes about every aspect of politics—from the candidate
himself to the press. "Before going on the plane, I thought it would be
a lot more glamorous. It's not. Edwards got, I think, eight hours of
sleep in three days," he blogged. "Keep in mind that almost all of
these candidates are rich. They could do something more fun with
their time. I found myself wondering if I had tens of millions in the
bank would I be working that hard? And, would I invite people on my
plane who could report every single move I made? I found that I was
far less cynical about the political process. Leave Edwards out of this.
Anyone who is doing this deserves a lot more support than we've been
giving political leaders. We treat politicians like scum, and I came
away with a lot more respect for the process and for the people who
put their ideas out in front of people." Just as he had once humanized
Microsoft with his down-to-earth language and honest takes on technology, Scoble now in 2008's first campaign was humanizing the candidates who had for a generation been just packaged television
personalities.

As part of his effort to get his ideas in front of voters and build support, Edwards met with local bloggers at each of his stops. The en-
counters were often videoed and posted to YouTube or to Scoble's
blog, Podtech.net, and Edwards fielded question after question from
the armchair pundits who would help determine whether he won the
nomination and eventually the presidency nearly two years down the
road. Edwards is hardly alone in using the new technologies available
to talk about the pressing issues of the campaign. Using these new
technologies, other candidates, too, tried to reach past the mass media to talk directly to voters and activists like bloggers who will help
decide this first campaign of a wired world.

To see how technology has already reshaped this presidential race,
look no further than the candidates' original announcements. In November, the night before her husband, Tom, announced his presiden-

tial bid, Christie Vilsack sent out an e-mail telling his supporters about the potluck dinner she and Tom had enjoyed their first night in Iowa in 1970. On the night before John Edwards announced his candidacy to the national press corps in New Orleans's Lower Ninth Ward, he sent out a text message to supporters' cell phones: "I have a special announcement. Please visit johnedwards.com now." A few weeks later, on a Tuesday morning, an e-mail arrived from Barack Obama saying that he was interested in running. Most people hadn't even read a news article or seen a television report about Obama's decision before they clicked on the link to his website and watched the three-minute announcement video showing him sitting in his study talking—talking to us, the voters. The same thing happened a few days later on Saturday from Hillary Clinton. In this election, the candidates' main audience is going to be less and less the mass media— instead they're reaching past the mass media to try to grab voters personally and let their own personalities shine. The American people clearly understand the challenges ahead and want to be reassured that the man or woman they elect will be able to face the future.

This shift is no inconsequential change. Since television started to nationalize our political discourse in the 1950s, electioneering became less about connecting with individuals and more a war for mass media attention. Thirty-second television ads and sound bites came to dominate. Now technology is reshaping that equation, returning the power to individuals. Not since the campaign of 1896—when an estimated five million people saw in person one of William Jennings Bryan's six hundred speeches as the country turned from an agrarian economy into an industrial one—have individuals played as big a role in an election as they will in 2008.

Together, the bloggers Edwards met on the trail, the voters at the receiving end of those e-mails and text messages, and the activists who watched those videos will play an unprecedented role in this election. They will have access to more information about the candidates in the first campaign than any campaign before. On the plus side for voters, the longer format of Web discussion, online videos, blogs, and e-mails helps allow for some more thoughtful and nuanced conversations on some of the tricky and complicated issues facing the United States today. Politicians don't have to boil down their ideas to a bumper sticker slogan for the evening news if they can talk directly to voters online. A four-minute YouTube interview is an eternity for politicians used to five- or ten-second sound bites.

The brand-new playing field of the 2008 election, complete with cell phone cameras, tech-savvy terrorists, and a global economy linked like never before, will help determine this uniquely important campaign—a campaign covered by people Tim Crouse never saw on the trail and focused on issues unimaginable to candidates of a previous era like William Jennings Bryan. The first campaign of a new era is upon us.

PART II

THE FIRST CAMPAIGN

ISSUE #1: INVESTING IN TWENTY-FIRST-CENTURY TECHNOLOGY

Appomattox, Virginia, is best known as a city of the past. Some 142 years ago, on Palm Sunday 1865, Robert E. Lee, the hero of the South, surrendered to Ulysses S. Grant in the stately living room of Wilber McLean. Three days later the rolling countryside and fields around the Appomattox Court House stood witness to a moving ceremony whereby some thirty thousand Confederate troops surrendered their arms and turned to head home in peace, ending for all intents and purposes the Civil War. The history in the area is rich and ever-present, the wounds of northern aggression still fresh for many. Farmers still find bullets in their fields, and thousands of tourists troop each year to the now-preserved national park. For me, though, Appomattox was the first stop in trying to understand the future and the challenges it holds for every community in the country.

Even though the presidential race was some twenty-six months

away and the "Macaca" moment that would rock the political world
still a year away, by September 2005 Virginia governor Mark Warner
already faced almost daily speculation in the press that the 2008 presidential race might shape up to be an all Old Dominion contest:
Warner versus the popular conservative Senator George Allen. Three
months before he left office, Warner traveled to Appomattox to celebrate one of his signature accomplishments.

After skimming over the treetops and fields that make up southern
Virginia at 120 miles per hour, the Bell 407 Virginia State Police heli-
copter pitched up and slowed as it prepared to settle on the lawn.
Crouched under the turning rotors, Warner jogged to a maroon Ford
Crown Victoria to drive the last few miles to the event site. It was a
beautiful fall day—one of the first with some crispness in the air—
and hardly a cloud was visible in the sky, which was bad news for the
crowd that had been standing in the sun for an hour waiting for
the tardy governor. As his car bumped to a stop near a dusty hay field,
he bounded out and headed right for the assembled schoolkids.

"What class you missing today?" he asked, looking inquisitively at
the kids as he grasped their tiny hands with his massive paw, smiling,
and making the students feel special with the practiced air of someone who's just wrapping up a term as an elected official.

"Business law," one boy replied.

"I might be able to get you a note from the governor." He smiled at
his own joke and the teens laughed politely.

The mayor of Appomattox, a rotund, dapper man named Ronnie
Spiggle—who had been mayor there for twenty-eight years as well as
serving as the local funeral director and who for the occasion of
Warner's visit wore a dark suit that could be useful in either role—
took the podium and began to sing the governor's praises. He boasted
that under Warner, Virginia was now the best-managed state in the
nation (according to *Governing* magazine) and bragged about how
Warner ran the government like a business. Then he turned to the
governor and said, deep from the heart, "You've never forgotten the
people of Southside."

Indeed, Warner didn't forget the rural residents of economically
depressed southwest and southside Virginia—communities like the
seventeen-hundred-strong town of Appomattox—that catapulted him

to office. He was deeply beholden to these people, who were won over in 2001 by his NASCAR truck, bluegrass music, and sportsmen campaigns. And so he came back again and again and again, trying to bring new jobs to a region hit hard by the collapses of the tobacco, textile, and manufacturing industries—those old economy industries long ago moved overseas even as the new economy set up shop on the other side of the Blue Ridge Mountains. In the last decade, this region, which once carried the weight of Virginia's industry and good-paying jobs, has been supplanted by the booming high tech corridor of northern Virginia, where companies like AOL are headquartered. The global economy giveth, and the global economy taketh away.

Taking the podium, Warner started in, talking as he often does like the shrewd businessman he is, a man now wealthy beyond his wildest imagination. "When I was a job applicant, I came down here and asked a lot of people to take a chance on me," he said. Now, he explained, he was here to give something back—a final thank-you for their trust and, as he might say, a down payment on a better future for the assembled students.

The project was the symbolic laying of broadband cable, a key part of one of the largest broadband initiatives anywhere in the country. Soon nearly seven hundred miles of broadband cable will connect nineteen thousand businesses and seven hundred thousand Virginians in six cities and twenty counties, much of that countryside rural. "Nowhere in the country will have better broadband access than Southside Virginia," Warner proclaimed, and he was soon drawing on the map displayed on an easel next to the podium—showing where the cable will go and explaining what a difference it will make. Broadband will be the railroad of the twenty-first century. "The communities on the railroad prospered. Those that weren't withered away," he told the crowd. Those communities that don't get broadband, though, will "face a level of challenge even greater than being left off the railway or the interstates." The money for the project came largely from the state's tobacco lawsuit funds, and so it was apropos in a way that the money was being invested back into the communities where the crop once flourished.

Warner, clad in jeans and a sea green polo shirt, clambered aboard a bulldozer and set about laying cable. He was supposed to ride only a few dozen yards with the trained engineer still sitting at the controls, but as his staff and the assembled crowd watched, he chatted it up with the cable-laying crew and the bulldozer steadily disappeared down over the hill, cable spewing out behind it. It was as if he wanted to wire the whole state himself.

A month after his stop in Appomattox, Mark Warner journeyed to Lebanon, a few hours farther west and even farther into economically depressed rural Virginia. In the town of thirty-three hundred, unemployment ran about double the average in the state. Lebanon, where cow pastures still surround the tiny high school, was about to become the shining example of Warner's futuristic Virginia. Apple pies came out by the dozens to celebrate the occasion.

Two major government contractors—CGI-AMS and Northrop Grumman—were poised to begin building multimillion-dollar facilities that would employ hundreds of software engineers, most hired locally out of the rolling hills and nearby colleges like Virginia Tech. The jobs would pay about $50,000, nearly double the local average, but—and here's where the companies themselves got really interested—still only about half the going rate for those jobs in the tight northern Virginia labor market. "This is the day southwest Virginia is transformed," Warner told the senior class at Lebanon High School as he stood next to the town's mayor, Nelson "Tony" Dodi. Dodi also served as the local high school principal, just as Appomattox's Ronny Spiggle doubled as the local mortician. "These are serious high-tech jobs that any city in Northern Virginia would die to get."

The jobs were possible in part because of Warner's efforts to wire rural Virginia for broadband technology. Lebanon was now as competitive in the global market as Bangalore. The other major factor, of course, was education: To help win the jobs, local officials pulled together data showing that 4,566 people had graduated with computer science degrees in the past five years from colleges within one hundred miles of Lebanon—including major institutions like Virginia Tech and James Madison University. Local community colleges came on board the effort too, offering to tailor courses to ensure the needs of the new contractors.

For the companies, locating jobs in rural communities with access to broadband technology and good education prospects is a middle ground between high-tech, high-wage markets like northern Virginia and sending those jobs to India or China; the companies call it "farmshoring." In fact, as the skilled labor market in India continues to boom, salaries between rural America and urban India aren't all that far apart.

When he was running for governor in 2001, Warner realized that he needed to meet rural Virginians on their own terms. He turned for help to a local political operative, Dave "Mudcat" Saunders, a proud, self-proclaimed redneck. Mudcat, as he's known to everyone, was a fifty-two-year-old, fast-talking, thick-accented, lifelong Virginian who'd visited Washington, D.C., only a handful of times in his life. He's the type of Southerner with a drawl that can turn "fuck" into a six syllable-long complete sentence, and he has a tendency to explain his approach on politics with phrases like, "You can jump all the rabbits you want but until you get 'em in the bag you got nothing." As Mudcat told me, he'd been initially wary of working for some tech millionaire from northern Virginia like Warner, but had come away impressed with the candidate's commitment to preserving the rural culture of the state. "We had a good horse," he drawls. "You can't win the Kentucky Derby with a mule."

As part of Warner's 2001 campaign, Mudcat, a huge bluegrass fan, came up with a bluegrass song that he got the well-known group the Dillards to play, and it eventually became an anthem of the campaign. The chorus included the phrase "Warner . . . to keep our children home." The phrase confused a lot of the city-dwellers who heard the song, but it was aimed squarely at communities like Lebanon, which were seeing a generation of children grow up on farms and in small towns only to be forced to abandon those already dying communities for jobs and opportunities elsewhere. Rural America and especially the rural South is being left behind in the global economy, partly due to their lack of educational opportunities. In the United States, the South is home to half the nation's rural adults who lack a high school degree.

At the end of the event in Lebanon, Michael Kiser, an eighteen-year-old senior at the high school, talked to *The Washington Post*'s technology reporter, Ellen McCarthy, who had made the long journey from D.C. down to the tip of the state to see the future of software development in the United States. "Before this, I always thought I'd have to move away," Kiser told McCarthy. "But I'd love to come back here . . . I want my kids to have the same experience I had."[1] The equation, in the end, was simple: Broadband investment plus solid educational achievement equals hope and opportunity for a new generation. Kiser's words, Warner would later say, were the proudest moment of his time as governor.

THERE IS NO MORE famous piece of historical theory in the United States than the thesis of Frederick Jackson Turner. He held that Americans are a restless people, driven ever forward (and west) by the desire for new frontiers. America was exceptional because it had never known boundaries. Even as the western land frontiers disappeared, the country has continued to be on the cutting edge of the frontiers of science, technology, and innovation. In the twenty-first century, we must choose to do the same.

At the dawn of the twenty-first century, the United States is still a nation unique for its innovation, ingenuity, and capitalistic drive. In *Forbes*'s 2000 survey of the 400 richest Americans, 263—roughly two-thirds—had created their own fortunes from scratch. Fewer than one in five people on the list had inherited enough to qualify.[2] Perhaps this drive is simply part of the genetic makeup of the restless pilgrims and hopeful workers who left behind their homelands in Europe to travel to the New World over a dozen generations ago. "There can be no doubt that if the United States is famous for its get-up-and-go, that is because Americans are descended from those who got up and came," argues economic historian John Steele Gordon.[3]

The combined encouragement of innovation and willingness to risk has over the course of the last century cemented America's role as the place where the future is invented. The internet as we know it today would never have happened without a two-century-old tradition of government investment in general research with unknown results. The United States succeeded in the twentieth century by being the country where the most exciting things happened and by attracting the restless thinkers who "got up and came."

In the new high-tech world today, we see signs of the importance of government-sponsored research all around us. American families cook dinners and reheat leftovers in microwaves that grew partly out of a Columbia laser research project sponsored by the Department of Defense. Tim Berners-Lee, whom we remember for inventing the World Wide Web, was working at CERN, a government research institute, when he revolutionized the way information is presented. Even the algorithms that serve as the basis for Google grew partly out of the work by the government-funded Digital Library Initiative.[4]

In fact, the United States, more than any other country, created the modern world economy—and it has benefited the country immensely. The internet? Primarily U.S. inventions. Netscape browsers and Google search engines? Primarily U.S. inventions. Travel to nearly any country in the world and one quickly finds signs of the United States—from a local McDonald's (maybe even with a drive-through) to a Gap to GM vehicles.

Now, though, the United States risks being overtaken in the world that it created. Some recent headlines paint a troubling trend:

- For the first time, in 2007, the world's best high-energy particle accelerator was outside the United States.
- The United States is no longer a net exporter of high-tech, going from a $54 billion surplus in 1990 to a $50 billion deficit in 2001.
- In 2005, out of the twenty-five largest IPOs worldwide, only one was held in the United States.
- Of 120 billion–plus chemical plants being built in the world, only one is in the United States, while fifty of them are in China.[5]
- Only three of the top ten recipients of U.S. patents in 2003 were U.S.-based companies.
- As a percentage of GDP, federal R & D dollars fell from nearly 2 percent in 1965 to 1 percent by 1990 to about 0.75 percent in the early 2000s.[6] Meanwhile, in the last decade, China's R & D investment by GDP has more than doubled to over 1.2 percent.

Addressing national problems like American competitiveness is supposed to be the task of our elected representatives, but by and large there's been little concentrated and focused effort to make the investments needed to ensure the continued success of American workers in a knowledge-based economy. Superficially perhaps this shouldn't be surprising. On many days, our elected leaders seem almost relics of the industrial age themselves.

The U.S. Senate in 2007 is the oldest it has ever been, according to the Senate historian, with the average age of members being sixty-two in the 110th Congress—including three of the five longest serving senators in the body's history.[7] Most of the leaders of Senate committees had graduated from college by the time television became widespread in American homes in the 1950s; the chair of the appropriations committee when the 110th Congress convened was Robert C. Byrd, who graduated from high school before World War II. Byrd, a talented and legendary orator and venerated member of the Senate, joined the body when he was well into his forties in 1959, at a time when television was just hitting the mainstream.

There are some exceptions. U.S. Senators Lamar Alexander and Jeff Bingaman saw the writing on the wall for American business soon after the 2004 election, and they asked the National Academy of Sciences to investigate the question of American competitiveness in the new knowledge-driven world. After their report, *Rising Above the Gathering Storm*, the leaders of the committee testified to Congress, "It is the unanimous view of our committee that America today faces a serious and intensifying challenge with regard to its future competitiveness and standard of living. Further, we appear to be on a losing path."

Of course it's one thing to diagnose the problem and something else entirely to actually fix it. The American political landscape is littered with abandoned solutions to once-pressing problems. The challenge for the country and its leaders today is to actually move forward with the investments critical to the prosperity of the next generation. The conclusion of the "Gathering Storm" committee appears to be right on. In dozens of conversations with academics, scientists, entrepreneurs, industry representatives, elected leaders, and government officials over the last year, I found a disturbing trend: Almost no one believed that the government understands what it needs to do to ensure that America remains the most innovative (and thereby competitive) country in the world.

John Chambers, the head of world IT giant Cisco Systems, sees the new international innovation playing field every day. As he says, "I talk to almost every major world leader on a regular basis. Not because I'm particularly interesting but because they understand the role that technology and the internet will play in the future of their country. And this goes from India to Australia to Japan, China, across Latin America and South America, Germany, UK, Eastern Europe, and almost all the Middle East countries. There's a common understanding today that regardless of your form of government, if you want to be successful as a leader you have to create jobs and economic stability. The key to that is a basis in education. The second key is how you create infrastructure. The old world infrastructure used to be electricity, water, and highways—not to say that's not important, they still are—but the new world is broadband."

Chambers, whose company is headquartered in San Jose, California, but has more than fifty-four thousand employees scattered across a score of countries on six continents, says he's only recently realized how important government is to the future of a successful business. "My view of governments used to be that the further we stayed away, the better it was, but boy was that naïve, because not only do we have the similar agenda as business but we have the same challenges that must be addressed in collaboration." And frankly, right now, he says, he's worried.

INNOVATION IN THE American economy began as the first settlers tried to scrape a living and permanent settlements out of the wilderness of the New World, but it wasn't until the beginning of the twentieth century that companies realized just how important innovation would be to their ongoing financial success. From the start, though, the government had an integral part in research and development—providing resources and insight and a home for research too broad for any single company.

During the 1800s, the government-funded land grant colleges grew into a national research network, and agencies like the Naval Observatory and the U.S. Geological Survey filled important niches. The government also supported promising technology when it could—the development of interchangeable parts by Eli Whitney was the result of his work at the Springfield Armory on the Connecticut River to develop rifles for the military; and the government made the first large-scale investment in Samuel Morse's telegraph by funding construction of a 40-mile link between the nation's capital and Baltimore in 1843. In 1890, it was work by the head of the census bureau, Herman Hollerith, that led to punch card–driven counting machines. Hollerith later sold his idea to what would become IBM. The Wright Brothers saw their conception of the airplane developed largely thanks to the patronage of the Army.[8] A century ago, the pioneer of a new model for business was Theodore Newton Vail, the mustached executive with sweeping, dramatic dark hair who took over as CEO of the struggling conglomerate AT&T in 1907.[9] The company had failed in an attempt to sell bonds and finance expansion, prompting J. P. Morgan's empire to acquire it and promote Vail to turn it around. At the time it seemed almost silly for a monopoly like AT&T to devote massive resources to research, but Vail recognized that the company would hold onto its monopoly only through continued innovation.

Vail thought Bell's facilities were subpar, and a year after taking over he proclaimed it essential to acquire "enough surplus to provide for and make possible any change of plant or equipment made desirable, if not necessary, by the evolution and development of the business." The team he began to assemble and the culture he created would cement decades of cutting-edge research long after he was gone. "As this strategy evolved, the expectational horizon of the enterprise pushed far into the future; eventually it came to be assumed within the Bell System that there would never be a time when technical innovation would no longer be needed or even when it would pay diminishing returns," explains Johns Hopkins historian Louis Galambos. Vail's efforts paid off handsomely for decades. Between 1947 and 1979, productivity in the Bell System increased an average of 3.8 percent a year, compared to just 1.8 percent in the domestic economy. Output per employee, meanwhile, increased 6.8 percent annually in Bell versus a stately 2.3 percent in the rest of the economy.[10]

Even though Vail retired in 1919, his work and legacy held strong for half a century—in 1924, Bell Telephone Laboratories became its own entity under Frank Jewett, and it remained a powerhouse of innovation well until the 1970s, when the "Ma Bell" model came under attack. For nearly sixty years, Bell Labs would stand as the epitome of solid and innovative corporate-backed research. Among many other things, the first experimental proof of the big bang that created the universe came out of a Bell Lab experiment.

During the 1920s and 1930s, an influential class of leaders in business and academia came to recognize how critical science and continued innovation would be to the economic success and national security of the United States, and in the early days of World War II, Franklin Roosevelt turned to one of the leaders of this group—Vannevar Bush, president of the Carnegie Institute—to direct the government's war-focused science efforts. Born in 1890 in Everett, Massachusetts, Bush had come of age as the United States transitioned from its agrarian roots to an urban, industrial nation. Based a few blocks north of the White House, Bush's Office of Scientific Research and Development grew to encompass the work of six thousand scientists—including roughly two-thirds of all of the nation's physicists. *Time* magazine, when it featured Bush on its cover, dubbed him "The General of the Physicists."

The war—and Bush's work in particular—would mark a sea change in the way government treated scientific research. Prior to the war, a small number of massive corporations had controlled most of the nation's research and development work. In 1938, just forty-five companies, from American Can to Chrysler to Eastman Kodak to RCA and Western Union, controlled half of all the research personnel in the United States.[11] Everything would change with the coming of the war. The next year, 1939, would mark the last year that U.S. corporations would outspend the government on R & D until the Reagan era, more than forty years later.

The war provided science with near-unlimited resources. The radiation lab at MIT got anything it wanted, including expensive equipment that, in peacetime, it would never have been able to afford. University administrators became increasingly concerned that the team of scientists assembled to combat Nazi Germany and Imperial Japan would balk at the heavy teaching loads and limited budgets of peace.[12] Something had to be done.

Midway through the war, West Virginia senator Harvey Kilgore began to push the government to examine how it would build on the war's scientific progress during peace. In November 1944 Roosevelt sent Bush a letter asking him to examine the federal commitment to science, writing,

> The information, the techniques, and the research experience developed by the Office of Scientific Research and Development and by the thousands of scientists in the universities and in private industry, should be used in the days of peace ahead for the improvement of the national health, the creation of new enterprises bringing new jobs, and the betterment of the national standard of living.
>
> New frontiers of the mind are before us, and if they are pioneered with the same vision, boldness, and drive with which we have waged this war we can create a fuller and more fruitful employment and a fuller and more fruitful life.

Bush's final report, delivered to President Truman just months after the death of FDR and titled *Science—The Endless Frontier*, became the driving force behind a generation of science and research investment in the United States. Eloquent and stately, Bush's report pulled together the work of four committees into a forceful recommendation for an unprecedented national commitment to science, research, and technology. It became an "instant smash hit" with the public and the press.[13]

"Science can be effective in the national welfare only as a member of the team, whether the conditions be peace or war. But without scientific progress no amount of achievement in other directions can insure our health, prosperity, and security as a nation in the modern world," Bush's report concluded. "To achieve these objectives—to secure a high level of employment, to maintain a position of world leadership—the flow of new scientific knowledge must be both continuous and substantial."

Bush laid out several commitments the government should make in order to ensure success—not least of all, forcefully advocating that government's role in science is critical. "It has been basic United States policy that Government should foster the opening of new frontiers. It opened the seas to clipper ships and furnished land for pioneers. Although these frontiers have more or less disappeared, the frontier of science remains. It is in keeping with the American tradition—one which has made the United States great—that new frontiers shall be made accessible for development by all American citizens. Science has been in the wings. It should be brought to the center of the stage—for in it lies much of our hope for the future."

Thanks in no small part to Bush's forceful call to action, the postwar era saw an explosion of investment and growth in science, technology, and research. The Atomic Energy Commission came into being in 1946; the National Institutes of Health was created in 1948 and expanded to a full eight different institutes by 1950 under Surgeon General Leonard A. Schele. Its budget soared from $50 million in 1951 to $81 million in 1955 and continued to grow from there.[14] Last, but hardly least, after years of back-and-forth with Congress, President Truman signed Vannevar Bush's idea into existence in May 1950, and the National Science Foundation was born. In signing the bill, Truman explained that the NSF was critical "to promote the progress of science, to advance the national health, prosperity, and welfare; to secure the national defense, and for other purposes."

The period from 1945 to the early 1970s would come to be known in America as the golden era of science. During the Cold War, scientists—especially physicists—were seen as national heroes. In the two decades after 1947, the federal budget for research and development jumped to $16.5 billion, more than twenty-five times what it had been before World War II.[15]

Another important advance in American innovation came with the growth of venture capital. In the 1800s, venture capital had been critical to the development of the railroads, steel, oil, and a few other enterprises, but in the first few years of the 1900s, venture capital began a century-long expansion that would fuel much of the American economy, and the expansion of business after World War II helped launch the modern industry.

Laurance Rockefeller helped fund the launch of Eastern Airlines and McDonnell Douglas in the late 1930s, and then in 1946 the first firm open to public investment started up, American Research and Development (ARD), which was founded by MIT president Karl Compton and Harvard Business School's General Georges F. Doriot, among others.[16] ARD's success in 1957 in turning a $70,000 investment in the Digital Equipment Corporation into a $355 million company helped encourage others into the field.[17] Much of the expansion of government contracting, research, and development during the postwar period was driven by venture capital.

In the late 1970s, the field of venture capital took off as the Department of Labor relaxed its "prudent man rule," which had governed pension funds and limited their ability to invest in high-risk groups like venture capital. Whereas in 1978, roughly $424 million was invested in venture capital, individuals accounted for a third of the investors and pension funds only about 15 percent. Just eight years later, more than $4 billion was in venture funds, and pensions accounted for fully half of the investment.[18] The expansion continued as technology blossomed in the world economy. Whereas venture capital didn't break the $5 billion mark until the 1980s (adjusted for inflation), by 2000, more than $60 billion was invested in venture capital.[19] In fact, according to economist Robert Atkinson, more money was invested in venture capital in 1999 and 2000 than in the prior twenty years combined.[20] It's not unrelated that the tech-heavy Nasdaq soared by 57 percent during the same period.

History has proved a strong correlation between innovation and venture capital. While it's a risky field, to be sure—many more enterprises fail than succeed—the willingness to invest start-up capital in new ideas in emerging fields has fueled some of the nation's greatest successes, particularly among the tech companies of the last two decades. One study that looked at investments from 1983 to 1992 estimated that venture capital was responsible for as much as 10 percent of the U.S. industrial innovations during that decade, even though the funding amounted to only 3 percent of corporate R & D.[21]

The expansion of funding, resources, and commitments from Vail through to the modern venture capitalist helped ensure that the United States for the first time in its history became an international center for skilled scientific talent. Whereas for generations scientists and scholars from the United States had traveled to Europe to be trained and to advance their careers, beginning in the 1930s the world's best now wanted to immigrate to the United States. Thanks to men like Bush and Vail and the government's willingness to invest in technology, America had established itself as the pinnacle of science—it was where exciting things happened and where innovation occurred.

IN A DIFFERENT ERA, under different leadership that recognized just how critical the looming question of American competitiveness would be to the country's future, Andrew Rasiej would have been a sort of modern-day Vannevar Bush—a respected industry guru tasked with strengthening public-private partnerships to combat the new tech-driven landscape. Instead, he's an independent tech entrepreneur and sounds like a present-day equivalent of Cassandra, the figure in Greek mythology who could predict the future but was cursed such that no one would ever believe her. Her gift of prescience thus became a constant source of frustration, especially as her warnings that Troy faced imminent destruction fell on disbelieving ears.

The challenge for the United States in the twenty-first century, says Rasiej, is that now we have a government that doesn't understand technology and the role it should have in our future. "Politicians don't know the difference between a server and a waiter. Sure, there are some examples of leaders who get it, particularly on the local level . . . but the average political professional has no clue how to integrate any of this new technology and culture into their lives," he explains.

Rasiej, who ran for public advocate in New York City on the platform of using technology and a wireless internet cloud to transform the way the nation's largest city is governed and improved, recalls a presentation he gave to the Democratic caucus in the U.S. Senate, where he discussed the digital divides facing the country and how Congress must act to address them. Then the questions came. "The first senator to be called on was Senator Dianne Feinstein, the senator from Silicon Valley, May 2001, she says, quote, 'Majority Leader Daschle, I don't believe the Senate should be on the internet until we get rid of pedophilia and pornography. The Senate should avoid the internet at all costs.' The second senator to raise his hand was Chuck Schumer: 'Hi, Andrew, good to see you. I get ten thousand e-mails a day. How do I get it to stop?' " Rasiej recalls. "It's as disconnected as you and I having invented a steam engine and we show it to a bunch of our friends who are farmers and ranchers and they look at it and ask, 'Can we use it to carry our horses to the fields?' "

Later, after 9/11, he successfully pitched Oregon senator Ron Wyden on creating a "National Tech Corps," whereby the government would identify people from industry leaders like Microsoft, Oracle, and Verizon, who would volunteer to respond to disaster areas to rebuild the technology infrastructure—people with unique database skills, cell phone and satellite phone specialists, network administrators, and the like. It passed the Senate 97–0 as part of the Homeland Security Act, with an appropriation of about $5 million—and has gone nowhere. "We still think that we need National Guard troops to fill sandbags if a river floods, but if those planes had flown into 60 Hudson Street, which is basically the northern end of the bandwidth hub for New York, Wall Street would have been destroyed. The economy would be massively hindered, and we wouldn't have had anyone who could rebuild it in a short period of time," Rasiej laments. "They just don't get it."

Nancy Scola is another Democratic technology expert and five-year veteran of Capitol Hill, who at the 2007 South by Southwest technology conference in Austin, Texas, pleaded to a room of laptop-wielding geeks for more experts in the new world to become politically active. "You can't really overstate how poorly understood technology is in Washington," she told them. She pointed to the example of the 2006 Deleting Online Predators Act, whereby 410 House members voted to prohibit social-networking sites like MySpace, Facebook, and Friendster from being used in libraries and schools so as to hinder the ability of child sex predators to gain access to them. It was a remarkably boneheaded bill that could have passed only in a body with no understanding of where the internet and online communities were headed.

By now, octogenarian Alaska senator Ted Stevens's bizarre explanation of the internet in the summer of 2006 is a cultural joke, but it underscores just how misunderstood technology is by the nation's aging and increasingly antiquated highest governing body. Rising as part of the debate over Net neutrality, Stevens said, "Again, the internet is not something you just dump something on. It's not a truck. It's a series of tubes. And if you don't understand those tubes can be filled and if they are filled, when you put your message in, it gets in line and it's going to be delayed by anyone that puts into that tube enormous amounts of material, enormous amounts of material." At another point, he said, "Just the other day, an internet was sent by my staff at 10 o'clock in the morning on Friday and I got it yesterday. Why? Because it got tangled up with all these things going on the internet commercially."

The moment was, in many respects, hilarious. Stevens's phrase "series of tubes" repeatedly made the rounds of the *Daily Show* and YouTube, and became the butt of many jokes by programmers, technology workers, and younger tech-savvy people. The utter sadness of the moment was lost on many: The president pro tempore of the U.S. Senate, who was fourth in line to the presidency, who had been the chair of the powerful Appropriations Committee until 2005, and was, at the time of his remarks, the chair of the body's Committee on Commerce, Science and Transportation, obviously possessed zero knowledge about the most powerful engine of the U.S. economy, the centerpiece of all of science and technology, and the most critical tool in the daily lives of millions of Americans. President Bush hardly has a better record. At various times he's referred to "the Internets" and admitted that he uses "the Google." What are the chances for thoughtful internet policies, major investments in future technology, and future research and development when policy making is being done by people who evidently don't even understand the difference between the internet and an e-mail?

Whereas past generations have turned to Vannevar Bush–like leaders to serve high-profile assignments, and government strived to attract the brightest minds it could, today the nation's best minds quickly end up in places like Silicon Valley or Wall Street, where their entrepreneurial spirit and lust for the new new thing is powering an economy increasingly disconnected from the government overseeing it. With the experts out of government, the government is out of touch.

This disconnect points to one of the biggest problems that the country faces today: the new economy lacks a political infrastructure. The older industries are the best organized and most entrenched and therefore the most powerful. They're able to land the meetings with officials that lead to government loans; it's their armies of lobbyists who can operate in back rooms, slipping in tax breaks and making competition for newcomers more difficult. In contrast to the legions of lawyers and lobbyists backing telephone and cable companies, when Google cofounder Sergey Brin—the sixteenth richest man in the world—came to Washington in June 2006 to speak with members of Congress he found himself on a humiliatingly disorganized journey and mocked in *The Washington Post* for being a "tourist." "We are a seven-year-old company. Having policy that really significantly affects us is kind of new to us. We are doing the best we can. I think we are putting in a pretty good effort, but we don't have, you know, thirty or one hundred years, or however long telcos have been lobbying Congress," he said. Across the board, the government is propping up the past rather than looking to the future. It's too easy to blame the closing steel mills and the collapsing manufacturing industry on the world economy. But as they say, when one door closes, another opens.

"Old economy stakeholders, whether in business and government or as consumers and workers, usually have more power than innovators. That is one reason these periods of transformation generally take 15 and 20 years, during which time economic growth usually stagnates. That is also why these transitional periods bring forth strong debates and arguments about the future and what kind of society is desirable," economist Robert Atkinson explains.[22]

Half a century ago, the Republican Party led the way on building the transportation infrastructure for the industrial age. Against strong opposition, President Dwight Eisenhower pushed through Congress a plan to build the interstate highway system, which he argued was necessary during the Cold War to help speed war matériel around the country but would also have huge benefits for interstate commerce. The national GOP, taken up with its small-government, low-tax ideology, has thus far showed little interest in investing in the future through technology like broadband and wireless connections. Beyond the lack of investment, though, Republicans in Congress in 2006 actively struck down a Democrat-led effort to ensure "Net neutrality," a complicated provision that would have ensured equal access to all for the internet. As going online becomes increasingly critical to people up and down the economy, the nation's telecommunications laws appear more and more a relic of the industrial age. Yet because the internet economy is so new, one 2006 study found that it's still being outspent on government lobbying by older firms by a margin of more than three to one.[23] The new economy, despite the wealth it has created and the wealth it can and will create in the coming years, is having a hard time getting its voice heard in Washington.

"People are just always very busy. When you're busy, you have your natural momentum, you're not making giant leaps," says labor leader Andy Stern. "You could be talking to the wind down here." He sighs, gesturing out his eighth-floor window at Capitol Hill off in the distance. "It's a disgrace that we built an interstate highway system as the basis of commerce in the post–World War II generation because that's what it took for a national economy, but we can't seem to build an internet infrastructure that's the basis of the twenty-first-century economy."

With the world at our heels, the United States can't afford to wait for the system to catch up—it needs to be acting now. "We are now equidistant from the New Deal as the New Deal was to the Civil War. You can't imagine Franklin Roosevelt looking at Abraham Lincoln's economy and saying we need to go back to the policies of 1865. It's hard to imagine going back to the policies of 1935. It's a fundamentally different economy on every level," explains Stern.

Maybe the solution lies outside Washington. Whereas nationally the small-government-minded Republican Party has shown little willingness to champion the massive infrastructure investments required for the twenty-first century, at the state and local levels, mayors and governors of both parties, such as Mark Warner in Virginia and Tim Pawlenty in Minnesota, are making investments to keep their constituents competitive. Ray Scheppach, the executive director of the National Governors Association, has seen an important evolution in the way state and local policy makers approach economic development. There's long been among officials, he said, a "pelt on the wall" mentality that concentrates on landing demonstrable economic development results today instead of focusing on the longer-term strategies. Stealing a factory or a new call center from a neighboring city, county, state, or (increasingly) country isn't as important as building an infrastructure that can support growth and jobs in the new economy. "Being a knowledge economy—it's about growing your own. That's a long-term strategy," Scheppach says. Sitting in his office just a block from the Capitol where the stately building fills most of the window, he says, "In this city, I don't think they get it yet."

Other countries understand that infrastructure investment today pays off tomorrow. John Chambers at Cisco explains, "Japan got that broadband is the highway of the future. It's not the solution, all they do is create the highways. Their broadband capability is twenty times the speed at one-twentieth the cost of our country's. The ability of tying broadband to economic advantages is something Senior Minister Lee in Singapore clearly understands. He's going to put something called a gigabit in every home in Singapore. A gigabit is only about a thousand to ten thousand times faster than what we have in our homes. That'll change his health-care system, create jobs. It'll allow them, a nation of several million, to compete in the global environment in a unique way."

Now London is rolling out a citywide wireless network, where anyone can get online for about £11 a month and keep the connection anywhere in the city. As Labour MP Derek Wyatt, head of the all-party parliamentary internet group, told the *Evening Standard*, "Such a large-scale project is an exciting prospect for communications in the UK, allowing people to send emails, make cheap phone calls, surf the internet, do business and even play games online, wherever they are."[24]

The United States is still lagging far behind in wireless and broadband investment; according to the latest numbers, we actually rank twelfth among the major industrialized nations for broadband penetration. As for the nation's internet penetration, the United States has actually fallen from fourth in the world in 2001 to fifteenth in 2007. When Rasiej ran for public advocate in New York on a platform of a citywide wireless network, he found that most of the city's policy makers didn't understand the transformative nature of the investment. "What I was running on was an idea to buy an entirely new structure for the city to run better, become more efficient, save money, and then in turn have money to solve other issues. When you build a wireless cloud, you can do far more than just get on the internet." Rasiej saw almost limitless possibilities "You can read meters, you can control traffic lights, social workers can have little devices on the refrigerator doors of elderly people that can send a message to the social worker if that door didn't open that day." Plans for citywide municipal Wi-Fi networks in cities like Philadelphia have run into strong opposition from cable and telecom companies, who see it as undermining their businesses, but as long as the costs for residential broadband and wireless remain high—$500 a year in some cities—whole classes of twenty-first-century workers will be left behind. As Rasiej says, "The reason that broadband needs to be available to everyone for $10 a month is because $500 a year doesn't allow a family to participate in the twenty-first century."

Just like Japan and England, other countries up and down the economic ladder are moving ahead with the investments they recognize they need to make. Toward the top of the economic pyramid, countries such as Finland, Sweden, New Zealand, Canada, and South Korea are making huge infrastructure investments to compete on the world stage. Farther down the pyramid are emerging economies like India, China, and Eastern European countries that recognize that investments in research, development, and infrastructure are their tickets to a better life in the twenty-first century.

In February 2002, Canada—the nation that proudly boasts it invented kerosene and five-pin bowling—announced a two-pronged national initiative to move the country to the forefront of innovation. "Achieving Excellence" focuses on investing in Canadian research and science while "Knowledge Matters" focuses on developing national skills-training necessary for the new economy. In announcing the initiative, the government pointed to statistics showing the wide divergence between educational achievement and job growth. Opportunities for those with a college degree or better grew 40 percent in the 1990s, while opportunities open to Canadians without a high school diploma fell by nearly 30 percent. The distance between the two paths, the government said, will only continue to grow.[25] As the nation's minister of human resources development, Jane Stewart, explained, "We now work in a labor market that demands we keep up with technological changes. We now live in a society that prides itself on continuous learning to get good jobs to support ourselves and our families. We now compete globally on the quality and quantity of our ideas."[26] As part of its effort, Canada has ambitious targets focused on R & D: double the government's commitment to R & D and raise its R & D investment from fifteenth in the world to fifth by 2010, as well as increase the amount of venture capital invested in the country to levels comparable to the United States.[27]

South Korea is fighting for the future too. In 1997 it set a national course to raise its R & D investment from 3.6 to 5 percent of the government budget—and almost made it, getting as high as 4.7 percent. A comparable change in the United States would pour more than $10 billion into R & D. Among industrialized advanced countries, Canada and South Korea are hardly the exception. In the decade from 1992 to 2002, for instance, investments in R & D as a share of GDP decreased in the United States while increasing in Japan (15 percent), Ireland (24 percent), Canada (33 percent), South Korea (51 percent), Sweden (57 percent), China (66 percent), and Israel (101 percent).[28]

Around the world, one of the biggest challenges facing the United States, its leaders, and the workforce going into 2008 is simply one of size. The United States, with its massive pool of 300 million consumption-heavy citizens, has long been the economic engine for the entire world. Globally, it has long won the size war: Japan is less than half our size and the entire European Union is only roughly the size of the United States itself. Not anymore. The two largest developing economies in Asia dwarf that of the United States, each with three to four times as many people as the latter has. While the United States certainly has a much larger pool of middle-class consumers, that lead is unlikely to last forever—if only because of the sheer number of potential Indian and Chinese consumers. To invest in their future, China and India have nearly endless reserves of talent. As the Chinese like to point out to their most talented students, even if, in China, you are a one-in-a-million talent, there are twelve hundred people just as good. India faces a similar talent pool. By another measure, 1.2 million Asian students graduated with science and engineering degrees in 2000, three times as many as the United States. The Council of Scientific Society Presidents estimates that if current trends continue, by 2010, midway through the next president's first term, more than 90 percent of all physical scientists and engineers in the world will be Asians working in Asia. To compete on such a grand scale, the United States needs every advantage it has and every advantage it can get in terms of technological investment to speed the country's way forward.

As China expert Ted Fishman points out, since China set about reforming its economy a generation ago, the country's official growth rate has been 9.5 percent a year, meaning that China is closing in on a thirty-year run during which its economy has doubled three times. Fishman says, "If the United States, which boomed in the eighties and nineties, had grown at China's rate since 1978, the U.S. economy would now be roughly its current size plus two Japanese economies added on."[29]

China, while still investing only about a third of the amount by GDP in research and development as the United States, has been increasing its investment by some 20 percent annually in the last decade, and that has helped to attract new investment from foreign companies. Whereas just a few years ago, U.S. companies spent almost no money doing R & D in China, they now spend upward of half a billion dollars a year in such research efforts.[30] The United Nations Conference on Trade and Development actually found that of foreign countries, China outranks the United States—with India coming in a close third—in terms of the most attractive place for offshore R & D. China similarly understands that its future lies in innovation and creation. In Beijing, Tsinghua University, the flagship Chinese campus, promised on its ninetieth anniversary in 2001 that it would be among the world's best by its one hundredth.[31]

The efforts are paying off, because a talented workforce and the necessary technical infrastructure are prerequisites to competing in the global economy. As Professor Richard Florida of the University of Toronto observes, "Companies have always sought to attract the best talent. The difference today is that instead of bringing that talent to their existing locations, companies are setting up facilities where the talent already exists."[32] In late March 2007, Intel and China announced that the company would build its first chip-manufacturing plant in the country. The project, "Fab 68" in industry parlance, was a massive $2.5 billion facility that would be Intel's first major production site in Asia and only its eighth outside the United States. Most are in the United States. "China is our fastest-growing major market, and we believe it's critical that we invest in markets that will provide for future growth to better serve our customers," Intel CEO Paul S. Otellini said at the time. As Patrick Wilson of the Semiconductor Industry Association explains, "A Fab—a fabrication facility—is the Holy Grail of economic development. There's nothing more valuable, period, than a greenfield virgin investment in a Fab. It's about $4.5 billion—to put that in perspective, it's about one third the cost of the Big Dig in Boston. It's about five Chrysler plants or four BMW facilities." Part of the reason a chip plant is so critical is that it feeds further investment and encourages other companies to locate nearby. Intel's Fab 68 was the country's first major chip plant, although, China hopes, not its last. The announcement, held in Beijing's ornate and important Great Hall of the People, launched what China hopes is a new chapter in its quest to become a world economic power. As Li Ke at the Semiconductor Research Center told *The New York Times*, "The Intel plant is very symbolic."[33] The new plant is also just the latest of many in China: Whereas in 1997 China had fewer than fifty research centers run by multinational corporations, it now has well over six hundred.

India and China know where their futures lie: Innovation for them is a matter of survival. It's hard when visiting India to miss the sense that history is in the making. The newspapers each day give the sense that India is on the cusp of greatness, that the Indians alive today are following their destiny. The cheerleading can be a bit overwhelming, but it's impossible to miss, and there are certainly great things happening: The Chennai newspaper's business pages one day this past winter featured the earnings reports of five Indian powerhouses—the annual growth rates the companies posted were 115 percent, 24 percent, 63 percent, 49 percent, and 116 percent. The only other major story that day on the business page? Sun Microsystems was expanding its Chennai operations.

It's also hard to miss the entrepreneurial spirit that infuses so much of India: Along with the comics, newspapers carry a page or two of quizzes—advanced math, vocabulary, and science questions to help people prepare for the rigorous college entrance examinations. Workplaces in the high-tech sector are dotted with inspirational signs. Slogans like "Try hard to get what you like or you'll have to like what you get" and "The harder you work the luckier you get" hang above the desks of the young professionals, many of whom are dressed in traditional saris, who plug away on PCs in the office of Sify, a Chennai-based internet service provider. "They are hungry. They have an . . . enormous drive to succeed. We pick them up and give them opportunities," Sify's David Appasamy explains.

As John Chambers of Cisco observes, "In the developing countries, interestingly enough, they're not going to follow the U.S. and be five or ten years behind. They're going to jump a generation in education, their infrastructure build-outs. They clearly understand that globalization has a tremendous number of very, very positive things but it creates opportunities for them and for us, as well as challenges."

Sify, which in October 1999 became the first Indian internet company to list on the Nasdaq, is busy rolling out a series of internet cafés and residential broadband access across India, which despite its high-tech reputation still remains remarkably low tech. Whereas in the United States there are about 950 computers per 1,000 people, in India the number is about 14 computers per thousand. The system that Sify is building, which relies on microwave-provided wireless connectivity, is so advanced that only a handful of U.S. cities could possibly compete with it. However, since many Indians still don't trust anything but cash—only about ten million of the nation's billion-plus people have a credit card—Sify, which is busy deploying an advanced state-of-the-art national twenty-first-century wireless system, must still send an eighteenth-century-style collection agent in person to each broadband customer to collect the month's fee in cash or by a paper check.

Indians today say they are excited to have children, to see the opportunities and changes that the coming years will bring to them and future generations. After all, to be alive at a critical moment in history is one of life's greatest gifts—it lends a sense of purpose and excitement to everyday life. There is certainly not that sense in the United States. There is a feeling that the United States might be at a similarly historical moment—but it's not a positive one. Overall there's a sense of dread of what the future might bring. For the first time, perhaps, Americans are scared of the future.

However, Americans shouldn't necessarily be afraid. As much as the sky may appear to be darkening for the United States, there's still a lot of blue sky—positive signs throughout our economy. The United States, according to the World Economic Forum, is the second most competitive economy in the world. It's first in technology and innovation, first in technological readiness, first in corporate spending on research and technology, and first with its research institutions. "China does not come within thirty countries of the U.S. on any of these points, and India breaks the top ten on only one count: the availability of scientists and engineers," foreign policy expert Fareed Zakaria points out.

Indeed, taken as a whole, there's a lot of good news for the U.S. economy, but that doesn't mean that we can be complacent as the developing world's economic growth explodes. "We're not playing catch-up. If anything, we're maintaining a rear-guard action," explains Bill Booher of the Council on Competitiveness.

According to a 2006 *BusinessWeek* study, sixteen of the twenty-five most innovative companies in the world are based in the United States, led by Apple, Google, and 3M. No other country has more than three companies on the list, and neither China nor India has a single company that makes the list.[34] That record of innovation is directly related to this fact too: The United States leads the world in universities and has more of the world's top universities than China, Japan, Germany, France, Canada, and Switzerland combined. There are also huge intangibles, just as there are in the developing world: In the United States those include a strong global brand, talented employees, and a deep and broad base of scientific research. Economists have estimated that there's as much "intangible investment" in the U.S. economy as there is "tangible investment."[35]

It's here—in innovation and entrepreneurship—where the United States has some of the best news for facing the new global economy. Overall, the United States has the most entrepreneurial workforce in the industrialized world. There are two kinds of entrepreneurs. What are known as "lifestyle" entrepreneurs start a company to employ themselves, family members, and perhaps a few other employees— these are your neighborhood bakers, café owners, boutique owners, plumbers, Web designers, and small consulting shops. The other category is "high-expectation" entrepreneurship, where people found a company to bring a new product or service to the market with the hope of expanding into a vast company—these are your Dells, Googles, and Microsofts. By percentage, the United States has more than double any other industrialized country in overall entrepreneurship and as much as three times as many "high-expectation" entrepreneurs as countries like Germany.[36]

"If innovation and entrepreneurship profoundly shaped the twentieth century, they will define the twenty-first," explains Bruce Mehlman. "Going forward, the nations with the most competitive technology-based economies will be those whose policies promote innovation, support entrepreneurship, and make sustained investments in scientific research and talent."

The U.S. is making some smart investments for the future: The pricey $3 billion project to map the human genome was obviously too large of an investment for any single company to make, but the government's support for it will transform the biotech and health-care industry for decades to come, spawning new industries, new companies, and new jobs along the way. Right now, though, the genome project is—like Mark Warner—the exception rather than the rule in U.S. policy.

Robert Rubin has watched the new world evolve and the twenty-first century arrive from two of the most powerful posts in American business, first as treasury secretary under President Clinton and now as an executive at Citigroup, the world financial giant. Although cautious by nature, he'd still bet on the United States in the years ahead. "The U.S. economy has enormous strengths—a dynamic culture, flexible labor market, a willingness to take risks, sheer size—and I believe that without question we could thrive in this transformative environment," he says in the guarded economistspeak so familiar to men like him and Alan Greenspan. "To realize that potential, we need to meet hugely consequential challenges, and the other side of this coin is that if we don't meet those challenges, I have this belief that in some time we could have serious difficulties. In that sense, the United States is at a critical juncture for the longer term, and what we do at this critical juncture will be enormously dependent on how well the political system rises to meet our challenges."

In this first presidential campaign of the twenty-first century, we must understand just how fundamentally our choices might affect the country for generations. Pundits often sum up elections as "change versus more of the same," and in this case "more of the same" won't solve any of our problems. Rubin says, "Moving forward in my judgment will require a political system in which there is a willingness to reach across partisan and ideological divides to find common ground, a willingness to acknowledge difficult issues and difficult trade-offs and finally a willingness to make tough political choices. And I believe our most fundamental challenge is to develop that willingness in our political system." So far, he says, it's not promising: "At the present time, in my view, in terms of meeting those challenges, we are far far from where we need to be on virtually every front."

The United States can't afford to let the issue of competitiveness continue to slide by under the radar. The issue of whether it will make the investments and decisions necessary to compete in the coming decades must be front and center in this first campaign. So far, there appears to be little serious discussion or focused debate on one of the subjects that will likely determine the fate of millions of workers in places like Appomattox or Lebanon, Virginia, and their new global competitors in Seoul, Chennai, Toronto, and Shanghai.

During a March 2007 conference he organized of technologists and political leaders, Andrew Rasiej took to the stage at New York's Pace University to ask a question and lay out a challenge: "Who will be America's first tech president?" Calling the internet the "dial tone of the twenty-first century," Rasiej explained that the next president must embrace the internet as a fundamental public good requiring ongoing government attention and investment—much like it currently invests in water, electricity, highways, and public education. As Mark Warner had explained to the crowd in Appomattox nearly two years earlier, those towns, counties, and states with poor internet connectivity will find themselves more economically disadvantaged in the twenty-first century than those towns the railroads bypassed in the 1800s.

At his conference, Rasiej outlined a six-point plan for what it will take to move U.S. policy into the twenty-first century, ranging from investing in broadband to wiring schools and better emphasizing teaching students to use computers, to finally creating the National

Tech Corps that would help rebuild critical national infrastructure after a disaster. Writing on their blog, Rasiej and Micah Sifry laid out the fundamental question about the internet: "As we prepare to pick the next President, we'd like to challenge all the candidates running to tell America: How should this public resource be used to make our country more competitive, more democratic, healthier, better educated, more secure and financially sound?"

If the United States has lost its edge on competitiveness a decade or two from now, it will be because the president elected in 2008 failed to understand the pressing global interconnected climate and failed to take action even while the United States could have done so easily. The last campaign in 2004 saw these issues come and go with nary a peep. The intervening years have seen the nation's leaders discuss using "the Google" and explain, helpfully, that the internet is "not a truck. It's a series of tubes." It's amusing for now, but it won't be for much longer, as China, India, South Korea, Canada, and a dozen other countries come racing up in the rearview mirror. The nation can ill afford to let the opportunity of 2008 pass by without action. This must be a campaign focused on the challenges of the future. Cisco's John Chambers believes the only thing holding the United States back is its will: "What is possible? Broadband to every house, every state in the country in what? Four years, six years, or ten years? I'd argue when that occurs is largely an issue of what objective we set and how hard we go after it to make it happen."

ISSUE #2: EDUCATING AND RECRUITING TWENTY-FIRST-CENTURY WORKERS

A few weeks after his journey to China and Tsinghua University to see the future of the twenty-first century, Mitt Romney traveled to Michigan to kick off his presidential campaign at the center of the aging industrial economy. Although he had many symbolic locations to choose from—including Utah, where he saved the 2002 Salt Lake City Olympics and his ancestors had lived for generations, or maybe Massachusetts, where he served for four years as governor—Romney chose to announce his presidential campaign at the Henry Ford Museum in Dearborn, Michigan, the state where his father, George, served proudly as an auto executive and three-term governor, and even flirted with a presidential run in 1968. Dearborn is just about twenty miles from the posh neighborhood of Bloomfield Hills where he grew up.

A few days earlier Barack Obama had stood outside on a cold morning to announce his historic presidential bid in Springfield, Illinois, where Abraham Lincoln had delivered his famous speech proclaiming, "A house divided against itself cannot stand." Dressed in a long dark overcoat buttoned up to combat the 12-degree weather, Obama told the crowd, "I recognize there is a certain presumptuousness—a certain audacity—to this announcement. I know I haven't spent a lot of time learning the ways of Washington. But I've been there long enough to know that the ways of Washington must change." In a twenty-two-minute speech that emphasized how he was a different kind of politician from a pre-1960s generation, Obama laid out how the country's leadership was failing to address the major problems of our time. "All of us know," he said, "what those challenges are today—a war with no end, a dependence on oil that threatens our future, schools where too many children aren't learning, and families struggling paycheck to paycheck despite working as hard as they can. What's stopped us from meeting these challenges is not the absence of sound policies and sensible plans. What's stopped us is the failure of leadership, the smallness of our politics—the ease with which we're distracted by the petty and trivial, our chronic avoidance of tough decisions, our preference for scoring cheap political points instead of rolling up our sleeves and building a working consensus to tackle big problems."

Obama's theme of a political system failing to address the major needs of the country would sound familiar to those in the audience at Romney's speech. The needs of the first campaign—the need for new ideas, new innovations, and new approaches for new challenges in a new age—were there in both speeches, even as they each evoked history of a different kind. Instead of the political history of Lincoln, Romney's speech bespoke history of the economic kind. On the Michigan stage, devoid of bunting and flags, that looked more like a corporate annual meeting than a presidential campaign rally, he was framed overhead by a silver DC-3, the commercial airliner that transformed aviation and helped save Berlin during the 1947 airlift. As props, a pea green Ford Hybrid that signaled the future was parked on his right, and on his left was a white 1963 Nash Rambler, the nation's first "economy" car, which his father had introduced as head of American Motors. It earned a then-stunning twenty-five miles to the gallon and helped save the company in the 1960s.

"Innovation and transformation have been at the heart of America's success. If there ever was a time when innovation and transformation were needed in government, it is now," Romney declared during his twenty-minute speech. "Even as America faces a new generation of challenges, the halls of government are clogged with petty politics and stuffed with peddlers of influence. It is time for innovation and transformation in Washington. It is what our country needs. It is what our people deserve."

Throughout his speech, Romney stressed the innovation theme, mentioning the word almost a dozen times. And he spoke like the venture capitalist he is, framing the campaign ahead as an effort to lead the largest business in the world—the United States and its trillion-dollar-a-year government. He was, after all, the only presidential candidate who had run a business and governed a state. "Throughout my life, I have pursued innovation and transformation. It has taught me the vital lessons that come only from experience, from failures and successes, from the private, public, and voluntary sectors, from small and large enterprise, from leading a state, from being in the arena, not just talking about it. Talk is easy, talk is cheap. It is doing that is hard. And it is only in doing that hope and dreams come to life."

It was, as presidential announcements go, a relatively good speech, perhaps better on paper than in his delivery, which rightly emphasized the challenges of the new world. However, Romney's choice of the Henry Ford Museum also drew attention to just how much the global economic landscape has changed in recent decades.

At the museum, tourists can study and learn about one of the greatest industrial complexes the world has ever seen and find out for themselves what American innovation had wrought in twentieth-century America. The museum began as Henry Ford's personal collection of historical oddities and now includes every kind of Americana, such as an Oscar Mayer Wienermobile and the presidential limousine in which John F. Kennedy was shot in 1963. Nearby is Greenfield Village, a 260-acre outdoor museum where Ford brought notable buildings from around the country, including Noah Webster's Connecticut house and the Wright brothers' bicycle workshop from Dayton, Ohio.

From the museum, tourists can also board a bus to tour the living artifact of a once-proud industry, the River Rouge Ford facility, which at its height employed one hundred thousand people in a sprawling complex that measured its dimensions in miles not acres and was unlike anything anyone had ever seen before. At its peak, Ford ran its own railroad over more than one hundred miles of track, generated its own electricity, processed its own ore brought in by its own fleet of ships, and, using more than a square mile of factory floor, turned raw materials into finished cars all in one place. The site—which over the years made the Model A, the Thunderbird, and four decades of varying Mustangs, among other models—belched smoke and flame, and long resisted unions, most famously at the bloody 1937 Battle of the Overpass. Today workers are represented by the United Auto Workers, which has seen its membership plummet amid rounds and rounds of layoffs, and signs in the plant's parking lot proclaim, "Ford Vehicles Only." There's more room in the lots than there used to be. Today the plant employs only six thousand workers. Within twenty-four hours of Romney's announcement, another testament to the struggles facing Michigan and its beloved auto industry arrived. Chrysler announced that it would lay off eleven thousand additional workers, some 18 percent of its North American workforce. Later in the spring, German auto powerhouse Daimler would happily rid itself of the struggling Chrysler brand altogether, selling it at a bargain rate to a U.S. private equity group. If only George Romney were still alive to help turn the industry around again.

If Romney's intention had been to look to the possibilities of the future rather than be reminded of our nation's past successes, he might have wanted to travel about forty-five minutes west to Ann Arbor, the site of the flagship campus of the University of Michigan. Presidents and presidential candidates have regularly used it as a stage for major new ideas. It was on the Michigan campus that John F. Kennedy first outlined his idea for the Peace Corps and where Lyndon Johnson outlined his for the Great Society in 1964. Known to sports fans for its Wolverine teams, Michigan is also one of the nation's best examples of a globalized international university. Today, it draws its forty-thousand-plus students from all fifty states and more than eighty countries and has more living alumni than any university in the world. Since the state of Michigan is home to one of the largest Muslim populations outside the Middle East—including about one in ten of the nation's Arab immigrants—the university's student body in the coming years will become only more diverse and more global and help to keep it on the front lines of Islam's global struggle with modernity and the West. According to *U.S. News & World Report*, the university is one of the nation's top three public institutions, and it emphasizes research and innovation like only a major university can: The government sponsors some half a billion dollars in research on campus annually, and industry pours in another $90 million. Michigan today has an office dedicated solely to technology transfer, which is helping its on-campus research move into the marketplace. In the last six years, Michigan has applied for nearly eight hundred patents and seen some fifty-five start-up companies spawned from its work.

During the twentieth century, River Rouge might have helped solidify American prosperity during the industrial age, but it was institutions like the University of Michigan—which built one of the first computer networks—that were laying the groundwork for the information age. Today, as Detroit seems to be running out of ideas, the answers for the coming decades are much more likely to arise from places like Michigan's optics or wireless microsystems research centers, its Life Sciences Institute, or its rare biosphere reserve. If the United States is to avoid being overtaken in the world it created, it will be because the country once again emphasized the power of education. If it *is* overtaken, it will be because places like Beijing's Tsinghua University, which played host to Romney in 2006, caught up with places like Ann Arbor's University of Michigan.

NEARLY EVERYONE AGREES that the American educational system currently fails to meet the challenges of today's economy. "Education has been allowed to be complacent," says William H. Schmidt, an expert at Michigan State University in East Lansing. "We are still teaching children to work in an industrial society." Something—or, in fact, many things—must change for education to enter the twenty-first century and help prepare students for a globalized, competitive job market. Addressing the problem will require a broader and longer-term view than education has today—one that begins before kindergarten and continues from the elementary basics through higher education and right through to on-the-job retraining. Long gone are the days when typing or shop class in high school would train students in a career for life. Today's workplace requires constant retraining and updating of skills. Today's brilliant innovation is obsolete tomorrow.

A key determining factor for companies looking to hire and expand in the twenty-first century is the availability of talent, and so this new economy is more and more pushing the United States into a global battle for a highly skilled workforce. In the last chapter, Mark Warner's plan to revitalize southwest and southside Virginia relied both on investment in technology infrastructure as well as partnerships with local schools and universities. The University of Michigan is successful partly because it draws top talent from around the world, understanding that the world's best talent can exist anywhere on the planet today. While the nation's immigration debate focuses heavily on the border fence with Mexico, its future relies on opening doors to more international students and then encouraging them to stay here to create the future. On all these fronts, from elementary education to recruiting the world's best minds, the nation is in danger of losing ground.

Since the 1980s, the United States has been steadily losing this ground educationally to other industrialized countries, until a recent survey showed it finished third to last, ahead of only Cyprus and South Africa. In 2000 George W. Bush, to a crowd in Florence, South Carolina, when he was campaigning for president, made the now infamous remark: "What's not fine is, rarely is the question asked, are, is our children learning?"

The answer appears to be a resounding no. By the time that students hit the fourth grade, they are falling behind their peers from other major industrialized countries. Each additional year they stay in school—or at least those who do stay in school—they fall further behind their new international competitors. By the time they reach high school, test results bear out that they are generally two full grades behind.

Intel chief Craig Barrett doesn't mince words. "The biggest ticking time bomb in the U.S. is the sorry state of our K–12 education system. It's the educational quality of our workforce that will determine our competitiveness," he explains. Right now the country's not doing so well, say industry leaders. Fareed Zakaria is blunt too: "We're losing interest in the basics—math, manufacturing, hard work, savings—and have become a postindustrial society that specializes in consumption and leisure."[1]

When the nation's annual "report card" came out in 2007 (covering the year 2005) it wasn't hard to see that the education system is failing everyone—and failing the nation's future. The report, technically named the *National Assessment of Educational Progress*, has tracked the progress of tens of thousands of students each year since 1969, and what it's found is a continuing and alarming trend beginning in 1990: American students are falling behind. The 2005 report found the lowest reading scores since 1992. While twelfth graders were taking harder classes and earning higher grades than they were fifteen years ago, they're still not learning the material. Only about one in three is able to read at grade level and even fewer—just 23 percent—were ranked competent in math.

Currently the United States ranks seventeenth internationally in high school graduation rates and fourteenth in college graduation rates, behind countries like Ireland, Norway, South Korea, Israel, and Russia. Even more striking is the historical perspective—whereas a few decades ago South Korea's graduation rate was only a third of that of the United States, it has increased almost four-fold while the United States' has stayed basically the same, and in fact is now significantly higher than the United States. The lead the United States once had with the Baby Boomers will quickly disappear as they leave the workforce.[2]

What's almost as troubling, though, is that the debate has been going on for as long as it has without noticeable progress. "We've had endless gubernatorial and presidential calls to action," laments Minnesota governor Tim Pawlenty. "Essentially the same discussion would have occurred in 2000, 1995, or 1990. Even though we've all made great speeches, upgraded our standards, the research has gotten better, the measurements, results appreciably haven't. In relative terms and in real terms we're not doing appreciably better—nothwithstanding three decades of the same discussion." He sighs with exasperation. "Some say we'll all be dead before this system at this rate of change fundamentally changes what needs to happen."

Indeed it's hard to see which half of the equation is more troubling: that America's schools are failing or that, despite numerous calls to action, nothing appears to be getting any better. The problem isn't necessarily a shortage of resources. Every year, nearly half a trillion dollars goes into public education, including some $80 billion spent just on the physical infrastructure. Most of the system still focuses on the cookie-cutter, mass-production model on which factories operated for most of the twentieth century: students entered, were taught the same thing, and then exited knowing the same things. Education expert Elwood Cubberly explained in 1934, "Our schools are, in a sense, factories in which raw materials are to be shaped and fashioned into products to meet the various demands of life. The specifications for manufacturing come from the demands of twentieth-century civilization, and it is the business of the school to build its pupils to the specifications laid down."[3] Such a model couldn't be more outdated or useless to a knowledge-based society, and yet education hasn't been forced to change.

The next president will face the same stalemate that caused educational progress in the United States to grind to a halt decades ago. Both political parties face tough ideological choices when it comes to education. Low-tax Republicans refuse in the short term to raise taxes to provide better schools and more opportunities for investments in education—even though such moves now would likely save money and lower taxes down the road in terms of jails not built and welfare not needed. Small-government Republicans too hate the idea of nationally dictated standards, of having Washington dictate local policies. Democrats, meanwhile, with their strong backing from the teachers' unions, won't allow the system to be changed to give administrators more flexibility to hire and fire teachers.

The good news is that the solutions to the education problems facing the United States are readily known and widely accepted: The country needs to reshape educational standards, better emphasize the teaching of STEM (science, technology, engineering, and math) skills, wire the country for broadband access, teach more foreign languages, and compensate teachers better—and, perhaps, embrace a truly radical idea: that better teachers should be paid better.

The first problem to address is the sticky flashpoint of local control. Education is closely held in the United States as a local issue, controlled by school boards and even individual principals in some cases—a dogged anachronism as the world gets more global and competitive. Governors fight local boards and in many cases don't have authority over their own state board of education. Nationally, the U.S. Department of Education is one of the Republicans' most hated government entities; they see it as robbing local municipalities of control and (rightly in many cases) of imposing unfunded mandates on local schools. No Child Left Behind was a start, but—like many educational programs before it—Congress and the administration have failed to fund it at levels where it could make a difference. "We still have fifty states acting as if they're independent from each other," explains Schmidt. "We're never going to solve this problem until we recognize we need to educate all of our children to the same high standards. We have the rhetoric. We talk it, but we don't walk it."

One example of the cost of America's mishmash of local standards among the fifteen thousand local districts is the shockingly heavy backpacks that schoolkids are carrying. Many students have switched to rolling backpacks to help lug around the pounds of reading material they're supposed to bring to school. "In other countries, no textbook is written that doesn't align with the national standards. In this country, without such standards, the textbooks . . . cover everybody's standards. They're 800 pages long in eighth grade—I'm giving you real data—they're 200 pages in the rest of the world," complains Schmidt. "This creates the chaos to the teachers and to students. They don't know what they're supposed to teach or learn. That's part of the problem. If we had a more national set of standards . . . the textbook companies would respond. If Michigan, Texas, Florida, Illinois, California—the big ones—put together a common set of expectations, guess what the textbook companies would finally do? They'd give you textbooks that focused on that."

There's evidence that some state standards aren't particularly rigorous. Idaho, for instance, reported that by its own state standards 90 percent of fourth graders were proficient in math, but the *National Assessment of Educational Progress* showed less than half that number passed the federal standards. As Schmidt says, "Why should the educational standards be different in Minnesota and in Michigan? Why should Alabama be different than California? There's no logic to that."

Former presidential candidate and U.S. Senator Bill Bradley puts it more starkly: "Many school boards don't appreciate the challenge of China, India, Russia, and other countries. Education has become a national security issue. Rigid local control doesn't make sense in a globalized world."[4]

So beyond national standards, what needs to happen to reform the American education system and ensure that our children are ready to compete in the twenty-first century? The basic building blocks are these: American schools need to teach students more thoroughly, relying less on facts and more on concepts, as well as introduce them to the skills they need to participate. It's no longer about rote learning, memorizing what year the Pilgrims landed on a rock in what colony. Today's schools are still relying on teaching "who, what, where, and when," when today's environment asks students to know "how" and "why." All of the other information exists at one's fingertips with Google. If a student for some reason needs to know when the Battle of Gettysburg was fought (July 1–3, 1863), Google knows. It's less important to know when Benjamin Franklin "discovered" electricity by flying a kite in a thunderstorm than to understand how an electric current works. Growth in the new tech-driven world comes at the edges of knowledge, not at the center. By teaching facts—not concepts or skills—American schools tend to undermine their long-term efforts. A pilot project in 2005 by the Educational Testing Service, which administers tests like the SAT, found that out of sixty-two hundred high school seniors and college freshman it tested, only half could judge the objectivity of a website.[5]

Additionally, the United States is still operating on an educational model adopted for an agrarian society where children were needed at home in the summer to work in the fields. Whereas a typical American school year runs about 180 days, students in Europe and Asia often attend school almost year-round—as many as 220 days a year—as well as a full workday of education, rather than ending at 2 or 3 p.m. Such differences add up to months of additional education each year and as much as two or three years of extra education time by high school.

As Schmidt explains, America's schools differ from those abroad in other major ways: Whereas U.S. schools typically see "advanced" courses as allowing students to move more quickly through information, gaining college-level AP credits in the process, high-performing school systems overseas often teach the same amount of material to advanced students but teach it in much greater depth. It's the difference, Schmidt says, between the U.S. emphasis on quantity and the foreign emphasis on quality. American standards, many critics charge, are a "mile wide and an inch deep."

THE NEXT PRESIDENT won't need to go very far to see the failures—and the success stories—of the current American educational system. Washington, D.C.'s young new mayor is fighting a hard battle to reform the district's failing schools. A 2007 study found that nearly a third of D.C. residents were functionally illiterate. The Bill and Melinda Gates Foundation is stepping into the district's void to help secure the future of D.C. children, 66 percent of whom currently fail to complete high school, and only one in twenty earns a college degree. The Gates Foundation's D.C. Achievers program will offer $122 million in college scholarships to students to encourage them to go on to higher education and a brighter future. Just across the Potomac River, though, is a shining example of a school turning out the students who will compete with the best Qatar, India, and China have to offer. Thomas Jefferson High School in Alexandria, Virginia, is a national powerhouse in science education; its students have won the National Science Bowl three times in recent years and it's a feeder school to the nation's top universities, like MIT. It and Montgomery Blair High School in surburban Maryland led the nation in Intel Talent Search semifinalists for 2007, together scoring nearly 10 percent of the country's three hundred semifinalists. The economic future of the United States requires a lot more TJs and a lot fewer of D.C.'s ongoing failures.

Nationally, the International Baccalaureate program, which began in 1968, has seen an explosion in the age of globalization and stands as a good model for what education in a global world should look like. The rigorous program is one of the toughest in the country and—this is telling—is supposed to represent what it means to educate children to an "international" standard. An IB diploma requires everything from passing tough classes to proficiency in a second language to a college-level four-thousand-word research paper to a community service project. IB programs have doubled in number since 2000 to more than seven hundred today—impressive, to be sure, but less so when one remembers there are fifteen thousand school districts in the country, most with many, if not dozens of, high schools.

Just as teaching needs to be brought into the twenty-first century during the course of the next president's term, he or she will need an agenda that helps bring American teachers themselves into the twenty-first century. The country must recruit better teachers, expand volunteer opportunities like Teach for America (a program which, by the way, more than 10 percent of Yale's class of 2005 applied to enter—the hunger to serve, to volunteer, and to teach is certainly there), and ensure that teachers get certified in the subjects they teach and that they get ongoing training throughout their careers. Right now, only 40 percent of eighth graders have a math teacher with a degree in math or who is certified to teach it. Fully 93 percent of science students in grades five to nine were taught by teachers who didn't have a degree or certification in the sciences. Our nation's future workers must be taught by those best equipped to provide them with the necessary skills. "They may be good teachers, but it's hard to really educate and inspire if you're not fully integrated into the subject," says Congressman Bart Gordon, who serves as the top Republican on the House Science Committee.

In World War II, when the Army Air Corps was training its pilots, the best in each class were held back to teach subsequent classes, and when a fighter pilot in Europe or the Pacific distinguished himself in the skies, he'd be brought back to teach. Why? Because it was critical that the best of one generation be used to teach the next. We must adopt a similar attitude in education today. To succeed, we must be willing to invest in teachers what our next generation is worth to us. Ray Scheppach, the longtime executive director of the National Governors Association, who has watched governors across the country wrestle with education for a generation, observes, "I don't think that we're willing to spend the money on teachers that we should."

Principals, the administrators on the front lines of this generational struggle, must be given better authority to police and staff their schools. Teachers' unions will argue about arbitrariness in decisions, but the truth is that the best teachers are well-known to parents, students, and administrators alike. They should be rewarded with bonuses and higher salaries. We should also recognize that certain STEM subjects require a higher skill level and more training than other subjects and pay those teachers accordingly. Money's a huge issue when it comes to teaching. According to Harold Levy, the former chancellor of the New York City schools, the difference in 1970 between the salary of a first-year teacher and a first-year lawyer was $2,000. Today the difference is more than $100,000. A starting teacher's salary sometimes is equal to the signing bonus offered by top firms.

One possible ambitious blueprint for the next president to address the creeping crisis of American education was laid out by the National Academy of Sciences' *Gathering Storm* report, which recommended that the nation embark on a program to educate 10,000 teachers and 10 million minds. The effort would annually recruit and help fund the education of 10,000 teachers who, in turn, would in the classrooms reach 10 million students. Modeled on successful programs like UTeach at the University of Texas, it would also offer bonuses to new teachers who chose to go to the most troubled and difficult districts. The second half of the program was 25,000 and 250,000: 25,000 annual scholarships to aspiring teachers in science, math, and engineering as well as summer institutes that would offer training and ongoing education to 250,000 teachers each year.

The next president must also help the nation's higher education system face many twenty-first-century challenges. Here again we see an impressive dominance by the United States, albeit one increasingly under threat around the world. The United States has more than four thousand colleges and universities, whereas the rest of the world combined has only in the neighborhood of seventy-eight hundred. California alone, with its sprawling UC system, has 130 institutions of higher education—a number exceeded by only fourteen countries in the world.[6] But other countries, like India and Qatar, are doing their darnedest to catch up, and while America's colleges and universities are the envy of the world, there aren't enough of them and they're harder to afford than ever before. Harvard, which now attracts students from more than 130 countries, is barely any larger than it was after World War II and yet there are now hundreds of millions more students out there. An American worker with a college degree during Jimmy Carter's administration could expect to earn 75 percent more than someone without a college degree. Since then, that number has leaped to more than 130 percent. Whereas a generation ago, there were jobs available for those who never went to college, such positions are increasingly scarce in the new knowledge economy. This "college premium" is making college more a necessity than a lifestyle choice.

At the higher education level, government has also fallen way behind in its support of individual students. In 1975, a Pell Grant covered about 80 percent of the cost of a public university and about 40 percent at a private institution. Today that percentage has fallen by more than half.[7] According to a College Board study, average 2006–2007 tuition is $5,836 at a state college or university and $22,218 for a private institution. Of course, the top private schools are much closer to $50,000. In the last five years, those figures have soared 35 percent for state schools and 11 percent for private ones. Despite extensions of various grant and loan programs, the average student borrower today graduates from college with more than $17,500 in debt—a massive burden for someone just entering a workforce to pay off over time. The rising demand for graduate school degrees in highly competitive fields only contributes to the debt. Simply increasing student aid isn't necessarily the answer, as much-quicker-than-inflation college tuition hikes have quickly consumed previous increases. Improved aid and support to community colleges and two-year institutions would help millions of students get a leg up and improve their lives on an ongoing basis through retraining.

Few investments pay off as handsomely as those in higher education, which fuel all types of economic growth, as the University of Michigan's technology transfer office can attest. According to the Council on Competitiveness, between 1980 and 2004, U.S. universities, hospitals, and research institutes spun out 4,543 companies based on licenses from these institutions. Graduates from MIT, for instance, have started more than eighteen hundred companies, generating $135.7 billion in revenues in 2003, while out in Silicon Valley, Stanford University students and faculty have launched more than twelve hundred start-up companies, ranging from small unknowns to Hewlett-Packard, Cisco, Yahoo, eBay, and Google. The effects of this higher ed–driven economic development are very localized, since entrepreneurs generally stay close to the schools; however, through further investments in higher ed and a wider spread of venture capital, the United States can foster research and start-ups at more schools around the country.

Additionally, the nation must recognize that in an information-driven economy, education can't begin with kindergarten and stop with a college diploma. Numerous programs around the country have demonstrated that everything from improved prenatal care to early childhood education programs can have a dramatic impact on a child's future. At ages as young as three years old, researchers have begun to see children fall behind, but the federal Head Start program, which requires that only half of its teachers have even a two-year college degree, should be just the start. One example for the next president to study is Michigan's innovative Perry Preschool program, which found that providing high-quality teachers in small groups to preschoolers could boost IQ test scores by eight to ten times that of Head Start, and reduce the chance that a student would need special education (down 43 percent), drop out before graduation (25 percent), or be arrested (50 percent). Nationalizing this initiative, upgrading Head Start to a more rigorous program like Perry Preschool, would require about $2 billion a year and save over time many times that from reduced need for social services.

On the other end of the education spectrum, a twenty-five-year-old today will be in the workforce for another half century. As skills evolve and change, as new technologies get developed, the U.S. government and U.S. companies need to develop a system that allows today's workforce to evolve and change with the times and develop lifelong learning programs—what educators call the extension of education from "K to 12" to "K to gray."

The winner of the presidential race in 2008 must understand that addressing American competitiveness requires a massive new commitment to lifelong learning and ongoing training. While the United States is a world leader in providing job training—about a third of the workforce has some kind of training in any given year—its workers receive much less total training than their counterparts in many other countries. A worker in the United States can expect to receive about seven hundred hours of training over the course of a career—about twenty hours a year—whereas a Swiss or Danish worker can expect to receive nearly double that.[8] The last major overhaul of the employment "safety net" was under President Kennedy in 1962, when the industrial mass-production economy was preeminent and America's economic power in the world unchallenged—meaning that the regulations and standards used are ill suited to a technology-driven world. In the new economy, companies are turning over faster than ever. According to Dunn and Bradstreet, from 1935 to 1981, around fifteen thousand businesses failed each year. By 1996, which is remembered as one of the Clinton-era boom years, seventy thousand companies failed. By another measure, the business landscape is also changing the fastest it ever has. In the sixty years after 1917, it took an average of about thirty years to replace half of the thousand largest U.S. public companies, but in the twenty years that followed—from about 1977 to 1998—it took only an average of twelve years.[9] Our ongoing efforts to develop and recruit human capital will be just as important as our investment in physical capital. "Despite the fact that the U.S. labor market ranks second to none when it comes to job turnover, the nation's safety net for easing job transitions remains one of the weakest among the wealthy economies," says the Brookings Institution's Lael Brainard.

In the twenty-first century, the makeup of the U.S. economy is changing entirely, and our systems and protections no longer reflect the reality of who's working where and who will be working where in the future. Whereas a half century ago 80 percent of U.S. jobs were "unskilled"—requiring nothing more than a high school diploma— today 85 percent of U.S. jobs are "skilled," requiring additional train- ing or a college education. The Bureau of Labor Statistics shows that every single high-paying, high-growth job in the next decade will require a college education. The only fast-growing jobs that don't require it are in personal care, food preparation, and building mainte- nance, all of which have the lowest average wages. Manual and rou- tine jobs are disappearing, while those that are growing require "expert thinking" and "complex communication," meaning that the jobs focus on areas where there aren't rule-based solutions to prob- lems or where workers must acquire relevant information on their own and explain it to others. As the Council on Competitiveness states boldly, "Generally, if a problem can be solved by a rule or a straight forward process, a computer (or someone using a computer in a developing economy) will be able to do it."[10]

THE REASON TO BE OPTIMISTIC entering the first campaign—as Mitt Romney and Barack Obama both were in their announcement speeches about the challenges and opportunities that lie ahead—is because at critical times in the past, the United States has met the challenge of education. The nation has certainly come a long way since Massachusetts in 1852 became the first state to pass a law re- quiring mandatory attendance for children between eight and four- teen for at least three months a year. Education gradually grew into a more and more critical responsibility of government as the country passed from an agrarian economy to an industrial one. The federal government began to step into education around the turn of the nine- teenth century, when the Smith-Hughes Act of 1917 provided for funding for teachers in certain fields like agriculture and home eco- nomics.

The transformative moment for U.S. education came in the 1940s, when Congress passed the GI Bill. The bill grew out of the work of the National Resources Planning Board, which was tasked by FDR to plan for the postwar economy, although the specific GI Bill was the idea of the American Legion, one of whose leaders, John Stelle, had received a letter from his son in the military asking for educational opportunities after the war. As FDR explained, "We must replenish our supply of persons qualified to discharge the heavy responsibilities of the postwar world. We have taught our youth how to wage war; we must also teach them how to live useful and happy lives in freedom, justice, and democracy."[11]

The groundbreaking GI Bill, which also was partly meant to spread out the flood of millions of veterans back into the private sector workforce, granted one year of education or training to veterans with at least ninety days of service, and an additional month of education for each additional month of military service, up to a maximum of four years. Under the legislation, all tuition and fees were covered—the maximum of $500 was more than any university was then charging—and veterans received generous monthly subsistence payments.

The program succeeded far beyond its founders' wildest dreams, even as the cost spiraled to $14.5 billion over ten years (more than $100 billion in today's dollars). From 1946 to 1947, the number of veterans in schools around the country soared from two hundred thousand to over a million, roughly half of all the students in the country. By the end of the World War II veterans' program, 7.8 million people had received education or training under the GI Bill—more than half of all World War II veterans.[12] To say that the bill transformed the Greatest Generation is an understatement. The extra education—studies showed a GI Bill veteran had an average of three more years of education or training than his peers—helped boost social mobility, radically increase standards of living and income in the 1950s and 1960s, and usher in the era of the suburban American dream. One study of the class of 1949 at the University of Georgia showed that 94 percent of the students had used the GI Bill and 90 percent considered it a turning point in their lives.[13] "Previously a man's job status had been determined primarily by the kind of job in which his father and grandfather had been employed. In the middle of the twentieth century, by contrast, many American men seemed to be experiencing dramatic upward mobility in this regard. Liberated from the more rigid occupational patterns of the past, they found employment in jobs with significantly higher statuses than those in which their fathers had been employed," explains political scientist Suzanne Metler, who has studied the impact of the GI Bill.[14]

The investment of $14.5 billion appears modest in retrospect as one considers the vast positive societal transformations that took place under the bill. From this knowledge base of GI Bill–trained veterans came countless political and industry leaders, as well as many of the scientific and industry advancements that helped move the world from the industrial age to the knowledge age.

The GI Bill's transformative effects were amplified a decade later when the Soviet Union launched Sputnik and Congress responded with the National Defense Education Act, which emphasized education in science and technology. As one example, the NDEA helped boost annual PhDs in math in this country from fewer than one hundred in 1961 to more than fourteen hundred a decade later.

Today we're seeing what amounts to a reverse GI Bill: an entire generation in danger of having their future standard of living radically lowered by missed educational opportunities. Beyond the simple numbers of the *National Assessment*, which measures high school seniors and how they're not measuring up on the world market, there are those students who never even make it to senior year to participate in the tests. In Detroit, where Mitt Romney announced his presidential bid, the public school system manages to graduate only about a third of the students who enter it as freshman. Nationally, 1.1 million students drop out of high school each year, all but a handful of whom will see a lifetime of opportunities dry up. Whereas twenty-five years ago, black men were three times as likely to be in college as in prison, by 2000, there were three black males in college for every four of their peers in prison.[15] The annual cost of maintaining a prisoner is roughly equal to a year's tuition at Harvard—but the social costs are much, much higher.

The failure rate of some of America's schools is shockingly high—and the pool of the worst institutions is shockingly small. Work by Johns Hopkins researchers Robert Balfanz and Nettie Legters has found that only 15 to 20 percent of the nation's high schools are responsible for more than half of all of the dropouts in the country.

These "dropout factories," where graduation rates often don't exceed 40 percent and therefore doom generations of children to low-paying, unskilled jobs, are heavily concentrated in fifty large and medium-sized cities and ten southern and southwestern states. Nationally, nearly half of the one hundred largest urban schools have a dropout rate exceeding 50 percent. This should be unacceptable—and politicians often tell us it is—but nothing seems to get better. The numbers are even more skewed when one begins to examine racial minorities: A June 2006 *Education Week* report found that only half of African-American students and roughly 55 percent of Latinos graduate from high school, compared to more than 75 percent of non-Hispanic whites and Asians. In the coming decades, the U.S. economy will increasingly rely on its growing pool of minority workers, especially Hispanics and African Americans, but these critical groups are almost always the farthest behind when it comes to educational achievement.

When examining incomes in the United States over the past twenty years, one other statistic stands out: Only those households headed by a college graduate saw their incomes rise. People who had not graduated high school, not attended college, or not graduated from college saw their incomes decline as much as 11 percent. In a globalizing and increasingly competitive world, education counts more than ever.[16]

While President Bush's much-touted No Child Left Behind program has brought some attention to the issue of education, it has been left starved for funds and attention in a budget increasingly pressed by the wars in Iraq and Afghanistan and the Republican-backed first-ever tax cuts in a time of war. Even as the world stage increasingly emphasizes it, education ends up an only occasional talking point for pundits and those leading the national debate. Someday the nation will rue its short-term savings on the massive Bush tax cuts for its long-term costs for a generation of youth who attended underfunded schools. Success in the coming decades will be largely contingent upon the ability of the president elected in 2008 to address education as a whole, from pre-K to worker retraining. That is a tall order, to be sure, given past reluctance to confront the higher taxes and powerful teachers' unions that have stood in the way of reform

before, but every year that the tough choices aren't made, every year
the battles aren't fought, will mean other countries have another year
to catch up.

One of the last dedicated and wide-scale attempts to remake education came some four decades ago under President Lyndon Johnson.
In January 1966, Johnson journeyed to the Welhausen Elementary
School in Cotulla, Texas, where he had once attended the Teachers'
College, and laid out the nation's challenge to its children. "Often
young Americans write to ask their President, 'What can we do to
help our country?' Well, this is my answer: If you want to help your
country, stay in school as long as you can. Work to the limit of your
ability and your ambition to get all the education you can absorb—all
the education you can take. What you are doing now is the most important work that you can possibly do for your country," he said. "If
your education falters or fails, everything else that we attempt as a
Nation will fail. If you fail, America will fail. If our schools and our
students succeed, we will succeed. If you succeed, America will succeed. It is just as simple and just as difficult as that."

DEVELOPING COUNTRIES ARE beginning to understand the sea change
under way and how their educational policies affect their economic
prospects. Whereas a country once rose and fell based on the toil of
its domestic industry, the new model of economic development is
more like *Field of Dreams.* If you build it, they will come. To see exactly what Thomas L. Friedman means when he says that India is racing the United States for the top, one need only examine India's elite
educational system. While most of India's schools, particularly those
in rural areas, are primitive and in many cases lacking even basic supplies such as blackboards, their national institutes of technology are
almost unparalleled in the global economy.

In mid-January 2003, a group of prominent alumni of the Indian
Institutes of Technology gathered to celebrate their alma mater's
golden anniversary and hear from the event's keynote speaker, Bill
Gates. The event, though, wasn't held in Kharagpur, the eastern Indian city where the first IIT opened, or any of the other six locations
that now have IITs. The event was held instead in the place where

IIT graduates have made one of their biggest contributions to knowledge and the global economy: Silicon Valley.[17] The group was hardly anomalous. More than twenty-five thousand IIT alums, hundreds every year, have migrated to the United States, and their combined brainpower has helped cement Silicon Valley's reputation as the center of the tech world.

India's first prime minister, Jawaharlal Nehru, had set up the schools to help the fledgling nation build up its stock of engineers for infrastructure projects like new power plants and dams. Ever since, even amid rampant corruption in other areas of the government, the IITs have remained a shining example of an incorruptible national institution. The tuition has remained affordable, but thanks to expansive support from the government, the professors and staff are paid handsomely and the students are the nation's best of the best.

The impact of the IITs on the economy is irrefutable—and proponents say that even having IIT grads move overseas, as about half currently do, is good for the country in the long run. Texas Instruments, which was one of the first international companies to set up a beachhead in Bangalore, did so after realizing how much of its research talent already came from IITs.

At Harvard, students typically joke that the hardest thing about the nation's premier learning institution is getting in. *The Boston Globe* famously revealed in 2001 that the majority of students graduated with an A record and with honors. Not so at India's IITs. Victor J. Menezes, who went on to lead Citigroup's corporate and investment banking branch, recalls the particularly challenging electrical engineering course taught by Professor M. S. Kamath at IIT-Bombay. Often, only one student in the class would get an A on a test. The second best student would get the test's only B, and everyone else would be rewarded for their long hours of studying with Cs, Ds, or Fs. "I used to tell my students, 'IIT is a center of excellence. I don't want you to be third-rate products,'" Kamath said.[18] IIT-Delhi graduate Vinod Khosla, who cofounded Sun Microsystems, also saw a world of difference between education in the United States and India. "When I finished IIT Delhi and went to Carnegie-Mellon for my Master's, I thought I was cruising all the way because it was so easy relative to the education I had got at IIT," he said.[19]

Of course, getting in isn't any easier. In 2007, three hundred thousand students registered for the joint entrance exams. Students often spend up to two years studying for the six-hour exams, knowing that only about 2 percent will be accepted. By comparison, Harvard's acceptance rate is four to five times higher. The culture of competition for spots at the elite educational institutions is so ingrained in India that many newspapers publish a page or two of practice exam questions in the back near the comics. And of those who actually secure a spot in the institutes, one out of five won't make it to graduation. To graduate from an IIT, though, is—as much as it can be at least—to have one's future secured. "It is impossible to quantify the value of Indian engineering talent as a brand," *The Wall Street Journal* wrote in marking the fiftieth anniversary of the IITs.

India still faces a hard uphill climb in education. Many critics have charged that India is shortchanging its citizens by investing so much in the IITs rather than the wider primary education system—the budget for the IITs, which educate only a few thousand, is about 15 percent as large as the entire educational budget for the millions of others. Philanthropists like B. Ramalinga Raju, the chair of Satyam Computer Services, are stepping in to fill some of the void, providing educational resources and computers to rural villages with open-air schools. Even the best IITs are not gleaming examples of higher ed—their dusty facilities and run-down campuses hardly lend themselves to the glossy viewbooks and brochures so popular in U.S. education. Currently only one in fourteen Indians age eighteen to twenty-four enters a university, according to the National Knowledge Commission, which is half the rate of much of the rest of Asia. The underfunded and crumbling nature of the infrastructure is one of the many reasons that so many Indians—one hundred sixty thousand at last count—go overseas for schooling.

With the recognition that the nation needs to provide as many as fifteen hundred colleges and universities to meet the growing demands, India is loosening its tough rules governing education and encouraging partnerships between U.S. schools and Indian ones. "In this country, education's the huge priority. People will go to great lengths to get a great education," explains Suri Venkat, an executive at the IT company Sify. "It's all we have to fall back on." His colleague

David Appasamy adds, "Aspirations are high and everyone knows progress is because of education."

As Madeleine Green, vice president for international initiatives at the American Council on Education, told *The New York Times*, India is "the next frontier" for American higher education. "The pull factor is the interest of India and the opportunity that India now presents," she observes. "The push is from American institutions saying, 'There's a world out there and we need to discover it. It'll make our grads more competitive.' It's part of their push to internationalize."[20]

Tiny Champlain College in Burlington, Vermont, has a satellite campus with THe INternational College (THINC) in Mumbai that offers degrees in subjects like hospitality management and software engineering. Giant Columbia Business School has joined with the famed Indian Institute of Management at Ahmedabad on student exchanges. California State University–Long Beach is working with Lucknow University in northern India on a four-year degree program. And Carnegie-Mellon, the U.S. engineering powerhouse, is developing an "outsourced" education, whereby students spend much of their education at the Shri Shiv Shankar Nadar College of Engineering before finishing their Carnegie-Mellon degree with six months in Pittsburgh.

It was precisely because of this new dynamic that Iowa governor and onetime 2008 presidential candidate Tom Vilsack found himself in an odd position in Hyderabad, India, in March 2006: He was leading a trade delegation to India to ask Satyam, one of the nation's leading outsourcing companies, to open its next facility in Iowa. The outsourcers were the new outsourcees. When Vilsack first took office in the twentieth century as Iowa's governor, Satyam was a small player on the world stage. Now, here he was in the twenty-first century, some ten thousand miles from Iowa, literally asking them for a job.

One of the odder truths of the "flat world" is that governors and mayors are the front-line public officials confronting it. Former House Speaker Tip O'Neill declared, "All politics is local," and that's never more so than in the global economy—governors and local officials must work harder than ever to shore up local economies, and they've discovered that their competitive field has fundamentally changed. "Economic development used to mean going to the next town or the next state and trying to steal their jobs," says Bill Booher of the Council on Competitiveness. "Now it's about going halfway around the world. Now the competition's between Peoria and Beijing, not just Peoria and Akron."

No governor in the United States can fail to see the impact of globalization every day in his or her state—in jobs lost and jobs gained and the role that education plays in that equation. Desperate for secure, good-paying twenty-first-century jobs at home and buffeted by massive layoffs in twentieth-century industrial dinosaurs like the auto industry, governors—Romney, Vilsack, and Warner among them—are increasingly heading overseas to see where the economic future is being created. In 2005 alone, thirty-five governors visited India on trade missions of one kind or another. In October 2007, Minnesota's Pawlenty planned a journey to New Delhi, Mumbai, and Bangalore as part of a trade mission to recruit more Indian companies to his state—he already has at least four Indian conglomerates operating in Minnesota, and wants more. Across the country, governors understand that their workers are now competing on a global stage and that their perspective must adjust as well. Governors and mayors constantly find themselves pitching companies on locating locally jobs, factories, and facilities. These are the kind of front-line business deals from which Congress and officials in Washington are often isolated and yet more and more demonstrate how the political landscape is changing thanks to expanding educational opportunities.

Patrick Wilson, the director of government affairs for the Semiconductor Industry Association, observes, "Governors get that. It doesn't matter what party they're in. And increasingly that question 'What do we have to offer?' is something that even the mayor of a medium-sized city, say fifty thousand people, might be competing with Bangalore or might be competing with Shenzhen or might be competing with Dresden for manufacturing investment and job creation. That's something they've felt because they've gone to meet with the teams from a company that are sent to do site selection and you can see who else is pitching. Oh, Stockholm, Sweden. It's like trying to win an Olympics."

Satyam Computer Services is a company few in the United States have ever heard of, but it's a powerhouse in India, on an explosive

growth path. After its initial deal with John Deere and the "Little India" it set up in Moline, Illinois, it went public in 1992 on the New
York Stock Exchange with about $1 million in revenues. In 2007, it's
expected to bank some $1.4 billion and has grown to thirty-eight
thousand employees. And company officials say they're just getting
started. All told, 71 percent of the global GDP is in services of one
kind or another, and almost all of that can be virtually delivered.
Satyam's opportunities weren't lost on Iowa's governor. Vilsack's group
of twenty-five Iowans—including his wife, the head of the Iowa farm
bureau, and a state representative from India—met with agriculture
officials, struck cooperation agreements between Iowa State University and two of India's top agricultural universities, and toured the Taj
Mahal. One of the centerpieces of the trip was the Satyam visit and
economic development pitch.

The drive up to the Satyam Technology Campus is a study in the
contrasts of India. Feral dogs and domesticated cows root through the
trash on the side of the road. Street merchants hawk fruit, food, and
goods alongside run-down hovels and tents. People bathe in the road-
side ditches and water from communal wells. Three-wheeled au-
torickshaws and lumbering native-made Tata trucks weave among
bicyclists loaded down with goods. Tarp-covered houses exist in the
shadows of billboards for country club developments.

But once inside Satyam's imposing gates one immediately sees the
difference that educational opportunities can bring to a country still
widely impoverished. Its giant campus could be anywhere in Silicon
Valley, and it boasts a golf course ("It's just nine holes, not the full
eighteen," says a tour guide, somewhat wistfully), swimming pool,
cricket pitch, fitness facilities and game rooms, and a helipad con-
structed for Bill Gates's visit in November 2002, as well as a me-
nagerie sporting peacocks, rabbits, deer, emus, chickens, and love
birds that borders on a wireless-enabled picnic area. On weekends,
horse and camel rides are provided for family entertainment since
more than six hundred critical employees live on campus. The conference rooms are named for globe-trotting pioneers like Albert
Schweitzer, and the sweeping drive in front of the company headquarters is lined with the flags of the fifty-three nations with which
Satyam works. Viewed from the front steps of the gleaming buildings,

where the spray from the decorative fountains cools the hot Indian sun, the level playing field granted by increased international educational opportunities seems pretty peaceful.

One of the keys to Satyam's success has been its focus on education, worker training, and drawing from the global talent pool. The first Western executives it hired—Virginians Ed Cohen and his wife, Priscilla—were tasked with setting up an executive training program and founding the Satyam School of Leadership to train talent for the hypercompetitive twenty-first century. The company is investing millions of dollars in cutting-edge training, leadership, and education research, and setting up its thousands of employees to compete against the best talent anywhere else in the world.

Near Satyam's campus in and around Hyderabad—India's version of Silicon Valley—twenty-nine IT parks cover a total of about fifteen hundred acres. There are eighty-four million square feet of IT offices already in existence and another fifteen million square feet rising from the rocky terrain. Hyderabad is home to Microsoft's only development center outside of Redmond, Washington, and Reuters's offshore development center employs nearly three hundred a few miles from the call center that handles Verizon's DSL support in the United States. Elsewhere in Hyderabad are offices for Google, Bank of America, Motorola, Dell, IBM, Nokia, UBS, and Amazon.com. All of it is thanks to India's investment in education and the Indian diaspora that, once educated overseas, is being lured home.

Indian cities, not unlike Iowan cities, are locked in fierce competition for new companies and developments. Each IT job created leads indirectly to four new jobs being created, government studies have shown, and so wooing new companies and operations is just as critical to the local government as it is to Tom Vilsack's Iowa. "Today there's huge competition between the cities," explains Gopi Krishna, the government IT secretary for Andhra Pradesh, the state that contains Hyderabad. "This will continue for some time. The competition is so intense." To compete on the global market, Andhra Pradesh, which has dubbed itself the "Land of Opportunities," is liberalizing some of India's bureaucratic rules; it's the first state in India to allow women to work the overnight shift, something that's critical to companies staffing for U.S. business hours. Krishna's office has prepared a PowerPoint presentation touting the economic and development incentives—from tax breaks to dedicated power supplies—available to new companies opening in Hyderabad. It wouldn't have been an unfamiliar presentation to the officials accompanying Vilsack on his trip. They have the same type of PowerPoint—and even many of the same incentives—to woo companies interested in opening in Iowa. Even "Land of Opportunities" sounds familiar. After all, Iowa's state slogan is "Fields of Opportunity."

Vilsack's visit, just eight months before he left office and declared his presidential campaign, brought home to the two-term governor the new reality American policy makers would face. "He's totally recognized the global framework he has to operate in," says Satyam's president Ram Mynampati. "He's not believing the rhetoric. He had to come here to see things for himself." The company was honored enough by Governor Vilsack's visit that they planted a tree to mark the occasion. Nearby are trees honoring visits by other technology and world leaders. At the rate they're visiting the Hyderabad campus, Satyam will have a thick forest in the not too distant future.

As Satyam, U.S. governors, and academics at places like the University of Michigan know, wrapped up in the issues of education and the global talent war is the question of immigration. To continue having the best-trained workforce in the world, the United States must recognize that means loosening the reins of citizenship to encourage the world's brightest minds to come here. The National Foundation for American Policy has shown that more than three out of five of the nation's top science and math students are the children of recent immigrants.[21] One way that China and India are competing with the United States is in luring emigrants back home—better than half of the Chinese Academy of Engineering staff and more than 80 percent of the Chinese Academy of Sciences staff returned from abroad to work in their native country. U.S. innovation has long been driven by foreigners coming here, but since 9/11 a crackdown on immigration has led to more potential immigrants staying home when they can't get visas. As Patrick Wilson at the Semiconductor Industry Association explains, competing for global talent will be expensive, but it's a contest the United States can't afford to lose. "For the longest time we've been living on past glory when it comes to high-tech investment because twenty years ago we had a huge advantage in terms of the location of smart people, risk-tolerant people, and capital," he says. "We became the Yankees of information technology because we bought up all the best talent, we made great investments, they paid off, and the basic advantages of an entrepreneurial culture made us all very rich. Now it can all go away if we're not careful.

"It's exactly like sports. You can't afford to let your competitor get that player. If they do, the whole dynamic of how the league works will change," Wilson continues. "Derek Jeter has to be with the Yankees or he'll play for the Red Sox, and you have to make that calculation: It's going to cost a lot of money to [persuade him to] stay here, but we don't want him to go there. That's how business works."

Foreign-born brains already compose a significant chunk of U.S. high-tech brainpower. Foreign-born scientists and engineers make up nearly a quarter of the science and technology workforce, and a total of 40 percent of all U.S. engineering professors are immigrants. Temporary visa holders account for half of all the graduate students in computer science and engineering mathematics.[22] For the United States to succeed in the coming decades, it must work hard to continue recruiting the best talents from around the world to study here, work here, and stay here to contribute their ideas to the U.S. economy. Instead, the post-9/11 travel restrictions and tightened visa requirements that have stretched the wait from days to months or years is beginning to affect the number of foreign students who are looking elsewhere—to Canada or Australia, for example—to study and then work. "The United States—and this point bears repeating—doesn't have some intrinsic advantage in the production of creative people, new ideas, or start-up companies. Its real advantage lies in its ability to attract these economic drivers from around the world," says Richard Florida, who points to the long line of foreign innovators who have come to the United States, from George Soros to Liz Claiborne to Adolphus Busch to Samuel Goldwyn.[23] Imagine, for a moment, how different our world would be today if Sergey Brin, the cofounder of Google, had remained in Russia rather than immigrating to the United States.

The National Academy of Sciences sounded the warning in its October 2005 report, *Rising Above the Gathering Storm*, saying, "The scientific and technical building blocks of our economic leadership are eroding at a time when many other nations are gathering strength . . . Although many people assume that the United States will always be a world leader in science and technology, this may not continue to be the case inasmuch as great minds and ideas exist throughout the world. We fear the abruptness with which a lead in science and technology can be lost—and the difficulty of recovering a lead once lost, if indeed it can be regained at all."

At times, the United States seems to be designing an immigration system specifically to keep out the most talented minds and workers. As Congress debated the new immigration bill in the spring of 2007, it included a provision that would do away with the special visa status given to people like Nobel Prize winners, world-class musicians, athletes, artists, scientists, and other "aliens of extraordinary abilities." Under that plan, if Albert Einstein applied to live in the United States, he'd be lumped into the same pool as everyone else. That's no way to sustain a world-class economy. While most of the debate over immigration in the United States focuses on the illegal aliens crossing the border from Mexico, we might do well to take a few cues from New Zealand, which is thousands of miles and a long flight from the United States but is proving to be a key competitor in the global battle for the best talents. As Pete Hodgson, the country's minister for research, science, and technology, explains, "We no longer think of immigration as a gatekeeping function but as a talent-attraction function necessary for economic growth."[24]

A half century after India began investing in its IITs, today other countries wishing to compete on the global talent market find no need to go through the lengthy, expensive, and intensive development of strong domestic educational institutions. When Qatar's emir set out to improve the country's education system in the mid-1990s, he founded the Qatar Foundation to attract the world's best universities. Instead of going through the arduous process of building great educational institutions and hiring world-class professors, it would simply recruit those that already exist.

The thriving twenty-five-hundred-acre Education City on the outskirts of Doha is steadily adding America's best minds. To launch its School for the Arts, the Qatar Foundation invited Virginia Commonwealth University to open a new Doha campus—the Qatar state would underwrite the cost, VCU would provide the courses. In 2002, Cornell University opened a new medical college, followed a year later by a branch of Texas A&M University and a policy institute run by the RAND Corporation. Carnegie-Mellon University opened its campus in 2004, and Georgetown launched a branch of its prestigious School of Foreign Service in 2005. In 2006, the brand-new Qatar Science and Technology Park opened, and next will come a teaching hospital and a communications and journalism school. All of the schools are models of liberal arts education and all the more impressive for fostering a culture of liberal tolerance and diversity within a Muslim nation—and all underwritten by the natural gas–rich nation-state at little or no cost to the participating U.S. universities. Nearby, the new $2 billion Doha International Airport, scheduled to open in 2008, will provide a gleaming welcome to the country. Qatar's approach to education—cherry-picking the best the United States has to offer and then using it to educate class after class of students equal in academic strength to any in the United States—is unprecedented and a model for public-private educational partnership in the globalized new economy. Whereas it once would have taken decades to build a world-class university, the Qatar Foundation made it so from day one.

Qatar's bet, of course, is that by churning out smart students, coupling higher education and research institutions with a science and technology park, and providing a first-rate airport and top-of-the-line health care, it won't have to wait for local companies to grow strong. Instead the strongest, most competitive companies in the world will beat a path to Qatar's door. Just as one can't doubt that India and China aren't racing the United States to the bottom but are instead battling for first place, don't doubt that Qatar plans to come after the U.S. economy, its jobs, and its best minds—it already is. If the next president fails to address education in a major way, waiting four more years or eight more years for a new advocate in the Oval Office might prove costly to the U.S. economy.

THERE'S ONE FINAL POINT on innovation and entrepreneurship, often overlooked in terms of economic development, that—if nothing else does—should convince Democrats to pursue a first campaign agenda in the 2008 election: New-economy jobs produce more reliably Democratic voters than even blue-collar labor jobs. Thus, if only for self-interest, Democrats should be pushing and prodding for a wide-scale economic and technical investment in education reform.

Richard Florida's work charting the "creative class" shows that there are three key determining factors for where new-economy jobs—that is, highly paid, highly educated creative positions—end up locating. He calls them the "three T's": technology, talent, and toler-ance. The first two make obvious sense, the last chapter examined the role of the first, and this chapter has traced the critical nature of de-veloping talent. The third "T" seems a bit strange at first glance. While tolerance for immigrants, racial minorities, and gays doesn't seem like it should foster innovation itself, it actually proves to be a great proxy for innovation. Communities that are tolerant and diverse almost inevitably end up doing well in the new economy. According to Florida, tolerance represents a low barrier of entry for new workers, new companies, and new ideas. A tolerant community doesn't care where a good idea comes from.

Smart business in the twenty-first century requires employers be open to all comers. Proctor & Gamble, the generally conservative soap behemoth headquartered in Cincinnati, withstood harsh criti-cism and a threatened boycott by James Dobson's Focus on the Fam-ily when in 2004 it came out in support of overturning a local ordinance that prohibited anti-discrimination protections based on sexual orientation. When pushed, the company asserted simply that the law was "bad economic policy" and made it harder for the city to attract and retain talented employees.

Given the current ideologies and the base of each party, "tolerant" independent voters still end up heavily in the Democratic camp, so it's no surprise then that of the twenty regions of the country that top

Florida's "Creativity Index"—regions that range from New York, Atlanta, and San Francisco to Albuquerque, Des Moines, and Raleigh-Durham—only three voted Republican in the 2004 election: San Diego, Boise, and Fort Collins, Colorado.[25] Even rural Virginia, as Mark Warner helped renew its economy through new higher-tech jobs that arrived as part of his broadband initiative, began to skew more Democratic as the jobs arrived—helping the Democrats to recapture the governor's mansion in 2005 and throw out a Republican incumbent in the 2006 U.S. Senate race.

As the country gets more and more online, and jobs rely on higher-skilled, higher-educated workers, the Republican Party will have to rethink its conservative base–oriented electoral strategy or face increasing marginalization around new-economy centers. Florida's research shows that in 1980 there was no electoral advantage to having "creative class" centers on your side, but by 2000, those that had benefited most from the new economy voted Democratic by a margin of 17 percent above the national average. In fact, the thirty-four cities and counties adjacent to high-tech centers—places like Salem, Oregon, Orange County, and Newark—went from being solidly Republican bastions in 1980 to being solidly Democratic by the dawn of the twenty-first century.[26] By running the first campaign and embracing the new economy through tech investment and education reform, the Democrats would be literally undermining the Republican base. Sometimes doing the right thing for the country also can be smart politics.

SO HERE'S WHERE we stand as we enter the first campaign of a global age: We know there are giant, systemic problems in the way our children are educated. We know we're not getting an acceptable return on our half-trillion-dollar-a-year investment. We know that every other major industrialized country is doing better than we are, with the possible exceptions of Cyprus and South Africa. We even know where the problems in education exist. Similarly, we know what the solutions are. We know where there are models for hope. We know what the future will bring in terms of greater global competition and challenges.

Intel chief Craig Barrett says enough is enough. It's time to act on education. "Every year that we debate these topics, we lose another graduating class. And as we lose another graduating class, we're really condemning those children to a lower level of professionalism in their careers. We need to recognize that, and either educate those children consistent with what the future will demand of them—and the future will demand that they be technically competent, be able to understand the technology that they are using, understand the technology and complexity of the society that they operate in—or they are going to be subjected to low-paying service jobs," he thundered during a speech at Intel. "The United States enjoys a wonderful, wonderful standard of living. That is based on the value-add that our workforce puts into the economy. That will only continue as long as our workforce is better educated than the rest of the world. And right now we are doing exactly the opposite to what we should be doing."

Ensuring that the United States can compete on the world stage will require the next president to act—the national consensus is there for action from CEOs like Barrett to the nation's governors like Pawlenty. Education can't be a local issue now that students don't have to compete in the workforce with peers in the neighboring town or county. The president must use the office's powerful bully pulpit to rally the nation around ongoing real reforms to education, but even before then, candidates in the first campaign must make these issues front and center—explaining that tough choices are ahead but that they are necessary for the United States to compete in the global age. As Barack Obama told the chilly crowd in Springfield, "Let us be the generation that reshapes our economy to compete in the digital age. Let's set high standards for our schools and give them the resources they need to succeed. Let's recruit a new army of teachers, and give them better pay and more support in exchange for more accountability. Let's make college more affordable, and let's invest in scientific research, and let's lay down broadband lines through the heart of inner cities and rural towns all across America." If Obama is wrong, and this generation doesn't accomplish those tasks, it will have dire consequences for all future generations of Americans.

In the 1964 presidential campaign against Barry Goldwater, Johnson's campaign ran the iconic "Daisy" ad, which would become the

most famous ad in political history, playing off the fears that Goldwater might lead the nation into nuclear war. It showed a young girl
picking petals off a flower, counting up to ten, where an ominous me-
chanical voice took over and began counting down to a nuclear explosion. Then as a mushroom cloud blossomed on the screen, Johnson's
voice was heard: "These are the stakes! To make a world in which all
of God's children can live, or to go into the dark. We must either love
each other, or we must die." Today, as we face the first presidential
campaign in a globalized world, we face a similar and equally ominous
challenge, but the danger is in books and bytes, not bombs. The outcome of the 2008 presidential race and the decisions made in the
next decade by the country's leadership will have a decisive impact on
whether the nation's children will have the skills for the twenty-first
century and whether the United States will make the decisions and
tough choices needed to remain an economic, military, and political
force in the decades ahead. From Satyam's Hyderabad campus to
Tsinghua's Beijing campus to Education City in Doha, there are
plenty of enterprising students and entrepreneurs ready to take up the
slack if the United States fails.

ISSUE #3: CARING FOR TWENTY-FIRST-CENTURY WORKERS

The challenge now is to practice politics as the art of making what appears to be impossible, possible.
—HILLARY CLINTON, WELLESLEY COLLEGE COMMENCEMENT, MAY 31, 1969

Andy Stern took the stage wearing his trademark purple shirt. This was his audience and his issue, and the 2008 Democratic presidential field was on his turf. Many on the left hoped that the popular and charismatic New Age union leader might enter the race himself—if not in 2008, then in 2012—flexing the political muscle of the "working poor," those in the new economy who might work forty, sixty, eighty hours a week or more for hardly more than minimum wage, a wage so low that in 2007 it meant you could barely hit the federal government's poverty line. The collapsing American health-care system has hit these workers especially hard. Since 2000 and George W. Bush's election, health-care premiums have increased four times faster than wages. Today, the average family insurance policy costs over $11,840 a year—or roughly $1,000 more than a full-time minimum-wage worker would earn in a year. With Stern's membership representing the nation's leading health-care workers' union, and with many of them struggling to afford insurance themselves, SEIU had brought the health-care issue to the front burner and intended through hook and crook to keep it there until progress was made.

It was early on a Saturday morning in a venue new to the 2008 campaign: Before the Democratic Party inserted the Nevada caucus up among the early voting states, the state hadn't had much swagger in the presidential race. Now, though, Nevada—Chris Dodd won points from the audience and moderator, *Time*'s Karen Tumulty, by correctly pronouncing the state "Ne-vaa-Da" rather than the more typical "Nuh-va-Duh"—was learning to swagger right along with New Hampshire and Iowa. The evening before, Richardson, Obama, and Clinton had gathered on the city's outskirts for a labor rally. The 2008 campaign would be Nevada's time to shine.

Stern launched in. On this subject, the numbers are both familiar and staggering. Premiums and costs were rising exponentially. In 2008, for the first time, experts predicted that health-care costs would exceed profits for *Fortune* 500 companies. It'd be one thing if those kinds of costs were delivering a system that was the envy of the world, but anyone who's gone to the doctor recently knows better. The United States currently ranks thirty-first in the world in terms of life expectancy and twenty-eighth for infant mortality. Nearly one in six Americans don't have any health-care coverage at all. All told, some forty-seven million Americans are without health insurance, including more than nine million children.

"It is not just a moral crisis but an economic crisis—an economic plan that will not work in a twenty-first-century global economy," Stern said. "The public now knows this. Polling in the four early primary states shows the cost of health care is the number one topic of concern among voters of both parties. The vast majority of Democrat and Republican voters believe everyone has a right to quality, affordable health care and they want fundamental, not piecemeal change . . . What are we missing? Leadership. Leadership in Washington, D.C. For the next president, here's the final point of our poll: Voters are saying they're not hearing from you enough about health care.

"The winds of change of health care are blowing," he promised. "It's up to us voters to keep the pressure on, to ask questions, but more importantly let's demand detailed answers about what they're going to do. America's future is not a matter of chance. It's a matter of choice. And every four years our choice, voters' choices, really do matter."

Over the next three hours, six of the men and the one woman hoping to be elected president in November 2008 took the stage as the opening chords of Bruce Springsteen's "Badlands" blasted in the auditorium and discussed how they'd address the issue as president. All agreed it was time to end the debate and get action. John Edwards: "What we have is a dysfunctional health-care system in the United States of America. What we need is big, bold dramatic change, not small change." Bill Richardson: "We Americans are in crisis today." Labeling the state of care in the United States a source of "collective shame," Chris Dodd thundered, "This is the United States of America, the most affluent country in the history of mankind, and we need to be doing a far better job of serving the American people when it comes to health care." Dennis Kucinich chimed in: "It's waiting for a candidate who will lead the way."

The noticeable absence from the health-care forum? All the Republican candidates. The entire GOP field had been invited by SEIU to participate, but not a single one accepted. Since Harry Truman first expressed a desire for a universal national health insurance system, health care has always been a Democratic issue, but now, it's become more than that: It's an issue critical to the nation's global competitiveness. In the first presidential campaign of a globally connected world, it's an issue ripe to be seized by the right candidate—as polling by SEIU and others show, reforming the spiraling cost of health care is one of the most critical issues for voters.

Barack Obama took the stage and laid down the biggest gauntlet: "What I think is most important [is] that we recognize that every four years we hear somebody's got a health-care plan. Every four years someone trots out a white paper, they post it on the web, but the question we have to challenge ourselves [with] is: Do we have the political will and the sense of urgency to actually get it done? I want to be held accountable for getting it done. I will judge my first term as president based on . . . whether we've delivered the type of health care every American deserves and that our system can afford." It was a not-so-subtle shot across the bow of the speaker who followed him, the speaker who more than a decade earlier had, as the nation's first lady, like Icarus, flown too close to the sun and gone down in flames when the Clinton health-care plan flopped.

When Hillary Clinton took the stage, she was so enthusiastic that she refused to sit with Tumulty, instead roaming the stage, fired up like she was leading a revival of some kind. "I know probably better than anybody how hard this is going to be. I've got the scars to show for it. I've been through it, but it just makes me more determined," she said, to cheers and clapping, referring to the 1993 health-care debacle. She gave herself a moment to gloat—"Now people are saying, 'Boy, we wish we'd done that back then' "—and then laid out a not-small challenge to the audience in the auditorium and those watching the event's live webcast. "We need a movement. We need people to make this the number one voting issue in the '08 election to send a message to the Congress and the special interests that we're serious and we're going to get it done this time."

The scope of today's challenge is well known but nonetheless staggering in its national pervasiveness. While roughly forty-seven million uninsured may seem like one of these numbers thrown around in government too large to comprehend, or perhaps even small in a country of more than three hundred million, it represents a population larger than that of twenty-four states combined. Even with politics at the national level as logjammed as it is, one can be pretty well assured that if the governors and congressional representatives of Kentucky, Oregon, Oklahoma, Connecticut, Iowa, Mississippi, Arkansas, Kansas, Utah, Nevada, New Mexico, West Virginia, Nebraska, Idaho, New Hampshire, Hawaii, Rhode Island, Montana, Delaware, South Dakota, Alaska, North Dakota, Vermont, and Wyoming woke up one morning and discovered that none of their constituents had health care, something would happen quickly to remedy the situation. If current trends continue, by the time of the next presidential election in 2012, another nine million Americans will have lost their health insurance, adding the equivalent of the entire populations of Alabama and South Carolina to the ranks of the uninsured, according to the Robert Wood Johnson Foundation's 2007 *State of the States* report. Addressing this issue can't wait.

Reforming the system will not be easy. Ever since Harry Truman, presidents have attempted to solve the health-care problem. It's been a "crisis" in the country for decades. So far the simple moral argument that health care should be guaranteed to every citizen has failed to advance the debate. Now, though, the framing of the issue is shifting in the public debate. The last time a president tackled health care, business was firmly against reform. In 2008, though, it will be the first campaign where business is solidly on the side of reform. Now in the global age it's also an issue of competitiveness. American business is finding itself falling behind its global competitors because of the country's broken health-care system. That has focused the attention of CEOs and business groups on the issue in a way that has never happened before—and that attention from business is helping to focus the attention of politicians in the 2008 elections. If the government won't do the right thing for the moral reasons, perhaps it will do the right thing for the economic reasons.

Whatever a final reform plan would look like, one thing is clear: There's never been a broader consensus across the groups necessary for reform—from the American people at large to the businesses and corporations that need this problem solved before they can compete on an even playing field with Asia, Europe, and even right here in North America with Canada. "There's a growing constituency that in the past was hostile to the idea of having a universal health-care plan that now understands the economics of this today better than they did fourteen years ago," Chris Dodd explains. "Let's sit down and get this done. The American people expect nothing less of us. We need to stop talking about it and achieve the results."

As former presidential candidate Bill Bradley explains, this consensus should be all that the nation needs to move forward. Change must happen. "The American people often give their leaders permission to take action by signaling agreement in principle while reserving the right to object strenuously to each and every specific sacrifice necessary to follow through," he says. "I have found that voters are willing to go much further to meet the crisis than most politicians assume is possible—but they are waiting for leadership."[1]

In today's economic and business landscape, the United States can't afford any more half steps or lip service when it comes to health care. The system needs sweeping, fundamental reform that guarantees quality, affordable health care that can't be taken away. This is a problem for government, and the nation needs leadership. The window for large-scale reform will be brief. Choices will only get harder in the coming years if the status quo remains, and in the meantime the health of millions of Americans (not to mention their productivity in the workplace and in society) will be impacted each year that health care remains out of reach. It's important for the nation's politicians to seize the opportunity for change in this campaign.

IT'S A HISTORICAL ACCIDENT that the United States ended up with employer-based health care at all. The first medical insurance in the United States was introduced in 1929 when Dallas's Baylor University Hospital offered a group of fifteen hundred schoolteachers up to twenty-one days of hospital care each year in return for an annual "premium" of $6. The hospital's idea was to even out its cash flow over the course of the year so it could budget better.[2] Later, the idea spread as government wage controls around World War II led companies to seek alternative ways of compensating their employees. Thus was born a system where health care ended up tied to one's employer. The percentage of workers covered by employer health plans more than doubled between 1940 and 1950, and rose steadily into the 1980s. Workers were rewarded because the health-care coverage wasn't taxed as income, and employers were rewarded because they could deduct the cost from their profits. Today, with health-care costs going up at double the rate of inflation, businesses are under extreme pressures to cut costs. The Census Bureau reported that the number of Americans covered by employer health-care plans fell by three million in the first five years of the decade, as the number of uninsured grew by 6.7 million—roughly the population of Massachusetts.[3] In all, whereas in 1979 as many as 70 percent of employees were covered at work, today only 55 percent are. Plus the idea of tying health care to one's workplace seems all the more outmoded in an environment where by their early thirties, workers today will have held more than nine jobs.

Contrary to public belief, the uninsured in the country are not people who "choose" not to be insured. In 2005, more than 80 percent of individuals without health coverage lived in families with at least one full-time worker. All told, more than a third of the nonelderly poor—that is, families of four with an income of $20,000 or less—are without health insurance, more than double the national average of 18 percent. The "near-poor" are only slightly better off: A quarter of the uninsured live in families with earnings between $25,000 and $49,999—a range that encompasses the nation's median income of around $46,000. Young adults just starting out their working lives comprise the fastest-growing segment of the U.S. uninsured population. Nearly a third of the uninsured are nineteen to twenty-nine-year-olds, a majority of whom report going without needed medical care because of their situation. Racial minorities continue to lack health insurance at stunning levels. Nearly one in three Hispanics is uninsured—including 40 percent of all Hispanic workers—as is one in five African Americans. These statistics taken together should be an outrage to the country, Obama argues: "If you're working full-time in this economy, there's no reason you shouldn't be able to access health care."

So what does it mean to be uninsured? It means making trade-offs between medical bills and essentials like food and heat. Research shows that more than one in three uninsured adults report that they choose not to pursue medically recommended tests, treatment, or medications because of the cost. Fifty people a day between the ages of twenty-five and sixty-four die because they don't have health insurance, a category the National Institutes of Medicine euphemistically labels "excess deaths." Again that doesn't sound like a huge number until one realizes that in the fourteen years since the failure of the Clinton health plan in 1994, 255,500 people have died because it failed.

Being uninsured also means stressful decisions like when to seek care for worsening ailments and what ailments are worth risking collection calls and possible bankruptcy over. In fact, health-care costs are the primary cause of bankruptcies across the country. Too many Americans can afford their sky-high health-care bills only by paying with credit cards, and end up paying interest rates of 18 percent or more seemingly forever. This problem isn't exclusive to those without health insurance. A Harvard Medical School study found that three out of four individuals who filed for bankruptcy due to medical expenses had insurance coverage at the onset of their illness. The study concluded "Unless you're Bill Gates, you're just one serious illness away from bankruptcy. Most of the medically bankrupt were average Americans who happened to get sick."[4]

Beyond the problem of the uninsured are the underinsured—those who buy health insurance but find that because of preexisting conditions, out-of-network services, and other insurance fine print they're not covered when they seek treatment. "There are a lot of people who think they have insurance except for when they need it," Hillary Clinton pointed out. "I met a woman in Austin, Texas, last week who said, 'I'm a teacher, Senator, I make $38,000, and I have insurance through my employer but last year I spent $19,000 out of my pocket'—half of her income—because she had a preexisting condition. We can't get to universal health-care coverage unless we end insurance discrimination once and for all." Insurance companies cannot be allowed to pick and choose whom they'll insure, or as technology advances we're going to find ourselves without any choices. Clinton continues, "We've now mapped the human genome and we're going to find we're all susceptible to something. None of us is going to be insurable if we don't change this system."

The Nevada forum came just days after the presidential race received a reminder about just how personal an issue health care can be. Two days earlier in Chapel Hill, John and Elizabeth Edwards announced that her cancer had returned. While he pledged his campaign would continue, he told the Nevada audience that he could do so in part only because his health-care situation was secure. "Look at all the millions of women who have had to struggle with the same sort of struggles Elizabeth has and many of them have had to struggle without what we've had, without great health-care coverage, without knowing that they're going to be able to get all the medicine and medications that they need," an earnest Edwards told the audience in his slow North Carolina drawl. "One of the reasons I want to be president of the United States is to make sure that every woman and every person in America gets the same kind of things we have, because it's not right that a woman—or anybody—has to go through this kind of struggle and has to worry about whether they can afford the medicine they need or get the health care they need. We don't have to worry about that and no one should have to worry about that."

This all takes place in a system that spends more on health care than any other nation in the world. At $6,697 per person, the United States has twice the per capita health-care bill of Germany and Canada. In fact, only one of the nineteen other major industrialized countries (Luxembourg) spends more than $4,000 per person. Nationally, health care represents 16 percent of the U.S. gross domestic product—about one dollar out of every six spent in the country goes to health care.

IT'S HARD TO remember today, but in 1993 it actually looked pretty likely that we'd have national health-care coverage. We now look back on Bill Clinton standing in front of Congress waving his "Health Security" card and see the defining failure of his administration: Big government, bureaucracy galore, and the 1994 Republican congressional sweep that it would help usher in a year later. At that moment, though, it looked liked Harry Truman's dream might actually become reality.

The problem had started two decades before—in 1970, *Business-Week* had labeled health care the "$60 billion crisis"—and accelerated through the 1980s. By 1990, health-care costs had jumped more than tenfold to $800 billion, and one sociologist warned, "Since 1980, health care has consumed an additional 1 percent of GNP every 35 months."[5] What had also happened in the 1980s was that after health insurance had gradually expanded to cover more of the workforce since World War II, the Reagan years saw coverage stop growing and the number of uninsured Americans begin to climb. It was also becoming increasingly fragile as the postwar social safety net became more stressed—one in four Americans went without health insurance at some point between 1987 and 1989.[6] By the time of the 1992 presidential election, the number of uninsured nationally had topped thirty-nine million.

As a critical political issue, health care first arrived on the scene in 1991 in the Pennsylvania special election to replace Senator John Heinz, who had been killed in a plane crash. Democrat Harris Wofford squared off in an uphill battle against Republican heavyweight Richard Thornburgh and, to the surprise of many, the defining issue of the race held amid the lingering economic recession became voters' health-care insecurities. In one ad, Wofford stood in a hospital emergency room. "If criminals have the right to a lawyer, I think working Americans should have the right to a doctor," he announced. "I'm Harris Wofford, and I believe there is nothing more fundamental than the right to see a doctor when you're sick."[7] As health care came to dominate, Thornburgh's seemingly insurmountable lead evaporated. Come Election Day, the Democratic candidate won by a stunning ten-point margin, and nearly a third of voters reported picking Wofford specifically because of his health-care championing.

President George H. W. Bush heard the message of the Pennsylvania election loud and clear. He promptly canceled a two-week Asia trip to focus on domestic issues. It was too late: Arkansas governor Bill Clinton would ride domestic issues into the White House a year later, thanks in no small part to his support for sweeping health-care reform. Just weeks before the presidential election—and almost exactly a year before he'd unveil his health-care plan to Congress as president—Clinton spoke at the Merck Pharmaceuticals plant in Rahway, New Jersey, surrounded by party leaders like Bill Bradley, Jay Rockefeller, and, not least of all, Wofford himself. He told Americans that we "are not getting the system we are paying for and nobody is paying as much as we are for health care." He recited story after story about working families struggling to make ends meet with growing health-care costs and promised, "This is a matter that is critical for the future of this country's survival."[8]

Contrary to how we remember it today, the Clinton health plan started out popular. After her husband appointed Hillary to head the effort, the first lady and Ira Magaziner spent months listening to experts, touring facilities, and interviewing people at all levels of the health-care system, as well as reading some seven hundred thousand letters sent to the task force by the public. Voters broadly supported her efforts, with one poll by Roper showing that 70 percent of Americans reported they liked what they had heard about the Clinton proposals.[9]

On September 22, 1993, Clinton took the rostrum in the House of Representatives and asked the country to work with him to "fix a health-care system that is badly broken": "At long last, after decades of false starts, we must make this our most urgent priority: Giving every American health security—health care that's always there—health care that can never be taken away."

He told the story of Americans on the front line of the problem, including Floridian Kerry Kennedy, who owned a small furniture franchise that employed seven people in Titusville and had been forced to end his company's health-care program when his elderly parents—the founders of the company who still worked in the store—proved too expensive to insure. "Millions of Americans are just a pink slip away from losing their health coverage, and one serious illness away from losing their life savings. Millions more are locked into the wrong jobs, because they'd lose their coverage if they left their companies. And on any given day over 37 million of our fellow citizens, the vast majority of them children or hardworking adults, have no health insurance at all. And despite all of this, our medical bills are growing at more than twice the rate of inflation," he said.

In the closing paragraphs of his speech, Clinton framed the debate as his generation's historical challenge—where the New Dealers banded together to provide Social Security and a way out of the Depression, and where the legislators of the 1960s assembled the pieces of the Great Society, the baby boomers would deliver this last piece of the social safety net. "It's hard to believe that once there was a time—even in this century—when retirement was nearly synonymous with poverty, and older Americans died in our streets. That is unthinkable today because over a half-century ago Americans had the courage to change—to create a Social Security System that ensures that no Americans will be forgotten in their later years. I believe that forty years from now, our grandchildren will also find it unthinkable that there was a time in our country when hardworking families lost their homes and savings simply because their child fell ill, or lost their health coverage when they changed jobs. Yet, our grandchildren will only find such things unthinkable tomorrow, if we have the courage to change today," he told Congress and the millions of Americans watching his speech at home.[10]

The first presentations of the plan were met with acclaim. A day after his speech, Clinton flew to Florida for a televised *Nightline* town hall meeting on the subject, where he held forth for nearly two hours on the critical need for reform. A *Time*/CNN poll showed that nearly six in ten Americans favored Clinton's health-care plan. "People feel he is trying," Clinton adviser George Stephanopoulos told *Time*. "Whether they agree with him or not, they feel he is doing big things."[11] *The New York Times* proclaimed ten days after Clinton's speech to Congress that on Capitol Hill, "The Clinton plan is alive on arrival."[12] Hillary Clinton was lauded for her tireless work; the *Times* said she was "breaking down the mentality that says there's a contradiction between being a warm, fuzzy mom and an expert on health care." Republicans were eager to work with her, with Senator John Danforth saying that he expected Congress to pass the bill within a year. The national debate quickly seemed to shift from whether reform should happen to focus on what reform should happen.

By late spring 1994, though, the plan had withered on the vine—the result of a concerted campaign by business, insurance companies, and Republican leaders like Dick Armey and rising star Newt Gingrich. The "Harry and Louise" series of TV ads pictured a middle-class couple at home, confused and frightened by the Clinton plan. Rather than offering their own solutions, Republicans blasted the plan for enlarging bureaucracy and threatening people's ability to choose their own doctors. Hillary Clinton was targeted and mocked. The Clinton team, which had pioneered the idea of a rapid-response "war room" in the campaign, had done a poor job selling the 1,342-page plan to Congress and the public. Many of the charges were unfair, but the simple matter is that the Clinton team didn't defend their baby until it was too late. By fall, the plan was dead and Republicans would take back the House of Representatives for the first time in a half century.

It wasn't the first time that national health care had failed because of strong grassroots outreach by opponents. When Harry Truman had first proposed national health care in the waning years of the New Deal era, the American Medical Association had sent more than a million pamphlets to doctors' offices to be read by waiting patients that proclaimed, "Compulsory health insurance—political medicine—is bad medicine for America!"[13] John Kennedy had also tried in the 1960s, only to be blocked by medical groups and insurance companies. It wasn't until that magical moment after his assassination when his successor, Lyndon Johnson, was able to usher in the Great Society that ensured the elderly and poor could at least receive health care.

What was important to note in the 1994 debate, though, was that the American people never abandoned their desire for a fundamental, sweeping reform of the health-care system. They simply, under enormous lobbying by special interests, lost faith in the Clinton plan specifically. In the heat of the battle in the spring of 1994, polling showed that while voters had been specifically turned off by the Clinton plan, they actually supported what it would accomplish. A *Wall Street Journal*/NBC poll showed that while 45 percent opposed the Clinton plan and only 37 percent favored it, when the same voters were asked about an unlabeled plan outlining the general principles of the Clinton plan, more than 76 percent reported that they thought it was "appealing," and it actually beat out the four other congressionally sponsored plans under debate at that point.[14]

It's on this last point where the political system most greatly failed the American people, observes political scientist Theda Skocpol, who studied the rise and fall of the Clinton health-care plan in her important 1996 work *Boomerang: Clinton's Health Security Effort and the Turn Against Government in U.S. Politics.* The public clearly supported health-care reform and some form of universal health care; they just couldn't navigate the complicated legislative choices to decide on a final outcome. That should have been the role of the nation's elected decision makers in Congress and the administration. The American people had spoken; the country's leaders should have delivered. "Public opinion in general never chooses among exact policy options; nor does it work out the details of policy innovations. These tasks are the responsibility of societal leaders and elected officials, ideally working within a general mandate given by voters and the public," Skocpol explains. The mandate was there. The nation's leadership in both parties failed to deliver.

Little in the public's mind has changed in fourteen years. Over the last decade, according to CBS/*New York Times* polls, the percentage of Americans who believe that "the federal government should guarantee health insurance for all Americans" has climbed steadily from 56 to 64 percent—an impressive and consistent consensus. Health-care reform remains a critical issue. Costs are still rising. The number of uninsured is higher than ever, and what was a $60 billion problem in 1970 and an $800 billion problem in 1990 is a $2 trillion-a-year issue today. Yet the nation's leaders still haven't delivered fundamental reform—they spend their time instead debating what the DLC's Will Marshall calls "capillary" fixes like a Patient's Bill of Rights. Other than on Howard Dean's campaign, health care was not a significant issue in the 2004 presidential election, and neither a Republican nor Democratic Congress has taken the lead in delivering one of the nation's most needed reforms.

Major changes have, though, taken place elsewhere in the American landscape, and as the nation debates who will next lead it, it's these other changes that just might finally cause fundamental health-care reform to move forward. Fourteen years after Clinton's first major effort failed, reform is all the more critical to the nation's future. Today American business is seeing its ability to compete on the world stage hurt by the creeping health-care crisis. In this global age, health-care reform doesn't seem quite the entitlement it did back in 1994 during the waning days of the industrial age. The United States is the only major industrialized country that relies on employer-based health-care benefits, and as costs spiral American companies are finding it harder to compete with international companies that don't have to put the price of their workers' health care in the price of their products. Whereas business hated the concept of health-care reform a decade ago, the effects of globalization since 2000 have caused a sea change in the way health care is viewed—government-led reform and cost controls are now critical to the future of many companies.

General Motors spends more on health care than it does on either steel or advertising; $1,700 of the price of a car manufactured in the

United States goes to cover health care, whereas that figure is only about $250 in Japan—meaning Japanese cars have an almost $1,500 advantage on the global stage when it comes to pricing. The Canadian automakers and the auto workers' union released a joint letter explaining that that nation's national health-care system saves its manufacturers four dollars an hour in benefits and this is a "strategic advantage" and an "important ingredient" in the nation's success in its "most important export industry." And where are those cars going? Into the United States, where health-care costs are much higher. "The rising cost of health benefits is the biggest issue on our plate that we can't solve," Bill Ford, Ford's CEO, told a Michigan business conference. "Health care is out of control—it's a system that's broken." GM CEO Rick Wagoner went to Capitol Hill in the summer of 2006 to plead for action on health-care costs. "They've just taken a complete pass on doing something about the health-care situation," he criticized. "It's driving jobs out of the country."

Howard Schultz, the CEO of Starbucks, which now invests more each year in health-care costs than in buying coffee beans, has been another leader on the issue. He sponsored the May 2004 "Cover the Uninsured Week" program and told *Fortune*, "We can't be the kind of society we aspire to be when we have 50 million people uninsured. It's a blemish on what it means to be an American." Starbucks has long offered health-care benefits to employees—a decision based partially on Schultz's experience growing up when his deliveryman father was fired and lost his health insurance when he broke his ankle. But with the company now operating in dozens of countries around the world where universal health insurance exists, Schultz lobbied Congress for changes in the way the United States operates—and, just like GM's Wagoner, came away frustrated by inaction. "It's all great when you're there," he says. "Then you leave, and nothing happens."[15]

The 2008 presidential campaign will be the first in an era where American business is among the strongest proponents of health-care reform. In fact, the first question at the Nevada health-care forum— the first presidential debate ever that focused specifically and only on health care—was from a small businessman who expressed concern over how health-care costs were impacting his ability to compete.

"We want to make American business competitive," John Edwards told the forum. "Something has to be done about our health-care system. It's making [businesses] increasingly uncompetitive with respect to the rest of the world. Universal health-care coverage done the right way, with the right choices and the right efficiencies will actually help American business, not just the 47 million individuals who don't have health insurance."

"The most important challenge for us is to build a political consensus around the need to solve this problem," Obama says. "The question is whether we are able to bring a majority of people together to solve the problem now? One thing that makes me feel more optimistic about this than I might have ten or twelve years ago is that now business is feeling the pinch. Large corporations realize that they can't be competitive on the international stage if their health-care costs are rising at a constant clip and their competitors don't have to pay anything because it's all covered by a government system. Small businesses know that their employees won't be as productive if they don't have access to health care. There's an enormous opportunity for the next president . . . to bring business, labor, consumers, and providers together and stay focused on it for a year, two years, however long it takes until it happens."

SEIU's Stern, whose members see the crumbling health-care system at work each day, is leading the way in building the consensus for national health-care reform. His approach in labor organizing—which has helped propel SEIU to be the nation's fastest-growing union—has always been to line up unlikely allies and to look at issues in a global frame. As he continues his lengthy health-care crusade, he says that in recent years he's noticed business coming around. February 2007 found him at probably the least likely press conference he'd ever expected: He stood next to Wal-Mart's CEO Lee Scott, the head of a company his union and the labor movement have spent recent years demonizing at every turn, to call for new approaches to health care. Scott had begun to take a public stance on the issue when he appeared on Charlie Rose's TV show in 2006, saying, "I think we're getting to a tipping point where this country is going to be willing to move on health care. Business and labor are going to have to participate and probably play even more of a leadership role than government . . . and then bring the political side along with them." That was music to Stern's ears.

The "Better Health Care Together" campaign—which brought together SEIU, AT&T, Wal-Mart, Intel, Kelly Services, and the communications workers' union—wasn't focused on specific policies but instead on changing the broader climate for politicians. "We can't keep tinkering, hoping that incremental change will fix our broken health-care system," Stern said at the press conference. "We need fundamental change, and it is going to take new thinking, leadership, new partnerships, some risk taking, and compromising to make it happen." Scott was more blunt: "We need to change the current system and we need to change it now."[16]

In health care, like many of the critical issues the nation's leaders are failing to address seriously, governors and states are moving ahead with their own reforms—and here, like on many of the other issues of the first campaign, there's leadership by Republican governors where there's no leadership from the national GOP. On one of Mitt Romney's first days as Massachusetts governor, the founder and former CEO of Staples, Tom Stamberg, came to his office with a message: "If you really want to help people, find a way to get everyone health insurance." Romney assembled a team to study the issue and made a series of improvements to cover the state's four hundred thousand uninsured—for one, he discovered that 20 percent of the uninsured were eligible for Medicaid but had never enrolled, so he set up an internet site where, if they sought treatment at a hospital, the hospital could sign them up. He also introduced and the legislature passed a law mandating health insurance just like auto insurance—people either had to have it through their employer or buy into a series of plans. As he explained, "We insist that everybody who drives a car has insurance, and cars are a lot less expensive than people."[17] The plan also included a clause inserted by the Democratic legislature that would force employers who didn't provide health-care coverage to pay a fee of $295 per employee to the state to help cover those workers. Even while the bill may seem to conservatives to be government meddling with the free market, Romney explained that it's anything but. "Some of my libertarian friends balk at what looks like an individual mandate. But remember, someone has to pay for the health care that must, by law, be provided: Either the individual pays or the taxpayers pay. A free ride on government is not libertarian," he said.[18]

Massachusetts is hardly alone. California governor Arnold Schwarzenegger wants to cover everyone in the nation's most populous state. Hawaii and Maine are trying to expand near-universal health care, and numerous states from Vermont to Illinois have nearly universal care for children. Less than a year after the Massachusetts bill became law, more than half the states had some similar major reform under debate. The states realized that in the current climate, leadership isn't going to come from Washington. "The federal government can't seem to get over the partisan divide," Martin Sellers, who runs a health-care consulting company that's working with a half dozen states on their reforms, told *National Journal* in 2007. "Governors are closer to the ground. [The number of uninsured] is more real for them. They think if they don't address this, it becomes a huge problem going forward."[19]

There are, at the core, two major related crises in American health care: outmoded practices and delivery of care along with spiraling costs and insurance premiums. To fix the problem, we must simultaneously reform the way the nation delivers and finances health care. Make no mistake: It will be a huge political battle but one that every day becomes more critical to win—and one, again, that plays to the strengths of Democrats.

For a presidential candidate in 2008 willing to run on a first campaign–type platform and embrace the realities of the health-care marketplace, the basic details of a national plan are pretty well established. The Bush administration's much-touted health savings accounts have proved they aren't the answer and less than 1 percent of Americans have bothered to sign up for one. The open market alone will not offer reform at the scale that is needed. Government intervention and participation are necessary. There has to be some sort of shared responsibility among employees, employers, and the government. A single-payer government-led plan seems unlikely given the objections of the insurance industry—no matter how smart a decision it might be—so the result is likely to be a hybrid of a public-private plan.

In fact, with the race under way, most 2008 candidates support some version of what Democrats have labeled "Medicare for all." One doesn't often hear these days of the federal government doing good, but in fact it actually administers two very successful health-care plans: Medicare, which covers elderly Americans and has some of the lowest administrative and bureaucratic costs in the country, and the plan for federal employees—including the president and members of Congress, as well as postal workers and cabinet employees—which provides a wide variety of private plans and options. As Chris Dodd stated, "I'm a United States Senator, I have a wonderful health-care program. I want every single American to have as good a health plan as every member of the United States Congress. That ought to be something that all of us stand and fight for."

To think that such reforms will be free is crazy. Even amid a general culture where politicians find the threat of raising taxes enough to end even promising careers, each candidate at the Nevada health-care forum admitted, in his or her own code words, that "additional revenue" would likely be needed for reform. "You don't get universal health care for free," Obama told the audience. Edwards is up front that his plan would cost the government between $90 billion and $120 billion a year, which he says he would finance by rolling back the Bush tax cuts on those making over $200,000 a year.

"The American people have heard so many politicians say for so long that 'Oh, we're going to have universal health care.' 'We're going to transform the way we use energy in America.' 'We're going to eliminate poverty in America.' 'And in the process we're going to eliminate the federal deficit,'" Edwards told the Nevada audience. "They've probably got a bridge in Brooklyn they want to sell you too. I don't think it can be done. I think it's really important, particularly given what's happened in the last six–seven years in this country, for the American president to be honest with the American people. And that honesty starts right here in the campaign."

Expanding coverage to forty-seven million more Americans will initially come with a steep price tag, although such a move would likely actually save money in the long run. The catch right now is that Americans are already paying for those uninsured and underinsured people in the country. Lacking regular access to doctors, these uninsured end up going to emergency rooms for chronic and basic needs alike, where their bills are passed along to taxpayers or other insurance plans. "It's already being paid for. They're in emergency rooms and we're already paying for it," Bill Richardson complained to the Nevada audience. In 2005, the advocacy group Families USA calculated that family health insurance premiums were $922 higher and individual health insurance premiums were $341 higher because of the passed-along cost of providing health care to those without insurance. All told, the Institute of Medicine estimates that the economic benefit of insuring all people might be as much as $130 billion annually because it would result in better health and longer lives of covered individuals, decreased Medicaid and disability payments, lower demands on the public health infrastructure like emergency rooms, and increased local health service capacity that no longer would be overwhelmed by minor cases. That figure is less than most of the 2008 candidates estimate their plans would cost, meaning that embracing health-care reform should actually be smart politics for both nurturing, family-friendly Democrats and fiscally conscious Republicans.

At the same time, though, other reforms are needed across the system. Democrats and trial lawyers like John Edwards may hate the mere mention of the idea, but any comprehensive health-care reform must address the skyrocketing litigation costs and malpractice insurance rates that are threatening doctors around the country. A dime out of every dollar in U.S. health-care spending goes to cover litigation costs and what is known as "defensive medicine," the extra tests and prescriptions doctors order to cover themselves from liability.[20]

Another critical part of any reform must be an increasing reliance on preventive care. Hillary Clinton points out that even as the country wrestles with an explosion of diabetes in increasingly younger Americans, the nation's health plans refuse to cover preventive measures like nutritionists or podiatrists to help ensure that people don't end up losing a leg—the irony of the current system, of course, is that only amputation, the most expensive and most damaging, is covered by most insurers. The much-debated obesity epidemic in the United States is alone costing the system more than $100 billion annually, and the long-term costs will be even greater. Chris Dodd phrases it like this: "The health-care system today deals with you when you get sick. We ought to be doing a far better job of making it possible for people not to become ill."

Pairing preventive care with better management of chronic diseases would be a big step too. According to what sociologists call the Pareto principle, 80 percent of a certain situation is generally caused by only 20 percent of the population. In terms of medical care, studies by the nonpartisan Congressional Budget Office have found that to be true in the health-care realm—roughly 80 percent of the nation's health-care costs are run up by only 20 percent of the population. These chronically ill people suffer from multiple serious ongoing conditions that together require annual hospitalizations, dozens of medical visits, and more than fifty prescriptions a year. In fact, according to medical studies, the chronically ill in the United States make up roughly 78 percent of total health-care costs, 76 percent of all hospital admissions, 88 percent of all drug prescriptions, and 72 percent of physician visits. And yet a *New England Journal of Medicine* study found that the average health-care consumer has only a fifty-fifty chance of receiving the correct care for a condition.[21] Better case management and holistic treatments could make a huge difference. As one examination of chronically ill homeless in Reno found, a single individual there had required over $1 million in emergency medical care over a decade—costs passed directly to the taxpayers.[22]

New Mexico governor Bill Richardson has fought the battle in his own state by pushing healthful lifestyle choices like banning junk food—which is helping to fuel the diabetes epidemic—in schools and a public smoking ban. "We spend 75 percent of health-care costs on chronic diseases and only five percent on prevention. That should shift," Richardson promises. In a culture where work is increasingly conducted behind a desk in front of a computer, he believes that companies should receive incentives to give their employees time for exercise and to promote healthful lifestyles.

Reducing the administrative burden would also save billions. Currently, nearly a third of the country's health-care bill goes to administrative costs and bureaucracy. Electronic medical records would be a big step in the right direction. "We are drowning and frankly people are suffering because we have a paper system in the health-care field. We don't rely on paper in any other big part of our economy anymore.

Because we rely on paper we are wasting money. We could save, by an independent assessment, $100 billion a year if we moved towards electronic medical records," said Clinton, who drew repeated, loud, sustained applause from the Las Vegas audience filled with health-care workers.

Last but hardly least, the medical community is increasingly aware of how environmental conditions can damage health. Addressing the way we use energy and treat the world around us will continue to have a major impact on our society's health in the coming years. One study of five thousand children in Los Angeles found that those living within 250 feet of a major roadway—of which L.A. has tons—had a 50 percent greater chance of contracting asthma.[23] We must recognize the links between the way that we impact our world and the way it impacts us in turn.

PERHAPS NO CANDIDATE in the race has so closely tied his or her political future to the issue of health-care reform as the woman who originally launched the issue onto the national stage during her husband's presidency. Hillary Clinton's health-care task force in 1993, with its endless deliberations, its secret discussions, and its overly complicated plan, came to symbolize what made so many wary of the Clintons' attempt at a "copresidency." The intervening years, though, have seen her remake herself, win election to the U.S. Senate twice with strong bipartisan margins, and win the friendship, support, and respect of many of her former adversaries in Congress. Yet at the same time she has continued to position herself as one of the nation's leading advocates for bringing the post–World War II health-care system into an information-based, globalized, and competitive world. She knows the issue's intricacies better than almost anyone else—the statistics, the pitfalls, the theories, and the dangers. She's quick to promise that her second attempt at national health-care reform from within the White House will have a different result, thanks, in part, to the ways the world around the White House has changed in the last decade.

Two days after the Nevada forum, Hillary Clinton was in Iowa to pick up the endorsement of former candidate and former Hawkeye Governor Tom Vilsack. Her first stop that morning, though, was at a town hall meeting about health care broadcast on *Good Morning America*. Speaking from the Science Center of Iowa to two hundred local activists, she explained how deeply she's committed to the issue. "We're going to have universal health care when I'm president—there's no doubt about that," she told the crowd. "I believe we're in a better position today to do that than we were in '93 and '94." The American people, she promised, would make health-care reform the primary issue of the race.

"We're going to get it done," she assured them. And the thing is, this time she might be right—thanks to the support of organizations as diverse as Andy Stern's SEIU and Lee Scott's Wal-Mart and the appearance that most of the 2008 presidential candidates seem ready to embrace the path necessary to address the twenty-first century. In this first campaign of a globalized, technologically reliant America, Harry Truman might finally get his wish and the United States might finally join the rest of the industrialized world in ensuring its citizens access to quality, affordable health care.

ISSUE #4: POWERING A
TWENTY-FIRST-CENTURY ECONOMY

Science, like any field of endeavor, relies on freedom of inquiry; and one of the hallmarks of that freedom is objectivity. Now, more than ever, on issues ranging from climate change to AIDS research to genetic engineering to food additives, government relies on the impartial perspective of science for guidance.

—PRESIDENT GEORGE H. W. BUSH, APRIL 23, 1990

A cartoon by *The Washington Post*'s Tom Toles, a few months before the 2006 election, said it all: It depicted, in six frames, a "public service announcement" from Planet Earth, seated at a desk and saying, "Global warming is now a crisis facing all of us. And despite NASA's suggestions otherwise, I, Planet Earth, am the only livable place you've got. The Republicans in power have made it perfectly clear that they have no intention of doing anything meaningful about it in the next two years. Two years we don't have. This alone is reason enough to vote against every single Republican running for national office in November. Thank you."[1]

Since taking office in January 2001, President Bush has done everything he can to ignore, downplay, and obfuscate the issue of climate change. Republican colleagues in the Senate and the House have followed suit, meaning that as other nations have forged ahead and confronted a problem that may well be a matter of life or death, America's leadership has been left behind.

Meanwhile, one of the leaders of the Democratic Party won an Oscar and a Nobel Peace Prize for his attention to and passion for the issue. The path to the Academy Awards for Al Gore began in the cold rain of War Memorial Plaza in Nashville, Tennessee, where on the evening of November 7 and in the early hours of November 8, 2000, he appeared to have won, then lost, then perhaps won again the presidency. The next summer he went sailing on the Ionian Sea, and at his wife's urging didn't shave his beard before he returned from vacation. The heavier, bearded Gore marked the launch of a new career as a crusader. A year after his sailing trip, in 2002, he called Beth Viola, who had served as his senior environmental adviser and was now a lobbyist in Washington. "Do you know where my slides are?" he asked.

In his early days as a congressman in the 1970s, he'd begun giving a slide show about the dangers of pollution and the perils of climate change. Over time it grew to be a complicated and technical performance, using three projectors at once. At one disastrous show in Tennessee he realized that he'd put in every slide backward. Climate change had first attracted his interest in college when he took a course taught by Professor Roger Revelle, who was the first person in the world to monitor carbon dioxide in the atmosphere. Revelle had found an alarming and ongoing rise in CO_2 ever since he began tracking it. Twelve years later, Gore asked Revelle to be the lead-off witness at the first congressional hearing on global warming. "Remembering the power of his warning, I assumed that if he just laid out the facts as clearly as he had back in that college class, my colleagues and everybody else in the hearing room would be just as shocked as I had been—and thus galvanized into action," Gore recalls in the introduction to his 1992 book, *Earth in the Balance: Ecology and the Human Spirit*.

Alas, it was not to be. Gore would spend the next three decades sounding warnings that went largely unheeded. *Earth in the Balance* became the first book written by a sitting U.S. senator to make the *New York Times* bestseller list since John Kennedy's *Profiles in Courage*. In his book, Gore argued, "We must make the rescue of the environment the central organizing principle for civilization." All through his eight years as vice president, Gore continued to pay attention to environmental issues and collect materials for his slide show. By the time he left office, the slide show had grown to three boxes full, which had ended up with Viola lest they get lost in the move out of the White House. She returned them to Gore, and he set to work updating them and presenting the slide show that he estimates he's now given more than a thousand times.[2]

Laurie David, whose then-husband, Larry David, is the star of HBO's popular show *Curb Your Enthusiasm*, saw Gore's presentation in 2004 in New York and was immediately struck by it. She put together a group to meet with Gore that included the billionaire founder of eBay, Jeffrey Skoll, and Lawrence Bender, who produced *Pulp Fiction* and other Quentin Tarantino films. They asked him to let them make a movie, and after some initial resistance from the man who introduces himself to crowds as "I used to be the next president of the United States," he agreed. The result, *An Inconvenient Truth*, won over the admittedly liberal-leaning crowd at Sundance in January 2006 and opened on four screens in New York City and Los Angeles on May 24, 2006, before going national on June 2.

That was where the incredible thing happened: Millions of Americans paid to attend a science lecture. In Washington, D.C., where I watched it at the independent E Street Cinema, all of the first night's shows on two different screens sold out. Audiences sat in rapt attention for the one-hundred-minute movie—essentially a long slide show lecture on the reality of global warming, souped up with some special effects, animations, and some history of Gore as a warm, funny, emotive human that few had ever seen. The documentary quickly climbed to be the third-highest-grossing documentary of all time. On February 25, 2007, he took to the stage to accept the Academy Award for the year's best documentary. He told the crowd, "My fellow Americans, people all over the world, we need to solve the climate crisis. It's not a political issue; it's a moral issue. We have everything we need to get started, with the possible exception of the will to act. That's a renewable resource. Let's renew it."

Perhaps no movie in the history of the country has had such an effect on the political landscape. In the days and weeks leading up to the movie's opening, the subject of climate change and global warming came to the forefront—where, inexorably, it has remained almost ever since. Gore's movie, the culmination of decades of environmental work and personal interest, broke through the noise and political clutter that had accumulated around an issue that the Bush administration and Republicans had pushed to the side. The consensus that action of some kind is required is strong enough that John McCain and Barack Obama are sponsoring the same climate change bill in the Senate.

Less than a month after getting his Oscar, Gore arrived on Capitol Hill to testify in front of the newly Democratic Congress on climate change. The line to get tickets to the hearing began a full day early when two professional line standers took their place in the Rayburn House Office Building—they're an oddity of Washington life whereby high-priced lawyers, lobbyists, and corporate executives will pay $75 an hour for someone else to wait in line for entrance to things like congressional hearings and Supreme Court arguments. The money was well worth it—by the morning of the hearing, the line stretched the length of the hallway. A half hour before Gore's hearing began, two executives from the Texas energy company TXU walked up to take their line holders' places at the head of the line.[3]

Gore didn't pull any punches. He held the feet of the panel to the fire for two hours, laying out the situation and pleading for action. He pointed to another movie then popular in the theaters, about the three hundred Greeks who died in the battle of Thermopylae defending a pass from the Persians but in the process saved democracy. "There are times—rare though they be—when a relatively small group is called upon to show courage . . . not only for themselves, but for all future generations. This Congress is now the 535; really and truly, it's one of those times," he told the packed committee room. "This is our Thermopylae."

Gore's testimony was an admittedly odd moment: When history recalls the two paths leading out of the 2000 election, the nation's response to climate change will be one of the clearest differences. For Gore, no other issue was as pressing as the changes taking place in the environment. For Bush, the candidate who won the Supreme Court decision that allowed him entrance to the Oval Office, climate change was and has been something to be ignored for as long as possible. In the intervening years, though, the American public has come to understand the issue in a personal and thoughtful way, ensuring that they're ready for action by the nation's leadership. Having rejected the path chosen by the president, they're now ready to be led—they want solutions and progress. Now the challenge in 2008 is to elect someone who also understands the difficulty and necessity of the tough choices ahead.

Climate change from CO_2 pollution is what economists like to call an "externality," a side effect, unintentional or otherwise, imposed on others by an "economic transaction." The original parties—the polluters—bear little, if any, of the cost of their pollution, while future societies will be hurt the most. Pollution, which once seemed primarily an issue addressed on the local level, is now understood to be worldwide. Our weather in the coming decades will be strongly affected by the new dirty coal plants coming online in China, just as Europeans will see their personal health and regional temperatures affected by pollution from the United States. Because CO_2 pollution and climate change are externalities, there's little incentive for the companies doing the polluting today to change their methods and clean up—especially as globalization connects us and intertwines the world's pollution. It's not a problem that the open market will solve on its own. Governmental coordination, intervention, and investment are required. This will be the first presidential campaign where global warming is understood to be a pressing issue, and the first where serious attention must be paid to its consequences.

While there are major decisions ahead for the next president in terms of economics, trade, education, and health-care reform, there's almost no issue as critical to the future of the country or the world as those the Oval Office will make in the coming decade on the increasingly interconnected issues of energy, the environment, and foreign policy. It won't be an easy road, to be sure, but the decision to act or not will have more profound implications than anyone can imagine. The challenge is that by the time true impacts begin to be felt, it may be too late. As Gore remarked on *The Daily Show with Jon Stewart*, "I do think that the situation that we're facing is outside the boundaries of what the political system is used to contemplating."[4]

That said, though, Al Gore explains that we as a nation know how to combat things that seem too massive to take on—we did it during the Cold War, defeating communism over the course of a half century because it was the never-forgotten focus of the government and its citizens. "What made this dramatic victory possible was a conscious and shared decision by men and women in the nations of the 'free world' to make the defeat of the Communist system the central organizing principle of not only their governments' policies but of society itself. This is not to say that this goal dominated every waking thought, or guided every policy decision, but opposition to communism was the principle underlying almost all of the geopolitical strategies and social policies designed by the West after World War II," Gore says.[5] And along the way, as previous chapters have shown, the United States got some incredible benefits—from the interstate highway system, built to speed war matériel around the country, to the National Defense Education Act, which in the wake of Sputnik brought tens of thousands of new scientists, mathematicians, and engineers into the workforce just as technology began radically reshaping our lives. Imagine the unknown and unforeseen things that a mass energy conversion campaign can bring to the country. Confronting climate change could be the engine that powers the nation's economy for decades to come.

IF THE CURRENT SITUATION is more than our nation's leaders are used to confronting, it's because energy, as it turns out, is a giant Gordian knot—wrapped up intricately, tightly, and inseparably from our national security and the health of our environment. The trade-offs and devil's bargains we've made over the last half century that have led us to today's situation became strikingly and blindingly clear in the days after September 11. The situation we're in today isn't really anyone's fault. The choices along the way all seemed to make sense at the time, but now, as we enter the first campaign of the twenty-first century, it's clear these choices landed us in some hot water—literally.

Our picture of the interconnectedness of national security, energy, and the environment has changed immeasurably in the last six years. Americans now see it sixteen billion times a year, forty-four million times a day, when they stop to buy gas.[6] Each $10 increase in the price of a barrel of oil sends another $50 billion a year overseas to countries that, by and large, wish the United States ill. Since industrialization, the country has built its entire economy around oil—which people now understand is both funding terrorism against the United States and destroying the environment at a rate faster than anyone had imagined.

Daily, the United States consumes upward of twenty million barrels of oil, a number that is expected to grow to twenty-eight million barrels a day by 2025. About eight million barrels a day of our oil needs are met with domestic production, and twelve million barrels are imported—one quarter from the Persian Gulf OPEC states like Saudi Arabia, a quarter from other OPEC members like Venezuela and Nigeria, and the rest from other oil-producing countries like the UK.[7] This reliance has led to some awkward situations: Our role in the Mideast is one of the key reasons for the jihadist resentment. Study after study of the Muslim world has shown that the United States isn't hated "because we're free" but because of a few specific U.S. policies, high among them our backing of the restrictive (but oil-rich) Saudi government.

Even though it had already begun to change after September 11, the energy picture began to evolve radically in 2003 as two major developments combined to reshape the world energy markets. First, the United States invaded Iraq, setting off a period of increased tension in the oil-rich Middle East that continues with no sign of abating in the foreseeable future. Second, China passed Japan to become the second-largest oil importer in the world as its GDP roared past $1,000 per capita, the Chinese began purchasing cars in increasing numbers, and its energy needs from power and industry soared. A country that had around 16 million cars in 2000—fewer than the number sold each year in the United States—had 27 million by 2004, and will have an estimated 56 million by 2010 and 120 million by 2020. In 2004, the country required a million more barrels of oil a day than it did a year earlier, and in 2005 that number went up another 230,000 barrels per day—roughly the equivalent of all of Chad's output.

And things are just getting started. To give some idea of the growth potential of the Chinese auto market, that country now has roughly as many cars per capita as the United States did in 1910.[8] "In the 1970s, North America consumed twice as much oil as Asia. [In 2005], for the first time ever, Asia's oil consumption exceeded North America's," oil expert Daniel Yergin explains. "The trend will continue: half of the total growth in oil consumption in the next 15 years will come from Asia."[9] By 2050, economists estimate that the number of cars in the world will have tripled. All that equates to a tighter—and pricier—oil market. As gas prices in the United States regularly hit highs of $2.50, $3, or even $3.50, it's an issue that Democrats have seized on, holding press conference after press conference in front of gas stations and their pricey signs, to focus public attention on the country's damaging energy policies—and one that families and commuters are responding to because they see the effect in their checking accounts each month. Even a family filling up its gas tank just once a week is paying $500 more a year now than before the Iraq war, not counting increased airfares and even in some cities taxi and pizza delivery fuel charges.

Thanks to the automobiles and broader industrialization, China is on a worldwide oil-buying spree that's placing the United States in an increasingly uncomfortable situation. As Chinese officials traveled the world to secure oil access, they promised Iran an auto plant and $70 billion in aid, Nigeria got $3 billion and a refinery, and Venezuela's dictator, Hugo Chávez, no friend of the United States, got over $700 million in aid. In 2005, China's state-run oil company even tried to outbid Chevron to buy the U.S. oil company Unocal, only to meet a storm of opposition. Our worldwide dependence on oil coupled with China's growth also forces us to make Faustian bargains with dictators. When the World Bank froze payments to Chad in January 2006 because its dictator, Idriss Déby, was spending the money on himself and arms rather than on economic development, all it took to turn on the spigot of funds again were threats from Déby that the oil projects currently under development by Exxon might end up in the hands of a Chinese oil company.[10] What even President Bush admits is an oil "addiction" is causing us to do things and make deals we'd never otherwise make, and it's killing us in the process.

So what exactly is the problem here? Quite simply, fossil fuels like oil are made up almost entirely of pure carbon—they are literally the liquid fossilized remains of carbon-based life like dinosaurs and other ancient creatures. Burning fossil fuels releases that carbon that has been hidden underground for eons into the atmosphere in the form of carbon dioxide. Over the course of recent Earth history, and we have data now going back millions of years, the amount of carbon in the atmosphere has stayed relatively stable. At the start of the Industrial Revolution in the 1800s, the amount of CO_2 in the atmosphere was about 280 parts per million, and even as recently as Al Gore's professor's first studies it was only about 315 ppm. Now, though, it's soared to more than 380 ppm and, depending on the study, will grow to somewhere between 600 and 900 ppm over the course of this century if left unchecked. Since additional CO_2 in the atmosphere serves as a blanket, trapping more of the sun's heat, the world faces an unprecedented warming trend of between 3° and 10° Fahrenheit this century—that speed exceeds the warming that ended the ice ages by a factor of thirty.[11] As Gore explains, "The human lung inhales oxygen and exhales carbon dioxide, and the engines of civilization have, in effect, automated the process of breathing."[12] Every gallon of gas sends 20 pounds of CO_2 in exhaust into the air, and in the United States we're burning 651 million gallons a day. It adds up.

The amount of fossil fuel America consumes is staggering. Americans use 1,143 gallons of gasoline per household per year, and the Energy Information Agency estimates that American petroleum use will increase by more than a third by 2025.[13] Each of the six billion people on Earth today is using about four times as much energy as a person did a century ago, and the burning of fossil fuels has soared sixteenfold over the same period. Energy needs show no sign of abating. In fact, half of the energy generated since the Industrial Revolution has been consumed in just the last twenty years.[14] Already we're struggling at the edge of the energy envelope. Pipeline capacity in the United States is running at 90 to 96 percent, and the investment needed to increase that to meet our annual 1.5 percent growth may require upward of a trillion dollars of pipeline construction by 2025 as well.

The signs of the impact of this additional CO_2 and the changes it's bringing to the environment are all around us, and they're getting frequent enough that we can't ignore them. The anecdotal evidence of warming is strong: At of the end of 2005, this first decade of the twenty-first century had already seen five of the six hottest years in recorded history—the sixth being El Niño–boosted 1998—so the next president will assume office in January 2009, one year before the end of what will be the hottest decade in the history of human civilization.[15] Ash trees are disappearing from New York City because the climate is now too warm and dry. Instead, city foresters are planting persimmon trees—the beautiful flowering trees abundant in southern cities. There's now grass growing on Antarctica's northern tip, and the continent's seven-hundred-foot-high Larsen B ice shelf, which was once the size of a small European country and had been stable for twelve thousand years, collapsed and broke up over just a few weeks in 2002.[16]

The future, on the current track, is not pretty. Once warming exceeds 4° or 5°, scientific models show massive, catastrophic changes to nearly every ecosystem in the world, ranging from the flooding of low-lying areas to the collapse of many agricultural regions and perhaps even a deep freeze for Northern Europe to even a doubling of the damage of hurricanes in the United States. The water supply will be affected and undermined for one-sixth of the world's population, and the poorest countries—those least able to deal with massive societal changes and population shifts—will be affected first, making very real the national security challenge to the United States. The greatest influx of refugees to the United States ever, the 1991 exodus from Haiti, was partly due to a collapse of the agriculture sector there.

Climate expert Joseph Romm predicts that "barring a major reversal in U.S. policies in the very next decade, come the 2020s, most everyone will know the grim fate that awaits the next fifty generations."[17] Scientist Peter Barrett, who has spent three decades studying climate and is now head of Victoria University's Antarctic Research Center, was more blunt when he received a lifetime achievement award in 2004. He used his speech to warn the distinguished audience about the dangers he foresaw after studying some forty million years of Earth's climate on Antarctica. He concluded, "A warming of this magnitude would risk the end of civilization as we know it by the end of this century."[18] As a point of comparison, the difference in average temperature between today and the last ice age—when glaciers covered most of the northern hemisphere and the oceans were hundreds of feet lower—is only 9°. It's frightening to consider what 9° more in the opposite direction would mean.

For starters, rising temperatures would speed the already-alarming melting of the ice sheets in Greenland and Antarctica, which have the potential over a century to raise sea levels worldwide by twenty to eighty feet. Climate change expert Tim Flannery suggests going to the beach and imagining what an eight-story building there would look like—and then imagining the waves breaking over the roof. Worldwide, the first few feet of sea-level rise alone will displace more than one hundred million people, largely in depressingly impoverished communities ill equipped to cope with hundreds of thousands of refugees. In the United States, all of the major Atlantic and Gulf Coast cities, or at least those we decide to protect and not abandon, would look like New Orleans—surrounded by levees to hold back the encroaching oceans. Conservative estimates show that Louisiana would lose a landmass equal to the size of Vermont, Florida would lose land equal to the size of Connecticut, and North Carolina and Texas would both lose land equivalent to the size of Delaware.[19]

Life in the interior would be radically changed as well. Left unchecked, temperature increases linked to greenhouse gases would dramatically alter life across nearly the entire country. A November 2005 study in the *Proceedings of the National Academy of Sciences* found that by the end of the century, temperatures in Washington, D.C., would exceed 98°F for more than two months out of the year; Oklahoma would see temperatures in excess of 110° for some sixty to eighty days a year—terrible enough, except that nearby Arizona would suffer temperatures of 105° or more for nearly a third of the year. "Hell and high water is not our certain future, but it is the future we should expect and plan for if we do not sharply reverse our energy and environmental policy in the next two decades," warns Romm.[20] Elizabeth Kolbert, whose lengthy series on climate change in *The New Yorker*, "Field Notes from a Catastrophe," won her a National Magazine Award, was more blunt: "It may seem impossible to imagine that a technologically advanced society could choose, in essence, to destroy itself, but that is what we are now in the process of doing."

As grim as that prediction is—and the science is increasingly sure that's where we're headed—it'll only get harder to address the longer we wait. We face a unique challenge in global warming: For the second time in the last hundred years, we confront a situation with the potential to end civilization. For forty years, the United States and the Soviet Union stared at each other during the Cold War, when pushing a few buttons could have launched thousands of nuclear missiles and decimated life on Earth. But the peculiar beauty of the Cold War was that someone needed to take affirmative action to end the world— each day that neither the United States nor the Soviet Union did anything was another day that the world went on happening. A day when no one did anything was a good day. Now, with global warming, we face the opposite: Inaction will bring about the end of civilization. We must act each day to change the situation and make the world better. A day when no one does anything is a bad day and makes every day afterward a little bit harder.

This is the situation presidential candidates in 2008 must confront: Every day that the U.S. government does not throw its considerable might, power, money, and intellect behind confronting global warming and climate change is a day when we gamble with the nation's future. If the candidate who wins in 2008 doesn't do it, it might be too late by 2012 or 2016. In the framework of the first campaign of the twenty-first century, we can't afford to not make this a top issue.

Already the world has largely squandered nearly three decades. None of the news is recent. As early as 1977, a report by the National Academy of Sciences warned that the continued uncontrolled emissions of greenhouse gases might raise temperatures across the world by 10°F and boost sea levels by twenty feet. Two years later, amid continued inaction, a 1979 academy report followed up with this grim statement: "[A] wait and see policy may mean waiting until it is too late." Fully a quarter century ago, an EPA report warned that "substantial increases in global warming may occur sooner than most of us would like to believe," with "catastrophic" results.[21]

And make no mistake: Scientists have developed a uniquely strong consensus that global warming is under way and that humans are causing it. The UN's Intergovernmental Panel on Climate Change's third report, in 2007, said that human-caused global warming was happening with a 90-percent certainty. The thorough review is an unprecendented effort—some four hundred experts reviewed twice by four hundred other experts, with more than thirty editors and a final report approved by more than one hundred countries.[22] The United States appears to be the only major industrialized country in the world in denial.

IT'S HERE, LOOKING at the interconnected issues of energy and the environment, that we see one of the challenges facing the Republican Party as it grapples with the first campaign of the twenty-first century. During the glory days of American science and research, Republicans were among its strongest backers; they understood that prosperity and economic growth stemmed directly from the research being conducted in our laboratories and universities. President Eisenhower created the President's Science Advisory Committee and named the first White House science adviser, James Killian, in the wake of the scare over the launching of Sputnik by the Soviet Union. It was a Republican, Russell Train, who helped found the World Wildlife Foundation in 1961, one of the first major environmental organizations, and who went on to be the second head of the EPA. Likewise, President Nixon was a major force behind the beginning of the environmental movement. He signed the Endangered Species Act in 1973 and strongly supported the Clean Air Act, which passed with the help of Republicans Robert Dole and Howard Baker, as well as Democrats Ed Muskie and Birch Bayh. In 1970, in a fancy ceremony in the White House's Roosevelt Room, as he signed the Clean Air Act, which would help combat smog in major cities, Nixon proclaimed, "I think 1970 will be known as the year of the beginning."

Over the coming years, though, the Republican Party's relationship with science would stretch and break. Nixon had a falling-out with his science adviser, Richard Garwin, after Garwin broke with him publicly over several issues, and as academics became increasingly vocal in opposition to the Vietnam War, Nixon threatened to cut off public funding for MIT even as his science adviser tried to explain that MIT was a critical part of the nation's defense infrastructure.[23] The split became wider under Presidents Reagan and George H. W. Bush. Reagan appointed a far-right surgeon general, C. Everett Koop, only to discover that Koop wouldn't let an ideological agenda get in the way of the science. Nevertheless, Reagan forbade Koop from speaking out about AIDS through the administration's first term. "I have never understood why those peculiar restraints were placed on me," Koop wrote later in his memoir.[24] Reagan also drew up an annotated "hit list" of scientists at the EPA, with notes like "a Nader on toxics" and "bleeding-heart liberal."[25] Reagan fought against taking action on acid rain, even after his own White House Office of Science and Technology Policy recommended that the nation take steps to curb it.[26] Under the first President Bush, NASA climatologist James Hansen found, a year after he had told Congress with "99 percent confidence" that a long-term warming trend was beginning, that the Bush administration edited his comments.

Nothing, though, has compared to the way that the current Bush administration has treated the issues of energy and the environment. The last seven years have seen an unprecedented level of animosity and distrust grow up between the scientific community and the Bush administration as the GOP's increasingly strong conservative wing has forced the administration to advance a social agenda over scientific progress. The Bush administration has ignored, downplayed, and outright lied about the issue at nearly every juncture. In one 2002 memo, Republican pollster Frank Luntz argued to the administration, "You need to continue to make scientific certainty a primary issue in the debate . . . The scientific debate is closing [against us] but not yet closed. There is still a window of opportunity to challenge the science."[27]

Through a movement calling for "sound science," the Republican establishment has advocated ever higher (and increasingly implausible) tests and consensus before acting on an issue. "To the Right, 'sound science' means requiring a higher burden of proof before action can be taken to protect public health and the environment. In other words, 'sound science' isn't really a scientific position at all," explains Chris Mooney, the author of the 2005 bestseller *The Republican War on Science*.[28]

To understand the dangers of "sound science," one needs to look no further than the December 2004 international conference in Buenos Aires on climate change, where Paula Dobriansky, Bush's un-

dersecretary of state for global affairs and the head of the U.S. delegation, blocked further action, arguing that it was useless. "Science tells
us that we cannot say with any certainty what constitutes a dangerous
level of warming, and therefore what level must be avoided," she declared. Such a standard is an impossibly high one that the administration has resisted on other issues—there was no such question, for
instance, on the Iraq war about "how many" weapons of mass destruction constituted a true danger to the United States. In the war on terrorism, Vice President Dick Cheney has argued that the United
States must pursue what journalist Ron Suskind outlined as a "one
percent doctrine": "If there was even a one percent chance of terrorists getting a weapon of mass destruction—and there has been a
small probability of such an occurrence for some time—the United
States must now act as if it were a certainty."[29] When it comes to
global warming, though, the administration suddenly believes it needs
a "one hundred percent doctrine."

To understand how thoroughly the Bush administration has sidelined science, one needs only to look at its appointments. Whereas
President Clinton's science adviser was confirmed just eight days after his inauguration in 1993, Bush did not get around to appointing a
science adviser—John Marburger, former head of Brookhaven National Laboratory—until October 2001, well after he'd taken public
stances on most important science subjects and delivered a major address on stem cell research—his first public prime-time address to
the nation. Unlike his predecessors, Marburger wasn't given the title
of "assistant to the president," and he was denied West Wing office
space. Meanwhile, the post of director of the National Institutes of
Health sat vacant for over a year, and Bush didn't get around to appointing a commissioner of the Food and Drug Administration for
nearly twenty months.[30] He has sidelined and forced out respected
Republicans like EPA chief and former New Jersey governor Chris-
tine Todd Whitman and Treasury Secretary Paul O'Neill, who wanted
to move forward on combating global warming and energy conservation issues.

On issue after issue, from global warming to AIDS to stem cell research, the Bush administration has gone against the consensus of
the scientific community to advance its social agenda under the ban-

ner of "sound science." In 2004, Eric Cohen, a consultant to the President's Council on Bioethics, wrote in *National Review Online*, "The promise of embryonic-stem-cell research is very real but wholly speculative. No human therapies of any kind have yet been developed or tested, and none are on the horizon."[31] His is a shockingly specious argument—saying that research shouldn't begin because it hasn't been proved yet. It's akin to someone arguing in 1900 that because no one had ever been able to fly before, research into human flight shouldn't be started and that the Wright brothers should be prohibited from venturing to Kitty Hawk.

"What we are seeing is the empowerment of ideologues who have the ability to influence the course of science far more than ever before. They say 'I don't like the science, I don't like what it is showing' and therefore they ignore it. And we are at a place in this country where that can work. The basic integrity of science is under siege," observes Alan Leshner, the head of the American Association for the Advancement of Science.[32] The new mantra of the Republican Party, says Democratic congressman George Brown, appears to be that "scientific truth is more likely to be found at the fringes of science than at the center."[33]

The administration has also repeatedly undermined environmental efforts in favor of the oil and gas industries. The Bureau of Land Management brought aboard five "volunteer" consultants to approve oil and gas permits, whose full salaries were paid by—no kidding— the oil and gas industries. The EPA has literally cheapened life: Whereas it used to value a human life saved at $6.1 million in weighing the cost-benefit analysis of toxic pollution, it lowered that number by $2.4 million under George W. Bush.[34] The administration's secret energy task force was the subject of a heated lawsuit when Vice President Cheney refused to release any information about who helped him draft the administration's energy policy, and the resulting energy bill passed by a Republican Congress did little but further embrace the oil economy and provide additional subsidies to companies that were already racking up record profits. Another opportunity for leadership on the issue of climate change was ignored.

The top Republican on the Senate's Environment and Public Works committee, James Inhofe, has repeatedly cast doubt on climate change, and today Inhofe aides e-mail around anti–climate change news clips each morning to a wide network of Washington insiders. In 2003, as chair of the committee, Inhofe moved to block a bipartisan bill by John McCain and Joe Lieberman that would have established the nation's first caps on greenhouse gases, blasting it in a twelve-thousand-word speech on the Senate floor and closing by saying that global warming might be "the greatest hoax ever perpetrated on the American people."[35] Republican congressman Dana Rohrabacher, who serves on the House science committee, has referred to global warming as "liberal claptrap."

Next to Inhofe, President Bush is perhaps the party's strongest dissenter on global warming. Bush avidly read *State of Fear*, Michael Crichton's 2004 novel attacking the underpinnings of climate change, and spent more than an hour talking in person with Crichton. Fred Barnes, in his biography of the president, wrote that the duo were in "near-total agreement." From time to time, President Bush will step into the issue and appear to be doing something. He often obfuscates by talking about greenhouse gas "intensity," which refers to "amount per unit of economic activity, as measured by the gross domestic product," and explains that greenhouse gas "intensity" will drop over the coming years. That's not what worries scientists. They are worried about the total, not its measure relative to the nation's economic prowess. The environment could care less how many trillions of goods and services the United States produces—it responds to the carbon dioxide.[36]

The confusion the administration has spread is real and pervasive—thanks in large part to a U.S. media that has abdicated its responsibility to hold leaders accountable to the truth. One study by Jules Boykoff and Maxwell Boykoff, *Balance as Bias: Global Warming and the U.S. Prestige Press*, looked at more than six hundred hard-news articles published from 1990 to 2002 in the nation's top newspapers—*The New York Times*, *The Washington Post*, the *Los Angeles Times*, and *The Wall Street Journal*. It found a disturbing 53 percent of the articles gave roughly equal weight to both views: that humans contribute to global warming and that climate change is a natural phenomenon. Only 6 percent—thirty-six of the six hundred articles—emphasized the scientific consensus that humans are the main cause of global warming. In an April 2006 poll by *Time* magazine, as part of its very realistic cover story "Be Worried. Be Very Worried," 64 percent of those polled thought there was disagreement among scientists about global warming. Only 35 percent thought scientists mostly agreed with one another on global warming's threat.

The Bush administration's decidedly mixed approach to innovation and renewable energy is perhaps best illustrated by Bush's 2006 State of the Union address in which he made his famous pronouncement that America was "addicted" to oil. He promised a massive effort to convert the country to renewable energies—but the realities didn't match his rhetoric. A few days later, to tout his State of the Union initiatives, he visited the National Renewable Energy Laboratory in Golden, Colorado, one of the country's premiere research facilities on the future of energy. The catch? Due to the Republican Congress and Bush administration's cuts, the lab had seen its budget slashed by $28 million, and just two weeks before the president's visit had laid off thirty-two workers, including eight researchers. An embarrassed administration quickly shifted $5 million back to the lab and rehired the staff. "I recognize that there has been some interesting—let me say—mixed signals when it comes to funding," the president told the lab workers when he visited. "You're doing great work here." Lab worker Tina Larney knew exactly where the problem lay: "There is technology available now, there is the know-how now. What is lacking is leadership on the large scale at the national level."[37]

The Republican leadership at the dawn of the twenty-first century is guilty of negligence for failing to address issues of global health like AIDS and climate change, a situation they have only recently begun to step forward and change. Make no mistake: As a nation, the United States has squandered the last decade, beginning with the failure of the Kyoto Protocol, and it has lost its world leadership position on the environment and energy issues. It's the unique kind of "leadership" on climate change that the national Republican Party has provided that led Toles to pen his cartoon pleading on behalf of Planet Earth just before the 2006 election. Luckily for Democrats and thanks in no small part to Gore's *Inconvenient Truth*, voters have begun to understand the magnitude of the issues we confront today. The new Democratic Congress has held numerous hearings on global warming and climate change—hearings that Inhofe, now the ranking member on the Senate environment committee, has mocked—but there's only so much that Congress can do without the support of the president. In 2008, the nation will get its first opportunity to change the leadership in the Oval Office, and neither the nation nor the world can afford another four or eight years of a president who won't address climate change.

THE UNITED STATES MUST be a strong international leader on the environment to encourage other nations to follow our lead. Thanks to missed opportunities like the Kyoto Protocol, the United States is already in a hole. As the environmental climate and the political climate both change around the world, there are strong economic reasons to ensure that the United States is a leader on international standards.

The United States also has a vested national security interest in ensuring that developing nations like China and India have secure access to energy. The United States should be leading international cooperation to develop clean, renewable, and sustainable sources of energy for the world community. The less China feels it's competing with the United States for oil in Nigeria, Sudan, South America, and the Middle East, the more secure both nations will be. The United States can't afford to wean itself off oil and leave China, India, and other developing nations competing for a scarce and vulnerable critical resource. The less competition for oil globally, the more excess capacity there is in the energy market, the cheaper oil will stay—ensuring not just that our troops (or worse, Chinese troops) aren't taken on around-the-world tours to secure oil fields. As Thomas Friedman's "First Law of Petropolitics" argues, the pricier oil is, the less free and more oppressive the Middle Eastern oil states end up. By working internationally to develop sustainable energies, the United States will help secure ourselves at home as well as do more to promote democratic institutions in the Middle East than we have achieved by having our own troops occupying the oil fields.

It won't take nearly as much effort as one might think. Experts believe that within three to five years of beginning a dedicated large-scale effort, we could achieve energy savings equivalent to all of the oil we import each day from the Middle East. To restate that, the United States could be free of Middle Eastern oil by the end of the next president's first term if it wanted to be and the leadership was there to get it done. The answer to that challenge lies in the hands of the next occupant of the White House. Will he or she commit the attention at the scale necessary to move the country forward? If the next president won't, who will?

Wrestling the nation from the clutches of its "addiction" to oil isn't impossible. The country's done this before and is continuing to make progress every day. Under President Ford and his successor, sweater-wearing Jimmy Carter, conservation laws cut America's per capita oil consumption by nearly a quarter between 1978 and 1983. Automobile efficiency increased 40 percent, as did that of home appliances and other energy-intensive products, and just thirteen years after the 1973 energy crisis first opened the country's eyes to its reliance on fossil fuels, the United States was producing every dollar of its GDP using a third less energy. All told, as much as three-quarters of the nation's increased energy needs since the 1970s have been met simply by more energy-efficient products. As oil expert Lisa Margonelli explains, "If the United States could increase its energy efficiency by just 3 percent per year between now and 2100 (somewhat less than the 3.4 percent yearly improvements the United States made between 1980 and 1986), the economy would grow dramatically while reducing the world's energy needs to half of their current level."[38]

There's still a lot more low-hanging fruit—easy things the nation could do to decrease its use of oil. The International Energy Agency estimated that a combination of telecommuting, carpooling, reducing highway speeds, and getting Americans to properly inflate their tires could save more than a month's worth of oil over the course of a year.[39] Industry and individuals can do a lot too. Starbucks rolled out coffee cups in spring 2006 that were made with 10 percent recycled postconsumer fiber. It doesn't sound like a big change, but that single move will save eleven thousand tons of wood and forty-seven million gallons of wastewater each year.[40]

One of the critical reasons the United States must address climate change soon and forcefully is that the rising industrialization of India and China is threatening to poison both countries—which would do little to increase either their national stability or their economic growth. Pollution in China, depending on the expert, is either the nation's "leading" killer or merely "one of" the nation's leading killers. In China's southwestern metropolis of Chengdou, the smog hangs heavy and low, as if the city were caught in a permanent fog. Locals have a saying, "When the sky's blue, the dogs bark." It happens so rarely that it spooks the local animals. "Many factors are coming together here: Our raw materials are scarce, we don't have enough land, and our population is constantly growing," China's deputy environmental minister, Pan Yue, explains. "This miracle will end soon because the environment can no longer keep pace. Acid rain is falling on one third of the Chinese territory, half of the water in our seven largest rivers is completely useless, while one fourth of our citizens do not have access to clean drinking water. One third of the urban population is breathing polluted air, and less than 20 percent of the trash in cities is treated and processed in an environmentally sustainable manner. Finally, five of the ten most polluted cities worldwide are in China."[41]

There's much more trouble ahead for China. It recently passed Japan as the world's second-largest consumer of petroleum, and even though the country is building one coal-fired power plant a week and adding the equivalent of Britain's entire electrical output every two years, it still has only about four-fifths of the energy it needs. In 2004, workers in Guangzhou and other cities had to work shifts overnight to even out power demands.[42] Overall, China's oil imports will need to roughly quadruple by 2020—to more oil each day than the United States currently imports—and China's population won't hit its estimated peak until 2030, meaning more demands for fewer and fewer resources.[43]

To see what international leadership on the issue of climate change looks like, Americans need only to look across the pond to the United Kingdom. As a counterexample to America's lack of leadership, Britain under Tony Blair demonstrated a strong commitment to recognizing the situation and acting. Its strong embrace of the Kyoto Protocol led to the creation of hundreds of thousands of clean-tech jobs, and its 2006 *Stern Review: The Economics of Climate Change* report, led by economics adviser Sir Nicholas Stern, is a model for a country realistically confronting the future.

"Climate change is global in its causes and consequences, and international collective action will be critical in driving an effective, efficient and equitable response on the scale required. This response will require deeper international co-operation in many areas—most notably in creating price signals and markets for carbon, spurring technology research, development and deployment, and promoting adaptation, particularly for developing countries," the report opens. "The effects of our actions now on future changes in the climate have long lead times. What we do now can have only a limited effect on the climate over the next 40 or 50 years. On the other hand, what we do in the next 10 or 20 years can have a profound effect on the climate in the second half of this century and in the next. The earlier effective action is taken, the less costly it will be."

The *Stern Review* concludes that the world is probably past the point where it could stabilize the amount of CO_2 in the atmosphere at less than 450 ppm. Instead, the best hope is to stabilize at 550 ppm, roughly double the amount at the start of the Industrial Revolution. Even that high number, which would undoubtedly commit the world to at least another degree or two of global warming, would require quick action: Global emissions would have to peak in the next ten to twenty years and then fall at a rate of 3 percent or more until 2050 and beyond. "There is a high price to delay. Delay in taking action on climate change would make it necessary to accept both more climate change and, eventually, higher mitigation costs. Weak action in the next 10–20 years would put stabilisation even at 550 ppm CO_2e [carbon dioxide equivalent] beyond reach—and this level is already associated with significant risks," the review reports.

To clarify, stabilizing global emissions must occur during the term of the next U.S. president, or the world might cross a point of no return. As Toles's cartoon warned, the United States doesn't have any time to dawdle if it's going to get this complicated issue right. And if, as the national party has demonstrated over the last decade, the Republicans won't do it, then Democrats will have to—and they'll have to put the issues of energy and climate change at the top of their national agenda. And make no mistake: Action on global climate change will not happen without strong leadership from the United States, and, in turn, international cooperation to help the booming developing economies address their own energy needs. The new power plants coming online in China and India will more than negate the effect of the Kyoto Protocol, and the United States is the leader for global emissions by a long shot.

Even if the national security and environmental reasons aren't enough for the United States to address its creeping energy crisis, one hidden line in the *Stern Review* shows another self-interest that should motivate the United States to act: "The transition to a low-carbon economy will bring challenges for competitiveness but also opportunities for growth."

Thankfully, as with health care and education and the other critical issues in this dawn of the twenty-first century, we're beginning to see an evolving climate ready for action—thanks, in no small part, to Al Gore's slide show and partly because of the *Stern Review*'s conclusion that there are jobs and opportunities to be had as the world transitions its energy needs for the future.

HILLARY CLINTON SAYS the United States needs to forge ahead with a new consensus. As she told the Apollo Alliance, a coalition of labor, business, and nonprofit leaders, in Washington in early 2007, "A clean energy agenda is a jobs agenda. We have to take that message and drive it home day after day." She continued, "The energy challenge is not, despite what we hear from the other end of Pennsylvania Avenue, a zero sum. It is not. By pursuing these opportunities, we can grow our economy and shrink our reliance on foreign oil. We can combat global warming and create thousands, I'd argue millions, of new good jobs. We can protect our security and our environment. This is what Americans do best—we're problem solvers."

The Apollo Alliance has been arguing for just that. The organization, named after JFK's ambitious and inspirational moon-landing program and not unlike the Strategic Environmental Initiative Gore first proposed in the early 1990s, insists that millions of good-paying jobs would be created in a national effort to develop alternative energy sources in the United States. By speeding the transition to hybrids and building a national energy-efficiency campaign, the alliance aims to generate millions of new jobs in developing industries and new technologies. Much as Kennedy's space challenge and the Apollo program invigorated science research and spawned new industries and products, the alliance's numbers show that a $300 billion national investment over ten years in an "Apollo-like" energy project would generate more than 3.3 million new jobs and nearly $1 trillion in personal income—as well as nearly $300 billion in energy savings. "If American economists agree on anything, it's that inventing new technologies and creating new industries is what America does best. Investing in a new generation of efficient and clean technology, and rebuilding a more modern national infrastructure can create millions of good jobs while making our communities more livable and more equitable. The moment is right for our nation's leaders to step forward on this important matter of national, economic, and environmental security," explains Bracken Hendricks, the executive director of the Apollo Alliance.

As Hendricks sees it, a thorough investment in a new energy environment would benefit nearly all sectors of the economy. Working on energy efficiency creates nearly twice the number of jobs as simply building new power plants. Investments in energy efficiency are good for manufacturing. More efficient consumption decreases demand (and therefore prices) for energy, benefiting consumers and industry. New energy technologies create new industries, new factories, and new jobs. Still, it's going to take a massive government-led effort to convert and rally the entire nation. The open market won't solve global warming on its own. "It's not going to happen unless America is prepared to invest in it," insists John Podesta, the head of the Center for American Progress and formerly Bill Clinton's chief of staff. "Like rural electrification, the building of the interstate highway system, and President Kennedy's Apollo program, there are some goals so costly, yet so vital to our national interest, that they simply can't be left to investment by individual companies alone."

So where do solutions lie? For one, in every U.S. car. If the United States just matched Europe's fuel efficiency standards, it could reduce its oil consumption by 25 percent—and have no need to import oil from the Persian Gulf. It's not as if the automakers couldn't do this if they wanted to or if the demand existed—they're the same ones building the fuel-efficient cars in Europe. Richard Wagoner, the head of GM, a company considered a leader in Europe in terms of fuel efficiency, was at the Geneva International Motor Show in Switzerland in early 2007 to unveil the new Opel Coursa OPC, which gets more than 30 miles per gallon. In fact, the fuel standards for Europe, where gas often hits $5 or $6 a gallon, will be in the mid-40s by 2008 and maybe even over 50 mpg by 2012. As GM's vice chair for global product development, Robert Lutz, explained it, American consumers just don't demand the fuel-efficient cars, and so they keep getting gas-guzzling SUVs: "There is one global GM serving a variety of different markets. We try to do whatever we have to do to succeed in each market."[44]

Lutz's point is an important one: Fuel efficiency standards aren't just about the environment and energy—they're an innovation issue. China is becoming a leader in automobile fuel efficiency, with its standards among the strictest in the world—in 2008 the standards will be about 50 percent higher than in the United States. Its national 863 Project, which focuses on high-tech research and development, champions the development and designing of electric, hybrid, and hydrogen cars.[45] These efforts aren't just part of a benevolent Eastern philosophy toward the world and the environment—they are a calculated economic plan to ensure that the world's newest and best technology gets directed toward Chinese needs. By having the toughest standards in the world and by being such a growth market saleswise, China is making sure that auto companies around the world are focusing their efforts on designing for the Chinese market and that domestically Chinese automakers will be able to export their cars everywhere. The United States, which lags far behind in fuel efficiency, will soon see that very few of its cars meet the standards for export to China. In the first round of standards, only one American SUV passed the Chinese tests.

The recognition of our innovation shortfall has created an environment where change is desired. While U.S. efforts toward sustainable energy fell off sharply in the 1980s under the Reagan administration and the nation saw a glut of cheap oil, other nations that forged ahead have a substantial lead on us now. "We are in such a threatening and emergent situation that, frankly, we need to start looking at the welfare of the country as a whole, and a tremendous weakness is our dependence on oil," asserts Southwest Airlines chairman Herbert D. Kelleher, who has publicly stepped up as part of a broad group of business leaders to argue that the auto industry must retool itself to provide more fuel-efficient vehicles.[46]

Business is now on board with change. "I sensed a shift about 24 months ago," says Paul Hawken, a consultant to corporations. "Suddenly CEOs were expressing genuine concern about this issue, not just 'can you get these people off our back?'" The story Hawken heard was generally the same: A CEO's daughter comes home from college and says, "Dad, we can't be that stupid."[47]

America's stalled efforts on energy reform—stalled with the full backing of the Republican Party—have allowed other countries to get the jump on us. Detroit's aborted experiment with electric cars was halted almost as soon as the Bush administration came into office, but the development program had sufficiently spooked Japanese automakers like Toyota and Honda that they kept at it and were first to market with mass-production hybrid vehicles. In the first three months of 2007 alone, Toyota sold 61,635 hybrids in the United States, which helped it almost overtake Ford as the second-largest car seller in the country and become the world's largest automaker—the first time that title has belonged to a company based outside of the United States. Honda and Toyota, whose sales are continuing to increase while Detroit's big three are continuing to weaken, both credit the hybrids and the overall greater fuel efficiency of their vehicles for the sales boosts. "The continued sales success of Honda light trucks and cars in this period of ever-increasing fuel prices shows the high consumer awareness of our excellent fuel economy," Dick Colliver, executive vice president of American Honda, told U.S. news organizations.[48]

Domestic politics often get in the way of new energy initiatives too. Brazil has stuck with the issue of sustainable energy, and now the country is arguably the world leader on alternative energy. Every gallon of gasoline sold contains 20 percent ethanol, and many cars operate on only sugar-based ethanol—a technology that, although available in the United States, isn't a political reality today because of sugar subsidies that artificially inflate the price of sugar beyond what would be usable for ethanol. The U.S. sugar producers are major forces in Florida politics, a critical state for any presidential candidate, so perhaps it's not surprising that Barack Obama backed the subsidies when they came up in Congress, despite the fact that sugar is a much more efficient and cheaper ethanol alternative than corn.[49]

The United States used to be a leader on solar energy, too, before it gradually gave up and let other countries get ahead to the point that we now import much of our solar technology. In fact, across the alternative energy spectrum, the United States has abdicated its leadership and innovation role for so long that, as John Podesta told an audience at Wayne State University, absent a strong commitment to new research and development, "any transition America makes to renewable energy sources will largely accrue to the benefit of industries in other countries, not the United States. For example, Japanese and European firms have increased their global market share of solar panels—technology American companies invented—from 25 to 50 percent. What's more, European manufacturers now dominate 90 percent of the world's wind turbine production . . . Unless we make a national investment in conservation and renewable resources, we are going to find ourselves importing this equipment even though we have idle factories and unemployed workers who can do the job in Detroit, Flint, Chicago, Toledo and dozens of other cities."

Into the federal void of leadership are stepping state and local leaders. Ironically, as much as the national Republican Party has refused to embrace clean energy in the last decade, the poster child for U.S. leadership is the Republican governor of California, who is using his unique "postpartisan," no-nonsense style of leadership to move the state forward. Arnold Schwarzenegger, who converted his signature gas-guzzling Hummer to hydrogen and biodiesel, signed the nation's first law to reduce greenhouse gas emissions, by 25 percent by 2020 and 80 percent by 2050, enough to arrest further global warming. In 2006, he declared, "The debate is over, the science is in, the time to act is now." He's labeled the U.S. position on energy and the environment "embarrassing," and if anyone would want to avoid that, it's the guy who once called his opponents "girlie men." Schwarzenegger signed agreements with Tony Blair to develop research, which given that California is the world's sixth-largest economy is no small promise. He saw the success that Blair had turning Britain into a hub of green technology industry, which has generated some five hundred thousand new jobs since the UK's adoption of Kyoto, and wants a piece of the action for California. He's also raised fuel efficiency standards by 2016 to the level that China will reach in 2008—about 50 percent higher than current U.S. standards—and more than a dozen states have said they'll adopt the tough California standards too. However, the Bush administration's EPA has attempted to block Schwarzenegger's tougher standards—meaning the federal agency in charge of protecting the environment is actually arguing against a state attempting to protect the environment. It's no wonder that Planet Earth, in its *Washington Post* PSA, asked for new national leadership.

Schwarzenegger's stance is winning him as many friends as it's costing him. He describes "a billboard in Michigan that accuses me of costing the car industry $85 billion. They say because of our new carbon fuel standards I cost them $85 billion. The billboard says 'Arnold to Michigan—drop dead.' The fact of the matter is, what I'm saying is 'Arnold to Michigan—get off your butt. Get off your butt and join us.' In fact, California may be doing more to save U.S. automakers than anyone else, because what we are doing is we are pushing them to make changes, to make the changes so they can sell their cars in California. And we all know—let's be honest—that if they don't change, someone will. The Japanese will, the Chinese will, the South Koreans will, the Germans will, they all will. So what I want to do is, I want to prevent that from happening. I want them to sell their cars in California. I believe strongly in American technology, and I think in the end it will be technology that will ultimately save Detroit."

Schwarzenegger's not alone. Local communities and companies are also taking the lead. In 2005, Republican governors Mitt Romney and George Pataki led seven (there are now ten) eastern states in developing a Regional Greenhouse Gas Initiative. Across the country, led by Seattle's mayor, more than four hundred mayors have joined the U.S. Mayors Climate Protection Agreement, which holds their cities to Kyoto standards. Cities and states have found that by switching traffic lights from incandescent lightbulbs to LEDs, which last longer and use less energy, they can save energy and money—$6.3 million a year in the case of New York City and $500,000 a year in Rhode Island. In

Austin, Texas, the city is making an effort to develop new houses that are "zero-energy-capable," meaning they are 65 percent more energy efficient and can, in turn, be powered by solar panels fed by the state's hot sun. Salt Lake City is offering free parking at any meter to hybrid owners. Many cities are moving ahead with planting more trees to cool paved-over areas and finding a strange benefit: Trees boost the local economy. It turns out that people are willing to spend more on products in an area with mature trees because they create a nicer shopping experience.[50]

Some business is moving ahead too, sensing opportunities in the new energy paradigm. "We've been talking about it from the perspective of cost to society, rather than the point of view of the opportunity for profit," says K. R. Sridhar, founder and CEO of Bloom Energy. "People are missing that this is a $4 trillion market for energy." And that's before China and India really get going energywise. As Sridhar predicts, "The country that figures out how to make that happen will be the leading economic power in the 21st century."[51]

In fact, there's evidence that converting an economy and saving the environment in the process is good government and good for development. Gamesa Corp., a Spanish leader in wind technology, is opening a Pennsylvania manufacturing plant where a steel mill once stood. The plant brings 1,000 jobs, including 230 long-term manufacturing jobs that will help a state hurt by traditional manufacturing losses. In Iowa, Siemens's new wind-turbine plant will provide 250 new jobs, and in Washington State the nation's largest biodiesel facility is opening in a region where paper mills are closing.[52] Bank of America's new billion-dollar Manhattan headquarters is the first "green" skyscraper in the United States, using about half the energy of a typical building, which over time will be good for the company's energy bills.

For larger-scale efforts, the entire country will have to be engaged—every person and every industry—and that type of undertaking comes only from ongoing presidential leadership. American business is largely waiting for a strong government commitment, even as it knows that some of its current products and policies are doing more harm than good. As GM's vice president of research and planning, Larry Burns, laments, "A government is not just a tax strategy! One of the important roles they play is to create collective will—like

Kennedy going to the moon. A government like China has a better chance than maybe a free country like the U.S."[53] That's how grim the situation is after only two terms of Republican leadership in the Oval Office—a vice president of one of the country's largest automakers thinks a dictatorial Communist country has a better chance of addressing the issue than the United States. American business is typically one of the most Republican voting blocks in the country, but it's unhappy, frustrated, and disgusted with the leadership its party has shown on energy and climate change, meaning that if in 2008 Republican candidates don't step up to embrace the issues, Democrats have a chance to create a new coalition for bold leadership in the twenty-first century.

The United States might have billions to gain from converting early. During the 1980s, adopting the worldwide protocol banning chlorofluorocarbons, the dangerous chemicals that were found to be eating away the ozone layer, actually proved to be a great economic boon: Early adoption gave the United States a jump start on new technologies, and some companies, like Nortel, which used CFCs as cleaning agents, found that they actually saved money by switching.[54]

So what could the future entail? Perhaps the best news here is that just like in health care and education, the solutions to our energy crisis are clear, well understood, and largely attainable—states, local communities, and countries like Britain are proving them. Briefly, they involve better hybrid vehicles, new energy sources, more energy conservation, and—here's the rub for many conservatives—some government regulation, taxes, and investment.

Why government regulation and higher taxes on things like carbon emissions? For one thing, since pollution is an externality, not shown in the costs or profits of an enterprise, businesses will continue to invest in the cheapest, most effective technology until shown they have a financial reason to do otherwise. Half of all U.S. electricity comes from coal, which is second only to oil in the amount of carbon emitted. Right now, 150 coal plants are on the drawing board in the United States to be built by 2030, but only 20 percent of them are planning to use the cleanest technology to date—the dirty technology is the low-cost option, the industry states. The setting of long-term goals in projects like energy conversion are important because it underscores to business how expensive polluting will be down the road and encourages investments today in cleaner technology. Right now there's more investment in coal than ever: Some 249 coal-fired power plants will be built between 1999 and 2009, half of them in China, which is moving forward at the rate of almost one new coal power plant a week. According to plans on the drawing board, a further 483 coal plants will follow by 2019, and 710 more between 2020 and 2030—about a third of them in China.[55] We must find new technologies to improve the way we generate electricity. Wind and solar are proving very effective in the rest of the world, and the winds of the Plains states would be more than enough to roll out massive productive investments in the United States, while the sun of the Southwest would be more than sufficient as new technologies allow greater generation capability. Nuclear fuel has to be part of the solution—the country has just over one hundred nuclear plants, but not a single new one has been built since 1973 because of public fears over the technology. The truth is that it's gotten more and more safe, and the largest current stumbling block is long-term storage of spent fuel.

Of course, there are some companies paving the way to the future. Seventh Generation, a Vermont-based maker of environmentally friendly cleaning products, has shown that there's plenty of opportunity for "first-movers" in the new arena. So far, GE's building of energy-efficient engines is paying off, as public campaigns to convert to energy-efficient products are resulting in more purchases. One of the amazing things about this is that GE is largely alone at the dawn of the twenty-first century—there are huge opportunities ahead and most U.S. companies, particularly the automobile industry, are fighting change tooth and nail. The automobile companies are suing the states over tougher emissions laws and fuel standards. For an example of how the opposite approach might work better, consider when the Federal Trade Commission revised its law about the minimum width between bars in baby cribs—kids were being injured by getting caught in the wider-spaced bars—the new rules applied only to residential cribs. But rather than fight the new approach, one smart manufacturer, Hard Manufacturing, went around and contacted all the hospitals in the country to explain that the cribs they were using had been deemed dangerous by the FTC for home-based use, so why should the hospitals be using them? Turns out that the public education campaign led most hospitals to replace their cribs and boost the market for Hard Manufacturing's products far higher than it would have been otherwise.[56]

Nothing would do more good more quickly than the next generation of hybrids—plug-in hybrid electric vehicles that allow people to plug their cars into a normal electric socket to charge and to travel much farther on battery alone. Former CIA director James Woolsey, who has become a strong proponent of electric vehicles and who signed up to advise John McCain's presidential bid, has testified that through a combination of lighter materials and plug-in hybrids, we could approach one thousand miles a gallon within a decade or two. Even so, as climate expert Tim Flannery explains, "The best evidence indicates that we need to reduce our CO_2 emissions by 70 percent in 2050. If you own an SUV and replace it with a hybrid fuel car, you can achieve a cut of that magnitude in a day rather than half a century."[57]

Raising the gas tax would encourage more switching to hybrids and fund tax incentives to do just that—boosting the federal tax 20 cents a gallon would raise upward of $28 billion annually, more than enough to fund massive tax incentives, fund the National Academy of Sciences' requested energy research efforts, and help ease the transition to energy-efficient models for Detroit's automakers.

As in education and health care, there's also a need for more national environmental standards. As one example, "flares," the excess chemicals burned off at oil refineries, are thought to remove 98 percent of the volatile organic chemicals in Texas, but go a few states over to California, and that state believes flares burn off 99 percent of VOCs. A difference of 1 percent doesn't sound like a big deal, but it means that a refinery in Texas "pollutes" twice as much as one in California.[58] National minimum standards of environmental quality are critical to measuring how much progress we're actually making. Local control makes less sense in a world where China's pollution affects us and where Michigan's pollution affects Vermont.

Similarly, energy conservation is a major part of any solution. Conservation and improved efficiency led the nation out of the last major energy crisis in the 1970s and 1980s, where from 1977 to 1985, the national economy grew by 3 percent annually while, thanks to better technologies, oil use dropped 2 percent each year. As Hillary Clinton points out on the trail, "Think about this: If we got back on that pace today, it would take less than three years to reduce oil consumption by an amount equal to what we import from the Persian Gulf." Switching lightbulbs, as many households and states are already doing, is a start, but most energy savings will come from technology and innovation. Major appliances have continued to improve in recent decades—from the mid-1970s until today, refrigerators have twice doubled in efficiency—and further innovation and development of more efficient technologies is critical to solving the crisis ahead.[59]

There's also a major public health component to this issue that the Bush administration has repeatedly stymied with its abstinence-only programs: We must stabilize the world population—and the difference between acting now and acting a decade from now is a difference in billions of people who must be fed, watered, and employed on an Earth ill equipped to handle too many more people. Third-world programs to raise literacy rates and education levels, as well as to make available birth control and improve public health to lower infant mortality rates, would mean fewer children, less AIDS, more stable families and states, and—here's our self-interest—fewer people using energy but more of them able to afford to participate in the global market. The UN's Millennium Development Goals aim to do just that across the world, and the money we invest in stabilizing and improving poor countries is the best money we could spend overseas—supporting the full goals would cost about $20 billion for the United States, less than a tenth of what we've spent in Iraq since 2003, and while costly, it would be a huge boon to our energy policies, counterterrorism policies, and economic and trade policies.[60] It would do more to expand the global middle class, which buys U.S. goods and services, and reduce the global underclass, which is the most susceptible to terrorist movements.

The United States has confronted lesser environmental challenges to society before under the leadership of both political parties. Smog was once such a problem that in signing the Air Quality Act of 1967, Lyndon Johnson explained, "Either we stop poisoning our air or we become a nation in gas masks groping our way through dying cities." Since then, smog has dropped by 50 percent. Ozone holes have begun to close since CFCs were banned. Acid rain has decreased since the Clean Air Act. Richard Nixon led the way on the creation of the EPA.

Global warming and climate change are admittedly huge world-wide concerns. Yet the problems are solvable—if we have the will. While the effects of climate change may seem far off in the future, remember that seven out of ten people alive today will likely live to see the year 2050—so this isn't a problem for future generations, it's a problem for us today, right now.[61] Moreover, confronting climate change and energy transformation is a great opportunity for the United States to renew its legacy of innovation and invention toward something that would save us and the world with it. There are exciting technologies down the road that we haven't even considered. "Conservation and energy efficiency are smart policies, but not enough," Fareed Zakaria says. "In the end, everyone realizes that innovation is the only real solution to the global-warming problem."[62]

One of the most promising aspects of the debate going into the 2008 presidential race is that the coalition of people willing to pitch in and help has never been broader.

As Governor Schwarzenegger told an audience at Georgetown University just after being featured on the cover of *Newsweek* as one of the nation's leading environmentalists, "As governor, I talk to scientists in our universities, I talk to CEOs that run major corporations. And let me tell you, those are not wacky people. Mainstream scientists are convinced, mainstream CEOs are convinced, and if you look at the surveys, mainstream Americans are convinced that global warming and climate change is real and we have to do something about it. So who are the fanatics now? Who are the fanatics? They are the ones who are in denial. They're in environmental denial, they're in economic denial, and they are in political denial."[63]

An unexpected recent addition is many of the leaders of the evangelical movement, who understand that protecting the Earth is one of humanity's greatest missions. Rick Warren, whose Saddleback Church helped found the megachurch movement and whose book *The Purpose Driven Life* is a continuing bestseller, signed a climate change petition in response to *An Inconvenient Truth*. So far these evangelical environmental leaders are not happy with the leadership they're getting from the national Republican Party—providing a unique opportunity for Democrats to win the support of increasingly critical evangelical voters. As Richard Cizik, the vice president for government affairs for the National Association of Evangelicals, describes himself, "I'm a Ronald Reagan sunny conservative, and I know that evangelicals are can-do, solution-oriented entrepreneurs." But so far he's amazed at the inaction he's seeing in the country: "We have to show leadership if India and China are to follow, yet we're at the back of the line; that's not American." For candidates ready to confront the problem and move toward a solution, they'll find that in this new framework of the first campaign, the right politics is also good politics.

Alfred Russel Wallace, the nineteenth-century British environmentalist, offered some words of wisdom that still resonate as we enter the first campaign of the global age—the first campaign in which climate change and global warming are established truths and accepted issues—and words that the cartoon Planet Earth Toles invented in 2006 would certainly applaud. "Vote for no one who says 'it can't be done,'" Wallace said. "Vote only for those who declare 'it shall be done.'"[64]

WEB 2.0 MEETS CAMPAIGNING 3.0

As the hour crept past 11 p.m., the entire city of Las Vegas was spread out radiantly some 850 feet below the windows of the Stratosphere Hotel. Mark Warner, former Virginia governor, was on the tiny stage, sandwiched uncomfortably between two Blues Brothers impersonators. They'd given him a hat and sunglasses and were striking up Wilson Pickett's classic "Mustang Sally."

Ice sculptures abounded, and around the corner from Warner, fresh-cut sushi and a flowing chocolate fountain entertained the eight-hundred-person crowd in between their trips to the open bars. Elvis was playing on the other side of the Space Needle–like Stratosphere, near a gift shop selling "I ♥ lap dances" T-shirts. A floor above Warner, on the outside observation deck, a group of bloggers debated a rational national energy policy, their backs turned on the gratuitously lit and energy-draining Las Vegas Strip.

The party could rival any of the soirees at a presidential nominating convention, but tonight it was all about the Democrats' newest interest group: the blogosphere. In fact, at the 2006 YearlyKos convention, the netroots activists who populate the progressive blog DailyKos lionize their outsider, insurgent status but at heart want nothing more than to be party power brokers themselves. The convention was filled with one thousand armchair ministrategists, all of them Mark Penns, Joe Trippis, and Celinda Lakes in training.

Who would have thought three years ago, as Howard Dean began his quixotic campaign for the presidency, that in the spring of 2006 he'd be chair of the Democratic Party, and bloggers, those great unwashed "pajamaudheeden," would be having a convention just like the dental hygenists' association—complete with box sandwich lunches, an exhibit hall, and lanyarded credentials, as well as eighteen workshops, ten roundtables, and twenty-four panel discussions? Even the convention's motto, "Uniting the Netroots," was written in the same font that Dean for America used during the 2004 campaign. This was the state of the blogosphere circa mid-2006: It even had a standardized font—Marydale—to demonstrate what was authentically "netroots."

Just three years earlier, DailyKos founder Markos Moulitsas Zúniga, who lent his name to the volunteer-organized conference, and fellow blogger Jerome Armstrong were the rebel outsiders leading party activists toward Howard Dean. Now the duo had penned the bestselling *Crashing the Gates: Netroots, Grassroots, and the Rise of People-Powered Politics*, and their movement had matured rapidly into a powerful force within the Democratic Party.

At the convention, there was no shortage of Washington insiders and party officials—the audience was peppered with staffers and consultants from PACs, campaigns, committees, and think tanks like the Center for American Progress. Bill Richardson, Howard Dean, Barbara Boxer, Wesley Clark, and Harry Reid all attended. There was even a pundit training session, where bloggers were taught how to do television. Markos, who appeared that Sunday morning on NBC's venerable talk show *Meet the Press*, admitted he was taking the advice. "If I criticize our side for not being put together, I figured I needed to be a bit more put together," he remarked.

The weekend conference displayed the new paradigm of U.S. politics: In the 2008 election, the four tools—online video, cell phones, blogs, and social-networking ties—provide unparalleled power to ordinary voters and together have created a new infrastructure for launching (and rebutting) political attacks. Add in the power of grassroots small-donor fund-raising—what allowed Howard Dean, John Mc-Cain, and Bill Bradley to challenge the establishment—and the 2008 election will be conducted on a playing field where the party establishment will have the least control of any election in American history. The four tools will also force campaigns to adapt, becoming ever more creative to win the eyeballs they were once able to purchase with a few network ads during the evening news and prime-time dramas.

Politics in this new paradigm will be markedly different from the politics of the past half century, and the rules of the game right now enormously benefit the Democratic Party and its candidates, for today there's much more energy and activity on the left than the right. And don't underestimate the power these bloggers can wield: We now live in a world where a blogger like Markos can drive a story as much as any traditional print journalist and where anyone, including, as we'll see, two guys who make videos about ninjas, has the potential to reach as many people and voters as *The New York Times*. Especially among younger voters who today make up the largest generation in half a century, new media technologies are far more effective than traditional advertising means.

At YearlyKos, there was scant humility visible amid a group that widely sees itself responsible for reinstalling a backbone in the cowed Democratic Party and holding a lazy and entrenched Washington press corps to account. Markos's Thursday night kickoff speech was celebratory and self-congratulatory; he gave those in attendance credit for building an online community that, he said, now attracted half a million readers a day. During a panel discussion on political journalism, moderator and blogger Matt Stoller began by chiding the national press in attendance: "It's all off the record except for this: It's all your fault."

At panel after panel—whose topics ranged from electoral reform to energy reform to "Building Progressive Infrastructure"—the tech-savvy progressives debated what needed to be done. Throughout the rooms and halls, attendees—who ranged widely in age and skewed more elderly than one might suspect—were perched typing furiously mostly on Apple laptops and surfing the Web to see what others were writing about the convention using the convention's free Wi-Fi network, named "n3tr00tz." It was the first time many of the bloggers had met their daily online conversation partners face to face, and many people introduced themselves both by their real name and their online handle, while others like DailyKos blogger "Hunter" stuck only to their pseudonyms. Marveling at the diversity represented among the crowd, one blogger said, "We're not at all geeks. Well, we are, but we're interesting geeks."

Further evidence of just how great a change the blogging community has brought forth in the Democratic Party was visible just a few hotels up the Las Vegas Strip at the Frontier, where the Young Democrats of America were simultaneously holding their national conference. Nevada 2006 Senate candidate Jack Carter, a son of the former president who in the fall would go on to lose to incumbent John Ensign by some 14 points, opened his remarks Sunday morning to the 150-person crowd of young enthusiasts by plugging his campaign blog and bragging that he even had a page on MySpace. Then, perhaps echoing the feelings of his party leadership at large, he laughed nervously and said, "I'll let you know I'm not entirely comfortable with that."

The truth is that few of the political elites in the country are comfortable with the new power being exercised online through blogs, social-networking sites like MySpace and Facebook, grassroots multimedia endeavors like YouTube, and the power of cell phones, which allow almost anyone, anywhere, to snap a candid photo and beam it around the world.

Politicians and their high-paid strategists have good reason to be wary. The game of politics no longer belongs solely to the professionals. If you fast-forward in the 2008 campaign exactly a year from the 2006 YearlyKos conference—this campaign, after all, seems to be stuck on fast-forward—and examine another example of the new netroots paradigm, it is clear that this election belongs to ordinary voters in ways that no election has in half a century. In June 2007, *The Sopranos'* long run as one of the most acclaimed shows in the history of television came to an unexpected and controversial end—in fact, creator David Chase left fans guessing exactly how it ended, whether mob boss Tony Soprano lived or died. No one knew what the ending actually meant. A few days later, Hillary Clinton's presidential campaign ended its monthlong online effort to select a new theme song for the campaign. The effort was a textbook study in the new online politics: Hillary's campaign understood that a mere press release or news conference wouldn't cut it anymore, so they turned the choice into a contest, e-mailing and texting supporters' cell phones to ask for suggestions. Then people voted using the website or cell phones. All along, the campaign posted a series of videos about the contest on YouTube. For the unveiling of the final song, the campaign shot a special online parody video of the *Sopranos* ending, complete with Bill Clinton and one of the show's actors reenacting the final scene while focusing on which song would win the campaign song contest.

The hundred-second online video was a creative and unexpected effort by the campaign's media team, and the creativity involved was a testament to one of the strangest side effects of the proliferation of new media: Ad makers now need to be good, smart, and creative online. No longer can they just put a thirty-second ad on television and be assured that everyone watching TV will see it. Instead, they recognize that online, no one has to watch anything, listen to anything, or read anything that doesn't grab their attention. The campaigns are competing for eyeballs, and that means they have to step up their efforts. In the case of Hillary's song, the extra effort was rewarded: The video almost immediately went "viral," being passed around the internet and (of course) posted on YouTube, where more than 250,000 people watched it. In the "last campaign," this anecdote would end right here—the campaign released something and it was over. But the story wasn't over. After all, Hillary's campaign didn't have a monopoly on creative energy. Far from it.

On blogs and in forums, people began to react, asking how Hillary could have picked a song for her campaign (Celine Dion's "You and I") that was sung by a *Canadian*. In California, two video bloggers, Kent Nichols and Douglas Sarine, who produce a popular weekly Web video called "Ask a Ninja," where a costumed ninja answers random questions submitted by fans, were inspired by the theme song contest to do their own parody of Hillary. They made a video of about the same length in which "Hillary Clinton" announced that she was going to have a theme song for every issue of her campaign. First up? The war in Iraq. "Many of you know I voted for the war but am now against it," the actress playing Hillary said. "I'm sure that together you and I can find a song that says that." Their low-budget video quickly went viral too (albeit on a smaller scale), receiving more than twenty thousand views in its first twenty-four hours. But again, the story didn't end there: In the comments on the ninja duo's parody video, hundreds of viewers weighed in, debating the video, its jokes, and its message. Their video was then posted on other blogs, where people continued the debate and discussed Hillary's original videos. In this "first campaign" environment, the creative energies and conversation just kept going—far, far away from the original song contest and far beyond the campaign's ability to control it. This final point, though, is the essence of the first campaign: The internet and the campaign are both about a conversation, and success in one realm is contingent upon success in the other.

THE 2000 CAMPAIGN first displayed the power of grassroots money to help boost Bill Bradley and John McCain, and then the 2004 election demonstrated how online grassroots organizations could help power a campaign as Howard Dean recruited nearly two hundred thousand Americans to join his Meetup groups in thousands of locations around the country. The history books will likely reflect that 2008 is the campaign of voter-generated content—when ordinary people seize the moment and use the increasingly powerful tools at their fingertips to create and spread information without any help from the campaigns.

Here it is important to say that since its inception, the internet has happened to candidates—they've always lagged behind in adopting new technology, failing to realize what it could do and thus being swept along with it as ordinary people step up and transform the process. McCain and Bradley didn't realize the financial power that the internet would bring them until it did. The Dean 2004 Meetup groups were already growing and swelling even before Joe Trippi put a link on the campaign's home page. When it comes to the Web, the campaigns themselves are more often than not getting yanked out of the station as the train pulls away.

Of course, some early evidence seems to suggest that many candidates don't get it. Hillary Clinton announced her presidential candidacy online in a video, which scored her some points among the netroots, but then her initial forays into the world online through a series of video "chats" were as wooden and stagey as any political event since Calvin Coolidge's first "photo op" eighty years ago. "If this was Clinton's idea of adapting to politics in a Webby way, she has a long way to go," commented Dan Gillmor, a pioneer of online media, who said that what we see right now is just the beginning. "Campaigns are always works in progress. So is governance. Embrace that reality, and help the public understand it. We'll all be better off."[1] By the time of the *Sopranos* parody, her campaign staff was beginning to better understand the medium, but there's a long way to go before campaigns fully accept or even understand the new world. To succeed in the first campaign, a candidate needs to be willing to let go of the reins and put trust in the voters—asking them for their help, for what matters, and addressing the most critical issues of this new era.

Another pioneer, Henry Copeland, who founded blogads.com, which provides income for bloggers to pursue their "hobby" as a full-time job, explains, "We're still just at the early stage of understanding what happens when you shift from a hierarchal society to a conversation-based one. The network is so much more powerful than this top-down stuff."

Copeland doesn't have the highest hopes for the 2008 campaigns, as they compete on a playing field so transformed that few truly understand the implications of the first campaign of the digital era. "It's just going to be brutal for these guys," Copeland says. "You can't predict what's happening. There's this astonishing level of cluelessness. Peter Daou at the Hillary campaign gets this, but when you're up against a whole swarm you need an entire organization that gets it. If your organization is hardwired otherwise, it's like sewing wings on a pig. It doesn't make it a bird." Copeland believes it might be ten years before a campaign truly adopts the internet and the power it can deliver. He explains that just as traffic has a memory—a minor car accident can ripple through a commute and cause tie-ups for hours after it's cleared away—campaigns have a memory too. There's a sometimes lengthy lag before new tactics are adopted. Tactics that won the last campaign are the ones most often the focus of the next one, even if the playing field has changed in the interim. In 2008, regardless of who wins, the senior campaign staff will be folks who came of age in the broadcast era of Campaigning 2.0. "The team that wins will be an old-school fuddy-duddy campaign, and then that'll live on," Copeland says.

Of course, as instances like the Hillary viral video ad, the George Allen "Macaca" moment, Meetup, and the 2000 infusions of cash to McCain and Bradley show, the campaigns themselves can't wait until they are ready to get it. The internet and its transformative politics is happening to them regardless; they're being swept along in the flood of new information and tools. When pressed to comment on the viral grassroots ad, Barack Obama admitted he was impressed. "You know, one of the things about the internet is that people generate all kinds of stuff. In some ways, it's the democratization of the campaign process," he told CNN's Larry King. "But it's not something that we had anything to do with or were aware of and that frankly, given what it looks like, we don't have the technical capacity to create something like that. It's pretty extraordinary."[2]

This transformed campaign landscape will be another huge challenge for the rules of the Federal Election Commission. Built over decades of scandals and mischief, the FEC rules are meant to prevent corporations and unions from playing outsize roles in the process, but they also have the effect of making it difficult for unaffiliated grassroots voters to get involved. Those ordinary people often have trouble understanding the rules that prohibit "coordination" between campaigns and outside entities. Zephyr Teachout, who helped run grassroots online outreach for the Dean campaign in 2004, had fight after fight with supporters who couldn't understand why she wouldn't help them with their little pro-Dean projects. How to "tax" and value free speech is another huge question in the FEC rules. In the wake of the passage of the McCain-Feingold campaign finance reform, a major scuffle erupted online between bloggers and Carol Darr, who runs George Washington University's Institute for Politics, the Internet, and Democracy, about whether bloggers' political speech should be regulated. Should procandidate posts be considered in-kind contributions? Should bloggers who receive money to run procandidate ads have to file FEC paperwork if they write positive things about the same candidates? Should campaigns be allowed to post materials like videos, photos, and speeches under the Creative Commons license, which would allow grassroots supporters to download them, remix or personalize them, and repost the new materials to the Web as commercials, viral videos, or flyers? Where's the line between a campaign contribution, political disclosure, and free speech, one of the most cherished rights in the country? The FEC provides for a "media exemption," but in a world where anyone can launch a free blog in a few minutes on sites like Typepad.com or Blogger, who counts online as a journalist?

"Bloggers aren't traditional columnists—they can write on any subject that they want, which means that as long as you've found someone who likes you, they can become a supporter," says Jerome Armstrong, the founder of MyDD, one of the early progressive political blogs. That difference helps to explain why a campaign like Edwards's would invite a technology blogger like Robert Scoble aboard his plane—politics may not be Scoble's forte, but courting Scoble might result in his reporting back to his niche-oriented readers, who, in turn, might tune in to Edwards's efforts.

Joe Hoeffel, who ran against Arlen Specter in the Pennsylvania Senate race in 2004, recognized that the world was changing when he found Mary Shull on his call sheets. Shull, a grassroots MoveOn.org member, had built an e-mail address list of fifteen hundred friends and activists, and Hoeffel felt he needed to call her just like any other local power broker to court support. "Ten years ago, somebody like Mary would be as interested as she is in politics, but her circle of influence would not have extended beyond her home or block or even voting precinct. Now she's got 1,500 other self-motivated and influential people at her fingertips and carries as much clout as half the people I've been calling," he explained.[3]

A similarly impressive example of the new breed of online campaigner came to the Dean campaign in mid-2003 when it launched a new program called Deanlink that allowed supporters to network with

one another. Nearly four thousand miles from the Burlington campaign headquarters, Jonathan Kreiss-Tomkins decided to get involved
in politics for the first time. As a fourteen-year-old middle schooler
living in Sitka, Alaska, he would have seemed to have limited options.
But he went online, found Deanlink, and quickly became the site's
top booster. Over the course of the campaign, he would come home
from school and spend hours working on the site, meeting people
around the country, and creating his own grassroots network of some
five hundred people. While he eventually attracted some fame for his
age, online it didn't matter that he was still a presidential term away
from being able to vote—although it did mean, under the FEC's ar-
cane rules, he couldn't participate in fund-raising.

Social Networking

Social networking sites are as old as the internet. But whereas in the
2004 election, sites like Friendster and Orkut.com had the field almost to themselves, by 2008 MySpace and Facebook had grown to
encompass tens of millions of users. Farouk Olu Aregbe was the coor-
dinator of student government services at the University of Missouri–
Columbia, when in January 2007 he started the One Million Strong
for Barack group on Facebook, a social-networking site started by a
couple of Harvard students that had blossomed into the industry
leader in its category. Within twenty-four hours, the new group passed
the thousand-person mark, and Olu Aregbe just watched as it took on
a life of its own and by May had some 325,000 members. To put that
number in perspective, at the end of 2003, Howard Dean's entire
e-mail list of supporters was a record-setting half a million, meaning
that the grassroots-founded Facebook group was actually larger than
most presidential candidates' e-mail lists ever get—and it had happened nearly a year before the first votes of the 2008 election would
be counted.

Meanwhile, MySpace, the social-networking site now owned by
Rupert Murdoch, had become such a phenomenon that it arranged to
sponsor a presidential debate. As the Obama campaign discovered,
the world of MySpace was a complicated one with rules all its

own. After seeing Obama speak at the 2004 Democratic convention, Joe Anthony, a paralegal in Los Angeles, started an unofficial My-Space profile for the soon-to-be Illinois senator. As Obama's popularity grew, so did his online presence, and Anthony found himself managing a massive online venture as Obama's "friends" surpassed the 160,000-person mark. In the spring of 2007, talks between Anthony and Obama's presidential campaign to work together broke down, and Obama's campaign asked MySpace to hand over Anthony's valuable URL, www.MySpace.com/barackobama, to it. Now Joe Rospars, who four years before had shown up to work for Howard Dean's presidential campaign blog and had sent the election morning-after e-mail that helped jump-start the former Vermont governor's DNC chair bid, had risen to be Obama's director of new media—and the former grassroots blogger found himself in the unlikely position of representing "the man" in the blogosphere. The resulting furor, eventually smoothed over, ended with both sides being cast in poor light online and damaged Obama's grassroots fervor, but it underscored a valuable lesson for 2008: Campaigns aren't the ones in control anymore.

As candidates and campaigns at all levels are finding, there are no easy answers to the question of how best to campaign online. There are also massive racial and socioeconomic differences a candidate confronts when moving a campaign online. Hispanics in the United States are oversubscribed to cell phones and text messaging and undersubscribed to broadband. An average thirty-something Hispanic male grew up with a cell phone and may have never had a landline in his house, whereas a white male of the same age group probably still has a landline. Two things are for sure, though: As we enter the era of Campaigning 3.0, the internet is forcing a level of disclosure and accountability with which candidates and elected officials have never had to contend and allowing ordinary Americans of all stripes to participate in ways that didn't exist before.

The new technology is also allowing an ever-greater number of people to participate in places where they never could have before. Barack Obama's podcasts have long ranked as one of the top political podcasts on Apple's iTunes music store. Thousands of people subscribe to get his latest speeches and reports from Washington, and the system's ease allows his messages to reach far greater numbers of people than he would otherwise. When he hosted a seventy-five-minute town hall meeting at Loyola University in Chicago, eight hundred people packed the room—a good crowd by most standards—but when the discussion was posted online, twenty thousand people listened to it.

This last point—that the revolution in online politics is about participation—is one reason that the Democrats outpace Republicans online. Today, the GOP lags far behind the Democrats in adoption of the internet and participatory online politics. So much so, in fact, that when the top three Republican presidential candidates—John McCain, Mitt Romney, and Rudy Giuliani—were asked at the end of the first quarter of 2007 to release how much money they raised online, they refused because the amounts were embarrassingly small. Meanwhile, Hillary Clinton, Barack Obama, and John Edwards proudly trumpeted the tens of thousands of people who powered their record-breaking fund-raising. "The trouble is not the internet strategists," said Michael Turk, who worked on the Bush-Cheney 2004 reelection campaign as an internet strategist. "It is a party that doesn't believe its people will up and participate if they are invited to do so. If you're cynical you could make an argument that it is a party that doesn't trust its people enough to let them participate."

As Peter Leyden, director of the San Francisco–based New Politics Institute, explains, open discussion and debate is the strength of the Democrats. "What was once seen as a liability for Democrats and progressives in the past—they couldn't get 20 people to agree to the same thing, they could never finish anything, they couldn't stay on message—is now an asset," Leyden told *The Washington Post*. "All this talking and discussing and fighting energizes everyone, involves everyone, and gets people totally into it."[4]

Online Video

While Virginia senator George Allen encountered a particularly devastating backlash with his "Macaca" moment, none of the 2008 candidates will escape the wrath of YouTube. The rules of the game have changed, and not in the candidates' favor. As Republican leader after Republican leader got up to speak at the Conservative Political Action Conference in February 2007—from America First–er Tom Tancredo to 9/11 hero Rudy Giuliani—two operatives in blazers and ties from the Democratic National Committee videotaped every word of their speeches from the back corner. It's easy to justify the enormous resources that political campaigns will pour into the 2008 video tracking, as one needs only a single "Macaca" moment to nail a candidate. This time the Democratic operatives hit pay dirt twice. First, conservative commentator Ann Coulter called John Edwards a "faggot" in her CPAC speech. Second, when the campaign of Mitt Romney, who had spoken just before Coulter, labeled her remark "offensive," video leaked—perhaps from the Democrats, perhaps from a rival GOP campaign—showing Romney and Coulter laughing it up together backstage. Of course, Republicans are not the only target. John Edwards saw a video parody of him primping for the camera set to the tune of "I Feel Pretty"; Hillary Clinton took a hit in a video made when, at a speech commemorating the civil rights march in Selma, Alabama, she affected a southern accent; Barack Obama's campaign found itself scrambling after a YouTube clip surfaced of him misspeaking about the number of people who died in a Kansas tornado (it was twelve; he said ten thousand). In the new world, candidates have to be prepared for anything they say to be around the world before they finish a speech.

An early example of the power ordinary people will have in the first campaign of the technological era was the pro-Obama remake of the classic *1984*-themed Apple commercial that launched the alternative computer company. The seventy-four-second ad, created anonymously and spread through left-leaning blogs and the right-leaning *Drudge Report*, rocketed around the internet, collecting over a million views in just a few days.

"YouTube really rewards risk-takers—the edgier the ad, the more likely it is to be viewed, forwarded, and echoed throughout the internet and into the mainstream media," says John Lapp, who headed the Democratic Congressional Campaign Committee's efforts to win the House in 2006 before entering the private sector as a media consultant. "The good news: It offers more ways than ever for people to impact campaigns, to influence the political dialogue. The bad news for candidates: The attacks increase exponentially, by land, by sea, by dark of night."[5]

The original Apple ad, famous to technologists and advertising executives—*TV Guide* named it the best commercial of all time in 1999—first ran on January 22, 1984, during a break in the third quarter of Super Bowl XVIII, which saw the L.A. Raiders dominate the Washington Redskins. The ad showed an anonymous heroine dressed in red shorts, red shoes, and a white tank top with a picture of Apple's new Macintosh computer running into an Orwellian world to throw a sledgehammer at a TV image of Big Brother, who was propagandizing to a room of dronelike people. The ad clearly was aimed at behemoth IBM as Big Brother. A voice-over explained, "On January 24th, Apple Computer will introduce Macintosh. And you'll see why 1984 won't be like *1984*." The 2007 Obama ad replaced the Big Brother imagery with Hillary Clinton, and the closing text read, "On January 14th, the Democratic primary will begin. And you'll see why 2008 won't be like *1984*." It then popped up a link to Obama's website.

The ad, which only later was discovered to have been made by a Democratic internet strategist in Washington and secretly posted online, started out on a few blogs, kicked around the Web for a week or so, and then took off like a rocket when it hit some of the A-list blogs and sites visited by hundreds of thousands of people each day. DailyKos, for instance, attracts roughly as many daily readers as the *Chicago Tribune*. The thousands of diarists—those who blog themselves on the endless group blogs of the site—spend an average of two hours a day on the site, debating, chatting, and gossiping about politics. Markos, the site's namesake, is one of the Web's new superstars—a "hyperinfluential." Popular works such as Malcolm Gladwell's *The Tipping Point* and Jon Berry and Ed Keller's *The Influentials* describe how certain "connectors" influence others about what to buy, where to eat, and for whom to vote. Berry and Keller, for instance, posit that one in ten Americans is "the Influential" among his or her peers. The duo's work on identifying "influentials" deeply influenced the approach of Karl Rove and Ken Mehlman to the 2004 campaign. They identified some two million "influentials" across the country to target for special attention and invited Berry and Keller down to the

Bush headquarters in Alexandria, Virginia, to make a presentation and hear the campaign's plans. As the two researchers left the nondescript office building after seeing the campaign's strategy, Berry turned to Keller and declared, "It's over. Bush will win."[6] And where can one find these "influentials"? Studies have reported that more than 70 percent of blog readers count as an "influential," meaning that getting on blogs is increasingly important to anyone hoping to spread a message.

Increasingly, even beyond the one in ten "influential," the Web's disaggregated nature has seen another layer—the one in one thousand person who is, like Markos, a "hyperinfluential." The impact that these major players will have on the race can be seen in how stories and events evolve online outside of the mainstream media. Matt Drudge, the founder of the popular gossip site the *Drudge Report,* whose attention to a story online can almost guarantee its pickup in mainstream media, may be more like a one in ten million online networker, but this top tier of bloggers is constantly evolving and changing. "The so-called 'A-List' is an open club. Anyone with talent can become a key influencer, no matter what community they inhabit," says Steve Rubel, who as an executive at Edelman Public Relations has built one of the best blogs on the new digital era, Micropersuasion.com. "There's also always a changing of the guard. New voices replace the 'fading stars.' Everyone has a chance to rise."[7] For example, there was no major leftist blog written by a woman until Jane Hamsher broke off from DailyKos to found Firedoglake.com, just as in the era before YouTube, there was no political blog that integrated video into its posts before John Amato launched Crooksand liars.com. The two sites are now among the most influential on the left. Hamsher and Firedoglake's team of "reporters" provided gavel-to-gavel coverage of the Scooter Libby trial, becoming some of the first bloggers admitted to cover a federal trial as their readership climbed to nearly one hundred thousand page views a day.

More than that, though, there are massive differences between the right and the left online. The left has a far more powerful, larger, and more popular blogosphere community, and its top bloggers differ especially in one key aspect—where top conservative bloggers like Hugh Hewitt and Michelle Malkin are pundits and talk show hosts in their day jobs who also happen to blog, on the left a new power structure of ordinary bloggers like Kos and Armstrong has emerged. The left's blogosphere has grown up in an era when Republicans controlled government, giving them a target and an ongoing battle to wage. The right's blogosphere has grown only in fits and starts within a party that's both in power and by its core nature more hierarchical. It's a situation remarkably similar to the atrophied communications structure that Terry McAuliffe discovered at the DNC after Clinton's eight-year reign. Now, though, the reins of power online are firmly in the hands of the Democrats, and it's the right that is struggling to catch up.

This is especially problematic for the GOP because between "influentials" and "hyperinfluentials" online, the internet is becoming ever more important in people's decision making. A 2006 Pew survey showed that about sixty million Americans reported that the internet helped them make big decisions or negotiate their way through major episodes in their lives in the past two years—from health problems to careers to where to live. Speaking just about politics, 15 percent of all American adults—double the number from the 2002 midterm— reported that the internet was the main source of their political news in the 2006 election, and even many of the people who cited newspapers or TV news as their main source of news admitted in the survey that they "read" the newspapers online or "watched" the TV news on a computer.

Winning Eyeballs

"There's an explosion—it's not glacial anymore," says Democratic consultant and tech campaign pioneer Will Robinson, who was one of the pioneers in campaigning online. "It used to be a glacier sliding away from broadcast. Now there's a whole new generation of people who don't have phones that plug into the wall, who don't read newspapers, who don't read their mail, and if you're under twenty-five you don't watch television all that much. You're just as likely to be on YouTube, making video, or text messaging friends as doing anything else. People receive information in ways that they've never received it before. Trying to break through that clutter is really difficult."

It used to be that a political campaign or a product sponsor could purchase ads on all three major networks and know that a sizable portion of the nation would see the ad—such a move was called a "roadblock" ad. As late as 1980, the total share (or percentage of TVs turned on watching) of the three evening news shows stood at 75 percent. There was no way to escape it. Now you'd need to purchase dozens of properties for the ad to reach that many viewers. Evening news in the 2005–2006 season slipped to 35 percent, continuing its steady decline of more than a point a year over the last quarter century. In that same July week when broadcast television achieved its lowest rating ever and Ned Lamont met Joe Lieberman to debate, the three Spanish-language networks—Univision, Telemundo, and Tele-Futura—garnered some 4.2 million viewers, and on cable, USA Network's *Psych* scored the highest premiere of a new scripted series so far that year—a whopping 6.1 million viewers. Long gone are the powerhouse evening shows that dominated the networks since TV's inception and allowed political (and corporate) advertisers to reach a broad swath of the public with a few targeted buys.

During John F. Kennedy's 1960 campaign, *Gunsmoke* ruled the airwaves—with a 62 percent share, it was watched each week by an average of 37 percent of all households with a television. By 2005, the top-rated show, *CSI*, barely covered a quarter of the market with just over sixteen million viewers. This splintering has being going on for years, but it has accelerated since 1990 as the cable market exploded and other distractions like video games came along. In fact, none of 2005's most popular shows would have made the top twenty list in 1988.

Campaigns and candidates are being forced to move to cable channels to reach voters. The Bush campaign in 2004 became the first presidential campaign to make widespread buys on national cable channels, totaling more than $3 million. The campaign realized early on through demographic research that to reach where its key voters were watching—Fox News, ESPN, and the Speed Channel, which covers NASCAR—they had to move beyond broadcast ads.

Now advertisers are just as likely to encourage their targets to not watch TV at all. When the U.S. Army evaluated its recruiting methods in the 1990s, it came to the conclusion that it was drastically lagging behind the entertainment industry. In 1999, after the recruiting numbers hit a three-decade low, the army decided it needed a different tack. On July 4, 2002, it released the results of a three-year $7.5 million production: a video game called "America's Army" that allows players to simulate being a soldier in the modern military. Distributed on CD or available online for free, the game first offers basic training and then allows teams of players to take on a variety of first-person shooter missions, from capturing targets to escorting VIPs to defending the Alaska pipeline from terrorists. The game has been a huge hit for the army—with millions of registered players and over two hundred million game hours—and the driving force behind the military's video age recruiting. At the industry's main gathering in 2006, the Electronics Entertainment Expo, the army's Golden Knights parachute team landed in the parking lot. "The Army is a brand now," John McLaurin, the army's deputy assistant secretary for human resources asserted. "The Army sells itself, but you have to know what the Army is. And getting that door open to communicate is difficult."[8] Now, the army estimates that a third of people of recruiting age have been exposed to the game.

But there's a problem with new technologies like this. The current political consultants don't understand it—and from what little they do understand, it's clear that they can't make their typical 10 or 15 percent commission off it. "What's going on right now is that there's a struggle in the political community about dealing with that because a lot of the people who are still in decision-making roles are still in the world where they read newspapers, they watch *Meet the Press*, they watch the local news," Will Robinson says. Such people are an increasing rarity: One Harvard study found that newspaper readership among eighteen-to-twenty-four-year-olds is down 57 percent.[9]

Robinson sums up the situation: "Besides the age and the technology divide, there's a profit divide. A lot of these older consultants are squeezing out every last fucking penny before the circus is over. I'm on the cusp. I don't think I can run out the clock on the old media. I think that the old media is changing exponentially. Two years ago, it would have been a nice slow gradual trend and now the Soviet Empire is crumbling," Robinson says. "There's going to be a whole bloc of voters who we're trying to talk to who won't be listening because we're using dead technology."

The new era requires the political professionals constantly to be incorporating new technology to hold people's attention. In 2004, a year after his daughter was born, Robinson was sitting in her pediatrician's office watching the man next to him playing *Raiders of the Lost Ark* on his Palm Pilot. After asking, he learned that the man had found the software to digitize video on the internet, downloaded it, and put the Indiana Jones classic on a memory card. A lightbulb went off in Robinson's head, and by the time he was back at the office later that day, the creative director was loading campaign commercials onto Palms. He took the idea to the Cleveland, Ohio, suburb of Parma, where he found that people really responded to the idea and the Palm videos. He says it became a "bright shining object" of the campaign season.

He was amazed at how interested people were in watching the anti-Bush videos he had on the Palm Pilot. "You know George W. Bush, his brother, his nephew, his mom, his dad, his other nephew, his twins, his dog, and even his mom and dad's dog's names. How much could one video do?" Robinson asks. "I'd be showing it three or four times because they'd get other family members to come to the door. It was still pretty novel. That will dissipate for people pretty soon . . . You're struggling to break through this cacophony and communicate with people in a way that's meaningful."

Michael Bassik became one of the pioneers of political advertising online in 2000 when he was a twenty-year-old University of Pennsylvania senior and was hired by AOL as a summer intern in the online giant's New York advertising office. After his senior year and a thesis on the effect of online ads in the 2000 election, AOL hired him to implement his thesis and build out AOL's educational, nonprofit, and political advertising divisions. He traveled around the country in 2002, working with campaigns on both sides, and was just settling in New York when a call from a political direct mail firm he'd never heard of landed him in Washington to found MHSC Partners' internet advertising division. Bassik's new job was created in recognition that technological changes were rapidly changing the political landscape. The traditional direct mail world, the source of much of the political and advocacy-focused fund-raising in the United States, is a relatively small and aging chunk of the country: It's generally estimated to make up about 6 percent of the adult population or about twelve million people, two-thirds of whom are sixty or older.[10] Now Bassik's staff has grown to ten people, and the division turns a profit. At almost every campaign, though, he faces a reluctance to embrace the Web's power for advertising. "Traditional consultants find it cumbersome and confusing—which it is. The internet is the least scaled advertising medium that exists. And so it's hard; it's not intuitive; it's time-consuming, unscaled, and not very profitable. Consultants making 9 percent or 10 percent on a $10 million ad buy—that makes sense to them. On the internet, a $25,000 ad buy is quite significant. A $100,000 ad buy is quite significant. So the amount one could make off online advertising given all its difficulties and scalability, it renders it not a top priority for consultants to bring to the table," he laments. "Whereas in TV, there's a commercial block and it's all the same time frames, on the internet, there are so many options. The overwhelming sense of difficulty outweighs the benefits."

As the Hillary Clinton *Sopranos* video shows, 2008's first campaign is forcing consultants to be creative again and break their traditional molds. Even as recently as the last campaign, a media consultant could have the most persuasive ad ever designed, but if it ran over a minute, it would never make it to air. Now online videos have removed the time constraints of television advertising while at the same time forever altering the balance of power: You can't *buy* people's attention as easily online; you have to *earn* their attention. After being left out of a presidential debate in early 2007, fringe Democratic candidate Mike Gravel bypassed the traditional media and went online— posting a three-minute-long video on YouTube in which he doesn't say a word. Instead, standing on the shore of a lake, he stares into the camera silently for over a minute before walking away and stopping to heave a large rock into the lake, before continuing on, disappearing into the distance. It was far from traditional, but it met the criteria for online success: it was amusing and compelling, and it made people want to talk about it and pass it along. It received some 200,000 views online. For decades, creativity has been an undervalued trait in a political industry that strives to offend the fewest number of potential supporters possible. Now it's essential to any successful online effort. "You can't push something on people if they're not looking for it," says Micah Sifry of techpresident.com, a website that's tracking the first campaign. "Go where the people are."

Done right, online ads are proving surprisingly effective. In 2004, the DNC bought a wide variety of ads online supporting John Kerry, especially right before the presidential election. Those who saw the ads, follow-up research showed, had higher favorability ratings for Kerry, were more likely to vote for him, and were more likely to contribute to the campaign.

Cell Phones

Three months after he campaigned with John Edwards, Robert "Scobelizer" Scoble and I were seated on the fourth-floor balcony of the Austin Convention Center. Inside at the South by Southwest Interactive conference were thousands of technologists of the first order— the geeks who hope to build the next YouTube, Google, or MySpace. They pondered what the "Web 2.0" movement, which seeks to connect blogs, podcasts, social networking sites like Facebook and MySpace, online games like "Second Life" and "World of Warcraft," and online video into ever more powerful connections, will bring in the future. In this insular world, packed with laptop-wielding entrepreneurs who wear T-shirts and corduroy pants to the office, Scoble was one of the convention's main A-list celebrities, as was Matt Mullenweg, who created the blogging software powerhouse WordPress before he turned twenty-one. Amanda Congdon, the first celebrity of the online video world thanks to her work on the site Rocketboom and, not unrelatedly, one of the small number of females in this world, turned heads wherever she went around Austin. Thanks to his eye-opening experiences on the Edwards campaign, Scoble was one of the handful of SXSW attendees pondering what Web 2.0 means for Campaigning 3.0. Politics, after all, has evolved from a prebroadcast world of marathon William Jennings Bryan–like stump speeches to thirty-second sound bytes in the broadcast era to who knows what in this increasingly postbroadcast era. With the networks hitting ratings lows, and TiVo and Web distribution of television shows taking off, the future of video appears to be a lot more like the Obama rip-off of the 1984 Apple ad than it does an expensive studio-produced sitcom episode.

Scoble, who has been a longtime blogging pioneer, explained blogging's origins as being rooted in a reaction against the flood of marketing facing Americans today. "We were sick of the committee-based marketing. Sick isn't the right word. We were becoming immune to it. You stand out in the middle of Times Square and you see four hundred marketing messages coming at you—they're all done by committee; they're all perfected; but none of them tell you anything. You might see a Sony camcorder ad and a Canon camcorder ad and they don't tell you anything about the product. You can't tell which one is better. We wanted to fight back against this corporate-perfected world . . . You can tell when someone's cleaned up the real world for you. The real world isn't clean. There are cigarettes on the table." He gestures at the full ashtray on the table between us. "There's mess. There's dirt. Corporate committees never like that. They'll get rid of the cigarettes.

"The world's collapsing. Thomas Friedman says the world is flat, but I say the world's in a conference room. I can talk with someone via Twitter or Second Life or e-mail or IM and I have no concept of where they are until they open their mouth and say, 'I'm in Shanghai' or 'I'm in Moscow' or 'I'm in Munich,'" Scoble says.

What had Scoble and everyone abuzz at South by Southwest was a recently launched site called Twitter, which allows people to create groups of friends and send regular 160-character updates to their computers, instant messaging programs, or even their cell phones. Twitter updates from conference attendees float across large flat-screen monitors set up around the convention center. As is often the case with heady new products, there seems to be nothing that Twitter can't do. One blogger explains how it can save lives in a disaster by aiding the response of emergency crews and rescuers. Scoble himself has attracted some one thousand followers on Twitter who subscribed to his miniupdates, creating a near flood of information about his whereabouts and their whereabouts. "What happens if you have a

Twitter group that just follows Romney through his day? People text in, 'Just saw him here,' 'Just saw him there,' " muses Henry Copeland, the founder of blogads.com and whose 2002 start-up has grown to a staff of twenty-two and allowed dozens of bloggers to make thousands off their Web traffic. Imagine the power, Copeland says, of a group of Twitter devotees tracking elected officials throughout their day and holding them accountable to how they're using their time. In countries like the Philippines, cell phones with their short messaging system (SMS) have been key in recent elections. "SMS has been a big part of political activity in Asia and Europe. Twitter is really showing that we're ready for SMS," explains Joi Ito, another tech pioneer.

A May 2007 government study found that nearly 30 percent of 18-to-29-year-olds in the United States used only a cell phone and don't have a landline phone at home. That number has profound implications for elections because pollsters aren't allowed to call cell phones—meaning that young people will be harder to predict as a political voting bloc—and most robo calls from campaigns don't include cell phones. At the same time, a growth in text messaging and the adoption of sites like Twitter allow campaigns to more easily reach cell phone–toting supporters.

Of course, the new technology may be second nature to teenagers and younger Americans, but it's still some time away from being embraced by the generation raised on rotary phones. When Speaker of the House Dennis Hastert set up a blog, he often faxed in his blog entries to his office. "It's one of the most interesting generational changes where you have people in the same room, live in the same country, who get their information in completely different places," muses Will Robinson. "It's like, 'Why would I watch local TV news and wait for some guy in a plaid jacket to tell me what the weather is when I can go online or check my cell phone?' "

"There's a whole group of people who are communicating in one direction and one way and that's getting smaller, and then there's a whole set that's communicating in a different way," Robinson said. "It's a struggle for politics to start communicating with these people in a way to reach them. The traditional ways of communicating with folks are dying." He held up a plastic bag filled with paper and gestured. "This is two weeks of mail. I went through it this morning and threw out half of it." Then he launched into what he hears in focus groups these days: " 'My roommate hasn't checked his mail in a year.' 'I pay my bills online.' 'The only time I deal with molecules is when my mom sends me cookies, and I'd rather she just e-mail me a gift certificate and I'll go off and get cookies here.' "

Robinson shook his head ruefully. "We sit in meetings around a table talking about this, and the principals are like, 'Text what?' " he recounted. "Usually what I say is 'While we're having this meeting, there are six of your assistants texting back and forth, "What a bunch of dinosaurs." ' I can hear the tittering in the background because that's exactly what they're doing."

John Edwards, for one, didn't wait to be targeted by a grassroots network of trackers. He jumped on the bandwagon early and sent in Twitter updates about what cities he was visiting and what he was doing on the campaign trail. At 12:43 p.m. on March 10, he Twittered, "Community meeting on healthcare in Newton, IA. Then 1hr1/2 drive to Burlington for a similar meeting. Later tonight, back in NC." Three days later, at 1:06 p.m., he updated, "Great to see my family. In NC today. Call with student reporters. Interview w Wolf Blitzer. College Tour Rally at Bennett in Greensboro." Barack Obama joined soon thereafter, and Hillary Clinton started her cell-phone text-messaging campaign by asking supporters to vote for their choice for the campaign's theme song.

The Twitter schedule updates aren't all that different from an effort pushed by Andrew Rasiej, the tech entrepreneur who ran for New York City's public advocate on a municipal wireless platform. Working with a new group, the Sunlight Foundation, he saw an opportunity for the Web to provide greater transparency and accountability for Congress. The organization is named after the famous quotation from Justice Louis Brandeis: "Sunlight is said to be the best of disinfectants." The foundation's "Punch Clock" campaign encouraged members of Congress to open up their normally tightly held personal schedules to the world. The text itself was simple enough: "I believe citizens have a right to know what their Member of Congress does every day. Starting with the next Congress, I promise to publish my daily official work schedule on the Internet, within 24 hours of the end of every work day. I will include all matters relating to my role as

a Member of Congress. I will include all meetings with constituents, other Members, and lobbyists, listed by name. (In rare cases I
will withhold the names of constituents whose privacy must be pro-
tected.) I will also include all fund-raising events. Events will be
listed whether Congress is in session or not, and whether I am
in Washington, traveling, or in my district." In the 2006 elections,
ninety-two candidates signed the agreement, and one—Kristin Gillibrand—actually won office. Gillibrand's staff immediately got concerned about her Sunlight commitment. As meritorious as her efforts
are, her implementation of the Punch Clock agreement met more the
letter of the agreement than its spirit. Her schedule is the last link at
the bottom of her website under the ambiguous title "Sunlight Report," and the page itself is replaced each day so there's no easily
retrievable archive of her past schedules. Gillibrand, like Jack Carter
and his MySpace page, may welcome the new era in which they
serve, but they aren't exactly comfortable with it—the new world
forces a degree of transparency and honesty and involves giving up a
level of control that campaigns have carefully massaged and manipulated for decades.

A key challenge for journalists and campaign professionals is that
in a world when anyone can report something, candidates must consider every person they meet and every person they see as a possible
"reporter." When Scoble decided in mid-2006 to leave Microsoft for a
start-up video-blogging venture, he told fifteen people at a conference
on a Saturday afternoon and—in a moment of shocking naïveté for a
pioneer of this new world—asked them not to tell anyone until Tuesday. He hadn't officially told his boss yet. By 7 p.m. that evening, a
small blogger Scoble didn't know reported that he was leaving the
software giant. That report was quickly picked up by another blogger
with a larger audience, and from there the spread started doubling almost every fifteen minutes, from one blog to two to four to eight in
the span of a quiet Saturday evening. By midnight the news had
spread to over two hundred blogs, and by the following morning the
news had hit the mainstream press. Within seventy-two hours, he was
on the front page of the BBC website. Waggener Edstrom, Microsoft's
PR agency, later estimated that the story was picked up by more than
130 newspapers worldwide, as well as on numerous TV reports, and

that altogether Scoble's departure generated 50 million media impressions. "Just because I quit a job," Scoble says with a laugh. "It shows that if you have information that people find fascinating, it'll get spread." Looking ahead to the campaign and the new environment facing candidates, he says, "A sex scandal could be broken on a blog with five readers, and I guarantee that they'll have fifty million media impressions in seventy-two hours."

Scoble says that as a blogger and avid blog reader himself, he starts out reading something on a blog with a high degree of skepticism. "If DailyKos reports that Hillary Clinton is going to do X or Barack Obama is going to do Y, I'm going to be skeptical about that because it's only in one source. DailyKos is usually pretty accurate, but sometimes they mess up," he says. "My skepticism starts out real high, but over the course of twenty-four hours it goes way down. If a campaign sees a rumor and it's not true, they should fight it instantly . . . If you're not media hip enough to understand that stories go from blogs with five readers to the front page of *The New York Times* in forty-eight hours, then you don't deserve to be part of this process—especially at the Super Bowl level."

Mitt Romney demonstrated a by-the-book response in the YouTube era when he was confronted with video of a debate from his 1994 Senate bid against Ted Kennedy. The clip showed him professing more liberal views and threatened his aggressive courting of social conservatives in the 2008 race. In only eight hours from the time the video surfaced on YouTube, Romney's campaign had posted a YouTube response: video of the former Massachusetts governor calling in to a conservative radio talk show to explain the video and place it in context. Showing the candidate on video himself explaining in his own voice was a critical point of the response, as it showed it wasn't just some staffer or flack apologizing in a statement e-mailed to reporters or posted on a blog. The lesson of the new campaign is similar to the Miranda rights offered to suspects placed under arrest: Anything you say can and will be used against you. Soon. At the same time, participating in the online conversation can help build trust. Romney combated the attack effectively by getting online quickly and forcefully, and by explaining what was going on. He treated the online audience (i.e., voters) as people who deserved his time and attention. In campaigns past that hasn't always been true—too often voters have been merely an afterthought in the political industrial complex—but Romney understood that his future depends on engaging people on their terms, not his.

Online Fund-raising

In the 2008 race, candidates are being watched at every moment. A clip of freshman senator Barack Obama campaigning in a poor Cleveland neighborhood appeared on YouTube. He told a crowd to contribute to his campaign. "Everybody here pony up five dollars, ten dollars for this campaign. I don't care how poor you are, you've got five dollars." It was certainly a "gotcha" moment—a brief moment when the candidate who espoused the hopes of the downtrodden seemed to mock their poverty—but it also illustrated how Obama and other less established candidates can compete on a campaign playing field increasingly driven by money. Iowa governor Tom Vilsack and Indiana senator Evan Bayh were driven from the 2008 race long before it really started simply because they didn't think they could raise the huge sums necessary to run for office. From 1996 to 2004, spending in the presidential race soared by 300 percent to some $718 million, and few would be surprised to see 2008 break the billion-dollar mark.[11]

While more of the money necessary is coming from the bundlers like George W. Bush's Rangers and Pioneers, more of it is also coming in the online era from small-dollar donations. In campaign parlance, these major fund-raisers are known as "whales," but to understand why Barack Obama was asking his Cleveland audience to donate $5, Will Robinson tells us to take a look at the real-life blue whale. Even at birth the *Balaenoptera musculus* is a beast to behold. When born, the calves are about twenty-five feet long and weigh 3 tons—larger than a Ford Excursion. Adult blue whales can grow to eighty feet and weigh up to 150 tons. They grow by feasting upon krill, tiny crustaceans no longer than two and a half inches. The whales force millions of gallons of seawater through their mouths, trapping the tiny krill in the netlike baleen that hangs from their upper jaws. During the summer, blue whale can consume more than four tons—roughly four hundred million krill. Internet fund-raising, says Will Robinson, is like a whale feeding. Tens of thousands or even hundreds of thousands of small donations add up to real money, and as credit cards and websites have transformed the transaction time of a donation from twenty days to twenty seconds, it makes sense to go after small dollars in a way it never has before.

Sites like ActBlue are allowing grassroots supporters online to become their own bundlers, and some blogs have successfully raised tens of thousands of dollars for candidates. Here, too, Democrats have a huge lead over Republicans: By the end of May 2007, ABC PAC, the conservative fund-raising site equivalent to the left's ActBlue, had raised only $385 for all the GOP field. Meanwhile, ActBlue, which draws upon the larger, more organized and powerful progressive blogosphere, had raised more than $3 million for John Edwards alone, and a total of some $22 million in online donations since its 2004 launch.

As the online fund-raising field evolves, though, one aspect of online campaigning is becoming clear: The thing that motivates someone to get involved and make a donation is the candidate himself or herself, the candidate's message and vision for a better world. This is, in essence, the critical point lost on so many people about campaigning on the internet: It's not really about the internet at all. "Two thousand four was the first time you saw people based on some offline action, something in their regular lives, go to Google, searching for the name of a candidate, clicking on an ad or clicking on a link, and giving money. User-driven fund-raising. Usually fund-raisers chase the donors. This was donors chasing the fund-raisers. 'I want to give you money, I'm going to seek you out and give it to you,'" explains Michael Bassik, the founder of MHSC's online advertising division. "Howard Dean's website wasn't what made Howard Dean a fund-raising phenomenon online. It was Howard Dean. He could have had a website that was a fund-raising page and a few 'About Us' pages. It wasn't about the fact that he had a blog, it was that Howard Dean spoke to so many people and that he spoke in a voice that so many people hadn't heard in four—if not more—years."

Bassik's view is almost universal among internet strategists. "If you look at the candidates who have all done well online—John McCain in 2000, Howard Dean in 2004, even Jesse Ventura going back a while—what they all had in common was they all had a core message that was really resonating with people," says Mark Soohoo, who oversaw the 2004 Republican National Convention website and was one of the early staff tapped for John McCain's 2004 internet team. "You become president because you have a vision, you have a message . . . You don't become president because you have a website. Howard Dean did well online not because he had a cool bat but because he had a good message."

Phil Madsen, who served as Ventura's webmaster, posted the same response after his candidate won. "While it's true that we could not have won the election without the internet, we did not win the election because of the internet. We won because our candidates, campaign staff, and volunteers engaged the voters in a number of meaningful ways," he wrote on jesseventura.org. "The internet is not about technology; it's about relationships."[12]

And herein lies the single most important lesson of the first campaign for candidates to remember: In this campaign, the candidate who succeeds online will be the one who succeeds offline. All of the fancy tools, YouTube viral videos, and Twitter updates won't help a candidate who doesn't offer a vision for a stronger, better America as it confronts the twenty-first century. If he or she doesn't offer a coherent vision or fails to follow through once in office, the blogosphere and online communities will be ready and waiting to hold the nation's leadership accountable. Creativity isn't just important for winning eyeballs online—the thought that goes into a well-crafted, attractive ad that makes people talk speaks to a larger desire to connect with ordinary voters on issues that matter to them is just as important. The internet, at its most fundamental level, is about opening up a conversation that has been dominated by elites for decades. In this era's first campaign, the candidate who best understands that the internet isn't an end to itself but merely a means to an end—a chance to pull people in and get them involved in the political process—will triumph.

"I think it's healthy for democracy to have leaders who understand how to listen to the people they're serving. I'm certainly attracted to someone who understands how to listen to the world," says Scoble, who, ever eager, almost trips over himself as he discusses the transformation. "That'll make this country a better place."

CONCLUSION: OUR COLLECTIVE FUTURE

We've stumbled along for a while, trying to run a new civilization in old ways, but we got to start to make this world over.

—THOMAS EDISON TO HENRY FORD, 1912

The presidential race today is as wide open as it was on November 30, 2006, at the campaign's unofficial starting point. Candidates such as Tom Vilsack have already come and gone; once invincible-seeming front-runners like John McCain have already stumbled, and new challengers like Fred Thompson have emerged; the front-runners have been through as much scrutiny already as they would have faced in an entire campaign eight or twelve years ago. Republicans and Democrats alike, though—and maybe even an independent or two—are struggling with how to campaign in the new environment of a globalized, interconnected world.

There is no telling whether the candidates in the general election will run the first campaign or run the last campaign all over again. But by midsummer there were the signposts of the first campaign—of how far we had come in the debate about the changes wrought by technology and of how far we still had to go—all across the country and around the globe. The various threads of the first campaign could be found all over the internet as well as in tableaus in places like Chicago, Charleston, South Carolina, and Manchester, New Hampshire. New reports came out touting how Japan's internet speed was nearly thirty times faster than that in the United States and how Americans in 2005 earned less than they did in 2000, and the 2006 annual census numbers showed that another 2.2 million Americans—more than the entire population of New Mexico—had lost their health insurance in the last year, making the total number a record high. Overseas, China kicked off its one-year countdown to the Beijing Olympics even as officials admitted that high pollution levels in the air might force some events to be postponed. Al Qaeda turned to the Web to publish its latest "ad," headlined "Wait for the Big Surprise"; it showed a digitally altered photograph of George W. Bush and Pakistan's President Pervez Musharraf standing in front of a burning White House.

Meanwhile, every day seemed to bring some new online development in the campaign. The dancing, bikini-clad "Obama Girl" had her brief moment in the sun on YouTube and ran into competition from the "Romney Girls" and the "Giuliani Girl." James Kotecki, a recent Georgetown grad who goes by the handle "EmergencyCheese," became the 2008 campaign's unofficial YouTube arbiter as his online commentary became a cult hit and he got to speak with candidates— including Ron Paul, who went to Kotecki's dorm room for the interview. Barack Obama hosted an intimate dinner with a handful of randomly selected online donors and posted the video on his website, where some fifteen thousand supporters had their own blogs going about the campaign. On his birthday in August, Obama's internet staff in their Chicago headquarters found themselves besieged by thousands of Happy Birthday messages from "friends" on the candidate's MySpace page. Mitt Romney found himself on the defensive after video of him forcefully arguing about his Mormon religion found its way online.

IN CHARLESTON, South Carolina, on the storied grounds of the Citadel military academy, the Democrats gathered for the first officially sanctioned Democratic National Committee debate—an authentic milestone of the first campaign. This was the first YouTube debate, pre-sented on CNN to an audience notable not just for its large size but for its relatively young age, and which sought video submissions from regular Americans for the candidates.

Out of more than fifteen hundred videos submitted, CNN eventu-ally chose thirty-seven. While some of the thirty-seven were a bit odd—including one with a talking snowman asking about global warming and one where the questioner wanted to know whether Arnold Schwarzenegger was a cyborg—the majority were something amazing and new in politics: Americans were asking powerful ques-tions of those who sought power. There was none of the false glory of a "town hall debate," but instead real Americans, from the comfort of their own homes, wrote with real problems. From the first question—when Zach Kempf of Provo, Utah, opened with "Wassup?"—it was clear that the first campaign was in uncharted territory.

The questions from "real" Americans made an impact that debate moderator Anderson Cooper, even with his abundance of gravitas, could not match. A Brooklyn lesbian couple, Mary Matthews and Jen Weidenbaum, asked whether candidates would let them get mar-ried—to each other. A question on Darfur came in from aid workers in a refugee camp close to the conflict. For a question on expanding health-care insurance, a thirty-something Long Island woman took off her wig mid-question to showcase the effects of chemotherapy: "I'm thirty-six years old and hope to be a future breast cancer survivor," "Kim" told the candidates. Later in the debate, one question—inspired by Bob Dylan's music video of "Subterranean Homesick Blues," in which the singer holds up signs with the lyrics printed on them—became what is surely the first presidential debate question ever with a guitar solo.

"See those flags over my shoulder?" one man prefaced as he asked about ending the Iraq war. "They covered the coffins of my grandfa-ther, my father, and my oldest son. Someday, mine will join them. I don't want to see my youngest sons' join them." It's much harder to dodge questions of accountability, sacrifice, and service in a setting like that—and it highlighted in a very direct way that the ones mak- . ing the decisions about the war aren't the same families making the sacrifices.

In a campaign environment where too many of the candidates' answers seem to be prepackaged talking points, the debate was a refreshing moment of authenticity, and it suggested that ordinary Americans could now get a response from power that they never could have gotten before. While some sites chided CNN for maintaining control over the choice of questions—the online community could have voted on which questions they wanted to see asked during the debate, and indeed a grassroots site sprung up that allowed them to do just that—the YouTube debate was a brave first step down the technological road and was a great experiment in participatory democracy. A few nights afterward, I was sharing dinner with Nicco Mele, Howard Dean's former webmaster, when he turned to me and, gushing about the changes the debate would usher in, asked, "Why would you go back? It's beautifully American."

The GOP didn't agree.

As the summer wound down and the Democrats and the blogosphere celebrated their small "d" democratic moment in the YouTube debate, there were signs that the GOP still wasn't ready to embrace the Web and still didn't yet understand how critical the internet would be to the party's future. In answering a question on the campaign trail, Mitt Romney, who with his high-tech background should have been the best informed of any candidate, didn't appear to know the difference between video-sharing site YouTube, currently the fourth most popular website in the world, and MySpace, the social networking site that ranked sixth in the world. Rudy Giuliani kept his MySpace page "private," meaning that it wasn't open to the public at large and people had to become his "friends" before they could see the page—raising a question of why he would bother pretending to participate in the Web 2.0 social networking revolution if he wasn't ready to embrace it. He wasn't fooling anyone, and the privacy setting on the site seemed a perfect metaphor for his party's reluctance: "We'll play online but only on our terms." Giuliani's approach was the exact antithesis of the twenty-first century's new ethos.

Beyond such minor issues was a much larger one: Even after the Democratic debate's rousing success on CNN, the GOP tried to scuttle its own YouTube debate. None of the top-tier candidates accepted CNN's initial invitation to the Republican debate, all citing "scheduling conflicts" for the September 17 date, and the debate looked like it might be an entire bust—until an online outcry started, and CNN rescheduled for early winter. The headline on the popular news site Digg.com read: "Grand Old Party Clings to Grand Old Media: Repub Candidates Refuse YouTube." Jeff Jarvis, one of the leading voices of the new medium, took on the GOP: "This is not only short-sighted tactically but also essentially insulting to the American people. We are on the internet. Come talk with us. What, you're too scared to? Big, tough terrorists don't scare you but we do? Come on, boys, we don't bite. But we do vote."

Within the GOP, top new media strategists (or, as the GOP calls them, "e-campaign advisors") like Patrick Ruffini, the former head of the RNC's Web efforts, and David All, who consults for numerous GOP congressional campaigns on their internet efforts, launched a site called SaveTheDebate.com to pressure their party's leaders to meet the country on the internet. As Ruffini explained, "There's no better time to start prioritizing online over older, increasingly less effective forms of political contact. And yet the response to stuff like this seems to be . . . crickets. This isn't a fringe Internets thing. We could lose because we don't correct this, in the same way that we almost lost in 2000 because we forgot door-to-door."

Andrew Sullivan, who was one of the first prominent conservative voices online, wrote on his blog, "For my part, the current old white men running for the GOP already seem from some other planet. Ducking YouTube after the Dems did so well will look like a party uncomfortable with the culture and uncomfortable with democracy." Indeed, coming on the heels of a party leader who speaks of "the Internets" and "the Google," it's a disturbing trend that GOP leaders seem so disconnected from the technologies that are changing the way most Americans live their daily lives.

It's still easy to dismiss the internet as a political tool, but as it becomes an ever-more critical part of the financing for expensive presidential campaigns, GOP candidates will be at a great disadvantage. Joe Trippi explained the importance of the energy created online during the primary season and how that carries over into the general election and beyond. Howard Dean's online campaign helped lay the groundwork for John Kerry to raise tens of millions of dollars online after being chosen as the nominee in 2004. This year's primary winner will see the same advantage—or disadvantage. "On the Republican side, there's almost no competition for supremacy on the 'net, which means the Republican nominee is going to inherit almost nothing," Trippi said, adding, "It's not just about the list, it's about the experience." By last fall, every single Democratic campaign had as one of its senior internet staff someone who got schooled in the internet either on Dean's campaign or at the DNC under Dean. The GOP, meanwhile, had such an anemic online effort that its candidates refused to even release internet fund-raising numbers because they were so low.

To see the impact that a strong online infrastructure could have, the GOP should have made the journey to Chicago in the week after the YouTube debate, when the progressive blogosphere gathered for the second annual YearlyKos convention—this one bigger, more professional, and more triumphal than the one in Las Vegas in 2006. The difference of only a year was evident throughout. A year before, the bloggers cum activists had come together amid a party in disarray and rocked by infighting and lacking control of any branch of government; but since the last convention, the Democrats had won a historic victory in the 2006 election and seen success in "red" states like New Hampshire, Indiana, Montana, and Virginia. Next to a lackluster GOP field where "none of the above" seemed to lead many of the polls, the Democratic Party had an electric field: Hillary, Barack, and John Edwards. Even "second-tier" candidates such as Bill Richardson, Joe Biden, and Chris Dodd were experienced and thoughtful leaders with strong online campaigns. While the week before, all the presidential candidates had skipped the annual gathering in Tennessee of the Democratic Leadership Council—the centrist group that had grown out of the 1984 Mondale defeat and helped catapult Bill Clinton into the White House in 1992, and today more than anything represented to the bloggers the ideologically corrupt Washington establishment—seven of the eight candidates showed up to court the bloggers. It was all the party faithful needed to see: They had arrived as a force in the party and represented the future of progressivism.

During the opening night of the convention, Howard Dean, whose campaign had first demonstrated the power of the blogosphere, returned for a victory lap. Seeming more mature and thoughtful than he did during the 2004 campaign, Dean spoke to the nearly fifteen hundred progressive activists, extolling the virtues of the new campaign paradigm and how the Democrats' embrace of it contrasted with the Republicans' online reluctance: "Traditional campaigns have relied on enormous amounts of TV advertising, thirty-second spots, aimed at you, telling you what we think, and what we think you ought to do. The new campaign, the two-way campaign is: we listen to you before we start talking, and we, throughout the campaign, have a dialogue between the people whose votes we're hoping to get, asking for their advice as we go through, and taking it to heart . . . This means real two-way campaigns where the views and opinions of the American people have an impact on the leadership, so leaders are *with* the people instead of seeking to lead folks that aren't interested in being led by them."

Assistant Senate Majority Leader Dick Durbin spoke also, opening with a joke about how Fox pundit Bill O'Reilly had spent the previous week attacking YearlyKos as a gathering of hate and how conservative pundit Bob Novak had recently described heaven as "a place where there are no blogs": "Well, you can understand why he might say that and why others, like our friends at the 'fair-and-balanced' Fox News, are saying the same kind of thing. But millions of other Americans see it just the opposite. They are looking at what's happening in our country these last few years and saying, 'Thank heavens for the blogs.'"

Durbin knew of what he spoke because he was, at that moment, experiencing the power of the internet firsthand. Using a new site called OpenLeft.com, Durbin had turned to the Web for help in writing broadband-access legislation and suddenly found himself with an unlikely new ally: the leading conservative blog RedState.org, which invited him onto their site to talk about the bill. As RedState.org blogger Robert Bluey wrote, "I don't see this as a Democrat vs. Republican issue. President Bush in 2004 called for universal and affordable access to high-speed broadband. Many conservatives welcomed his goal as a way to spur innovation, new jobs and economic competitiveness." Echoing the absence of the first-campaign agenda among the 2008

Republican candidates, leading Republican tech strategist David All chimed in on the Durbin discussion, writing, "Frankly, I'd like to see more Republicans and conservatives step-up-the-plate and support broadband access measures. It's sad to think that many go without that which we all rely upon and utilize so much."

All's final point is a sad fact of the 2008 campaign: Despite all the energy online at the YouTube debate and at gatherings like YearlyKos, this first campaign more likely than not is going to be a series of missed opportunities—like when the GOP candidates tried to skip their party's own YouTube debate. History will someday judge us on how we tackle the myriad challenges facing the United States as we elect candidates for a new age. Unfortunately, the American political system responds too often only to intense stimuli; the rise of Islamist terrorism, for example, sat on the back burner until 9/11. But we can't afford to wait for our politicians to be startled into action.

During the Charleston YouTube debate, among the hundreds of reporters covering the event *The Washington Post*'s Jose Antonio Vargas, who perhaps more than any other "mainstream media" reporter has dove headlong into the new online territory, alone journeyed the mile and a half from the Citadel debate site to Cooper River Courts, a rundown public housing project, where YouTube, the internet, and the flood of information and opportunities they provided were rare luxuries. He talked with fourteen-year-old Tiara Reid, who lives a thirty-minute walk from the public library, where she can use the internet only two hours a day. The "digital divide" and the country's reluctance to wire its citizens to participate in the information revolution was on full display. The need for investment in tech infrastructure was readily evident in a city where only 40 to 45 percent of the people have access to broadband connections. "At one level, the YouTube debate shows that the Web has really become a centerpiece of American political culture," Lee Rainie, the director of the Pew Internet and American Life Project, told Vargas. "At another level, it also shows that the debate is not for everybody. It's certainly not available to all Americans." Andrew Rasiej argues that the digital divide, a great buzzword for a decade or longer, is worse today than it was when the issue first arose because so little has been done to address it even as Fortune 500 companies wire their employees to be online 24-7. Until

Reid has the same economic opportunities as the people of southwest and southside Virginia that Mark Warner wired, she'll be left behind in the new economy.[1]

We'll never wake up one morning and see wall-to-wall coverage of the education crisis or the health-care crisis. We won't see twenty-four-hour coverage from towns that don't have broadband access or from factories that have closed. *The Day After Tomorrow* movie notwithstanding, it's unlikely we'll see a massive global change overnight. There's not a single day when these issues will become an immediate crisis. Instead, they will creep along day by day, as they already have in recent years. Even the collapse of the I-35W bridge in Minneapolis, which could have focused the nation on the crumbling infrastructure of the industrial age and the need to upgrade it and invest in a new generation of infrastructure for the decades ahead, garnered only a few days of front-page news before Iraq and fears of terrorism shoved themselves back to the fore. But the lack of a focusing crisis doesn't make the need for a change of agenda less important. Indeed, the historical reputation of the next president will likely ride on his or her response to the challenge of globalization more so than on any other challenge of the coming years, just as we remember how the two Roosevelts, Teddy and FDR, brought our country through the economic changes of generations past.

People—voters—are paying attention, and they're not happy with what they're seeing from the candidates in terms of a first campaign–type agenda. Frustration with this new modern world and the political response to it seems to be boiling over among voters on the campaign trail, both online and offline.

In early August, Mitt Romney found himself under verbal attack at the Red Arrow Diner in Manchester, New Hampshire, from a voter who was tired of all the talk. It had been an ordinary campaign event at one of the iconic sites of the Granite State's first-in-the-nation primary circuit, with Romney talking about the global fight to stop AIDS, when Michele Griffin, a waitress who's worked at the diner for twelve years, broke in, shouting, "What about our nation? How 'bout the USA? C'mon!" Romney tried to reply, but Griffin wasn't having any of the platitudes. "We pay over a thousand dollars a month for our insurance. Then we have co-pays. Every time you go to the doctor, it's fifty dollars a visit. Then you have co-pays for our prescriptions. Can you tell me what your co-pay is?"

"Yes," Romney said, still off-balance. "Ten dollars for each prescription."

"That's very nice, isn't it?" shot back Griffin, who has two daughters, one diabetic and one with Crohn's disease.

"Yes. What are yours?" Romney asked.

"Mine are like thirty dollars to fifty dollars. I have three sick children."

As Griffin later complained to a reporter, "They all talk about health care till they get in there. But they all have health care, don't they? Do they have to pay outrageous co-pays? No."

The whole scene seemed to hearken back to when John Andrew accosted Treasury Secretary John Snow in 2003 outside a custard stand in Wassau, Wisconsin, and was met with the unreassuring message from the leader of the nation's economy: "Just wait."

Just wait isn't going to cut it anymore. The country has already pressed its luck by waiting this long.

On the other side of the presidential primary, at the AFL-CIO debate in Chicago in August, the Democratic field was confronted with the evidence of how neither party was meeting the challenges of the new world. Steve Skvara, a retired Indiana steel worker, stood on his crutches and, his voice breaking and his eyes filling with tears, asked a question that captured the anxiety now gripping the country's workers: "After thirty-four years with LTV Steel I was forced to retire because of a disability. Two years later, LTV filed bankruptcy. I lost a third of my pension and my family lost their health care. Every day of my life I sit at the kitchen table across from the woman who devoted thirty-six years of her life to my family and I can't afford to pay for her health care. What's wrong with America and what will you do to change it?"

The audience at Chicago's Soldier Field went wild with cheers, and it was nearly impossible to see the pain and sense of betrayal on Skvara's face without tearing up—here was a man who had given his entire life to the American dream, working a good union job for the promise of a social contract that was never fulfilled. Chris Matthews, during the post-debate analysis on MSNBC, replayed the clip and asked, "I wonder if that wasn't a moment that's gonna change American political history."

The moment perfectly summed up the challenge of this campaign: What Skvara asked was a simple question and touched on the fact that America doesn't seem ready for today's world. *What will you do as president to ensure it is ready for the future?* As Andy Stern points out, the agricultural revolution took some three thousand years to transform the world, and the industrial revolution lasted three hundred years, from the first move toward industrialization to the peak mass-production economy of the post–World War II era. Today, though, in a span of some thirty years—barely a generation—Americans and citizens abroad are seeing their world transformed into a tech-driven, information-heavy economy.

THERE ARE A MYRIAD of issues to be dealt with in the decades ahead that have received little or no attention in this book—from the looming crisis of entitlements to intellectual property enforcement and reform, to realigning the tax code, to immigration, to balancing the budget and changing the country's out-of-control culture of debt. The threat of Islamist terrorism hardly gets a mention here, partly because it is already such an overarching focus of the government (many people far more knowledgeable than I have written at great lengths of the challenges it poses), but mostly because for the past six years it has already distracted the country from the many other challenges ahead, costing us the better part of a decade that we needn't have lost. Overall, I believe that while many other issues require attention, if the United States doesn't get right the four issues laid out in the preceding pages and invest in changes to the country's technical and energy infrastructure, and reform its education and health-care systems, it won't matter whether we fix Social Security, correct the tax on capital gains, seal the border with Mexico, or spend the next decade in Iraq.

Success in the decades ahead will not come by chance. It will come only because the nation, from the president on down, actively tackles the future over the next decade and meets the challenges of the new century. We can't afford to wait another four or eight years. This must be the first campaign. In the choices we make in the 2008 election, we'll begin to determine whether the country will rise to the occasion, as it has done so many times before, and take on the future, or whether we will continue to push off into the horizon the moment we recognize how fundamentally the world is changing. The choices that the 2008 presidential candidates make will determine whether the country will see—as it should—the first campaign of the twenty-first century, where the challenges and opportunities of globalization and technology are front and center, or whether they run the last campaign all over again.

OVER THE COURSE of more than twenty years as the director of the National Governors' Association, Ray Scheppach has studied the work of hundreds of state chief executives. To be great, he explains, a governor needs to provide the moral leadership necessary to change the game. The best governors, Scheppach explains, change the expectations of their citizens. Lamar Alexander came into office in Tennessee and rallied the state around education, such that the people of Tennessee came to believe it was important for teachers who taught well to be rewarded. Howard Dean, in Vermont, came into office and rallied the state around health care, encouraging the citizens of the state to think of health care as a right, not a luxury. Our next president must be one who can dream and rally the nation around a common set of ideals, goals, and aspirations that can lead us forward—to change the expectations of the nation to better reflect the needs of a digital, interconnected, global age, where discoveries are made out in the heavens and in labs under microscopes, where bytes and bits fly around the world faster than our faster jets, and where one can talk to a friend in Bangalore as easily as to a friend on the next block. Our expectations of the world have changed, and so must now our expectations of government and society.

To address the challenges ahead, we must again recognize that the future of the nation is not preordained to success or to failure. History will show that the United States today is only as exceptional as its people and the leaders we choose. Our votes over the course of 2008 for a presidential candidate will be only the first step. This is a generational struggle, not unlike that experienced during World War II or

communism, and everyone from school boards to mayors to congressmen have a role to play. Too many Americans, particularly younger
Americans, don't vote because they don't think it's important. Our
leaders must do a better job explaining why the choices we make on
Election Day do matter. We have billions of individual decisions to
make too—about where to shop, what to support, and where to work
and what education to seek. Our generation, faced like generations
before us with new, unforeseen challenges, must do our individual
part to keep the United States truly exceptional.

No part of the road ahead will be easy, but these pressing questions
must be answered. As former Virginia governor Mark Warner used to
promise on the stump, "It's not about left versus right. It's about future versus past." The future success of our country will be shaped in
no small part by the individual actions of more than a hundred million
Americans as they walk into the voting booth in November 2008. I'm
looking forward to casting my vote for the candidate I believe will best
meet the challenges ahead. From this stage of the race, I can't tell
who that will be, but I know we need to figure it out—and fast. We,
as a nation and as a people, can't afford to wait much longer.

NOTES

Introduction: A Period of Consequences

1. Dan Balz, "Vilsack Announces 2008 White House Bid," *The Washington Post*, November 30, 2006.
2. Richard L. Florida, *The Flight of the Creative Class* (New York: Harper-Collins, 2005), 29.
3. Zachary Karabell, *The Last Campaign: How Harry Truman Won the 1948 Election* (New York: Knopf, 2000), 8–9.
4. Joe Trippi, *The Revolution Will Not Be Televised* (New York: Regan Books, 2004), 38.
5. Theodore White, *The Making of the President 1960* (New York: Atheneum, 1960), 279, 283, 290.

PART I: THE LAST CAMPAIGN
The Rise of the Anxious Class

1. Jeff Ubois, "We the People: Electronic Bulletin Boards and the Political Process," *Midrange Systems*, Vol. 5, No. 19, October 13, 1992.
2. Robert Kuttner, *The Life of the Party: Democratic Prospects in 1988 and Beyond* (New York: Viking, 1987), 21.
3. Ibid., 83–85.
4. Ibid., 161.
5. Michael Schaller, *Right Turn: American Life in the Reagan-Bush Era, 1980–1992* (New York: Oxford University Press, 2006), 87.
6. Jon F. Hale, "The Making of the New Democrats," *Political Science Quarterly* 110, no. 2 (1995): 208.
7. Joel Rogers and Thomas Ferguson, *Right Turn: The Decline of the Democrats and the Future of American Politics* (New York: Hill and Wang, 1986), 197.
8. Hale, "Making of the New Democrats."
9. Timothy B. Clark, "Promises, Promises—the Presidential Candidates and Their Budget Plans," *National Journal*, March 10, 1984, 452–57.
10. Ibid.
11. Fred Barnes, as cited in Jon F. Hale, "Making of the New Democrats."
12. Kuttner, *Life of the Party*, 59.

13. Paul Tsongas, *The Road from Here: Liberalism and Realities in the 1980s* (New York: Knopf, 1981), 254.

14. Of course, it wasn't quite that simple—nearly half of the founding class of House DLCers were liberals, according to Americans for Democratic Action. Hale, "Making of the New Democrats," 216.

15. Kuttner, *Life of the Party*, 11.

16. Ibid., 110.

17. Ibid., 189.

18. Joe Klein, *Politics Lost: How American Democracy Was Trivialized by People Who Think You're Stupid* (New York: Doubleday, 2006), 102.

19. Hale, "Making of the New Democrats," 227.

20. Kathryn Marie Dudley, *The End of the Line: Lost Jobs, New Lives in Postindustrial America* (Chicago: University of Chicago Press, 1994), 131.

21. Terry F. Buss and F. Stevens Redburn, *Shutdown at Youngstown: Public Policy for Mass Unemployment* (Albany: State University of New York Press, 1983), 60.

22. Dudley, *End of the Line*, 133.

23. Louis Uchitelle, *The Disposable American: Layoffs and Their Consequences* (New York: Knopf, 2006), 5.

24. Ibid.

25. Robert B. Reich, *The Work of Nations: Preparing Ourselves for 21st-Century Capitalism* (New York: Knopf, 1991), 55.

26. Ibid., 64.

27. Dudley, *End of the Line*, 24.

28. Ibid., 27.

29. Reich, *Work of Nations*, 115.

30. Ibid., 3.

31. Ibid., 8, 162.

32. Ibid., 119.

33. Uchitelle, *Disposable American*, 154.

34. Ibid., 155.

35. John F. Harris, *The Survivor: Bill Clinton in the White House* (New York: Random House, 2005), 353.

36. Andrei Cherny, *The Next Deal: The Future of Public Life in the Information Age* (New York: Basic Books, 2000), 129.

37. Ibid., 34, 8.

38. Trippi, *The Revolution Will Not Be Televised*, 56.

39. Mark Halperin, *The Way to Win: Taking the White House in 2008* (New York: Random House, 2006), 229.

40. Gregg Russell, "Pandora's Web?" *CNN Interactive*, January 30, 1998.

41. Elizabeth Shogren, "Candidates' Efforts Clicking on the Net," *Los Angeles Times*, February 10, 2000, A20.

Google and People-Powered Politics

1. John Battelle, *The Search: How Google and Its Rivals Rewrote the Rules of Business and Transformed Our World* (New York: Portfolio, 2005), 143.
2. Jonathan Chait et al., "Debating the Netroots," *New Republic Online*, May 10, 2007.
3. Terry McAuliffe with Steve Kettmann, *What a Party! My Life Among Democrats: Presidents, Candidates, Donors, Activists, Alligators, and Other Wild Animals* (New York: St. Martin's Press, 2007), 290.
4. Ibid., 285.
5. Ibid., 279–80.
6. Ibid., 288.
7. Institute of Politics, John F. Kennedy School of Government, *Campaign for President: The Managers Look at 2004* (Lanham, Md.: Rowman & Littlefield), 99.
8. Ibid., 103.
9. Ibid., 73–75.
10. Thomas B. Edsall and James V. Grimaldi, "On Nov. 2, GOP Got More Bang for Its Billion, Analysis Shows," *The Washington Post*, December 30, 2004, A1.
11. Joe Klein, "Public Life," *The New Yorker*, November 11, 2002, 67.
12. David Von Drehle and Dan Balz, "Seeking Big Ideas to Break a Deadlock," *The Washington Post*, October 30, 2002, A1.
13. Ibid.
14. Elizabeth Warren, "The Middle Class on the Precipice," *Harvard Magazine*, January/February 2006.
15. Thomas B. Edsall, *Building Red America: The New Conservative Coalition and the Drive for Permanent Power* (New York: Basic Books, 2006), 216.
16. Institute of Politics, John F. Kennedy School of Government, *Campaign for President*, 239.
17. Ibid., 230.
18. Elizabeth Shelburne, "Inside the Dean Campaign," *Atlantic Unbound* (online), April 8, 2004.

The Democrats Reboot

1. Institute of Politics, John F. Kennedy School of Government, *Campaign for President*, 23.
2. Edsall, *Building Red America*, 16.
3. Ibid., 187.
4. Halperin, *The Way to Win*, 308.
5. McAuliffe and Kettmann, *What a Party!*, 385.

6. Ryan Lizza, "The Outsiders," *New Republic Online*, February 4, 2005.
7. "Political Insiders Poll," *National Journal*, June 17, 2006, 8.
8. Naftali Bendavid, *The Thumpin': How Rahm Emanuel Learned to Be Ruthless and Ended the Republican Revolution* (New York: Doubleday, 2007), 88–91.
9. Ibid., 207.

2008: The Lay of the Land

1. Scott Helman, "Romney Looks to Boost Résumé with Asia Trip," *The Boston Globe*, December 2, 2006.
2. Steven Greenhouse and David Leonhardt, "Real Wages Fail to Match a Rise in Productivity," *The New York Times*, August 28, 2006.
3. Kurt Andersen, "American Roulette," *New York*, January 7, 2007.
4. "Bush Economic Team Faces Tough Questions on Midwest Tour," *Minnesota Public Radio* (online), July 29, 2003.
5. Elisabeth Bumiller, "Like a Cloud, Economic Woes Follow Bus Tour," *The New York Times*, August 4, 2003.
6. Tim Dickinson, "Truth on Tour," *Mother Jones* (online), September 22, 2003.
7. George Packer, "Knowing the Enemy: Can Social Scientists Redefine the 'War on Terror'?" *The New Yorker*, December 18, 2006.
8. Dudley, *End of the Line*, 2.
9. Ted C. Fishman, *China Inc.: How the Rise of the Next Superpower Challenges America and the World* (New York: Scribner, 2005), 105–106.
10. Ibid., 1.
11. Ibid., 40.
12. Todd Bishop, "China Visit: On the Menu at the Gates House," *Todd Bishop's Microsoft Blog*, April 14, 2006.
13. Mike Lewis, "Gates Is a Big Draw for Visiting World Leaders, Including China's Hu," *Seattle Post-Intelligencer*, April 17, 2006.
14. "Corus Accepts £4.3bn Tata Offer," *BBC News* (online), October 20, 2006.
15. Dudley, *End of the Line*, 11.
16. "When the Chain Breaks," *The Economist*, June 15, 2006.
17. *Competitiveness Index: Where America Stands* (Washington, D.C.: Council, 2006), 2.
18. Ibid., 15.
19. Bruce Mehlman, "21st-Century Policy Challenges for American Innovation Leadership," remarks before the Georgia Institute of Technology, Atlanta, GA, October 23, 2003.
20. *Competitiveness Index*, 76.

PART II: THE FIRST CAMPAIGN
Issue #1: Investing in Twenty-first-Century Technology

1. Ellen McCarthy, "Mining Coal Country for Tech Workers," *The Washington Post*, January 2, 2006.

2. John Steele Gordon, *An Empire of Wealth: The Epic History of American Economic Power* (New York: HarperCollins, 2004), 418.

3. Ibid., xvii.

4. Robert D. Atkinson, *The Past and Future of America's Economy: Long Waves of Innovation That Power Cycles of Growth* (Northampton, Mass.: Edward Elgar, 204), 270.

5. Committee on Prospering in the Global Economy of the 21st Century, *Rising Above the Gathering Storm: Energizing and Employing America for a Brighter Economic Future* (Washington, D.C.: National Academies, 2007).

6. Brian Friel, "Science Scare," *National Journal*, January 14, 2006, 36.

7. John Bresnahan and Jonathan Martin, "Senate Shows Its Age," *The Politico*, January 25, 2007.

8. Atkinson, *Past and Future of the American Economy*, 270.

9. Louis Galambos, "Theodore N. Vail and the Role of Innovation in the Modern Bell System," *Business History Review* 66, no. 1 (Spring 1992): 95.

10. Ibid., 98, 104, 105.

11. Daniel Lee Kleinman, "Layers of Interests, Layers of Influence: Business and the Genesis of the National Science Foundation," *Science, Technology and Human Values* 19, no. 3 (Summer 1994): 264.

12. Daniel J. Kevles, "Passing the Buck," *The New Republic*, September 30, 2002.

13. Ibid.

14. Ibid.

15. Ibid.

16. Kenneth W. Rind, "The Role of Venture Capital in Corporate Development," *Strategic Management Journal* 2 (1981): 170.

17. Paul Gompers and Josh Lerner, "The Venture Capital Revolution," *Journal of Economic Perspectives* 15, no. 2 (Spring 2001): 146.

18. Samuel Kortum and Josh Lerner, "Assessing the Contribution of Venture Capital to Innovation," *RAND Journal of Economics* 31, no. 4 (Winter 2000): 676.

19. Gompers and Lerner, "Venture Capital Revolution," 148.

20. Atkinson, *Past and Future of America's Economy*, 8.

21. Gompers and Lerner, "Venture Capital Revolution," 165.

22. Atkinson, *Past and Future of America's Economy*, 27.

23. Declan McCullagh and Anne Broache, "Silicon Money: How Do Tech Firms Buy Influence in Washington?" *CNETNews.com*, March 27, 2006.

24. "Wireless Internet Zone to Cover City of London," *thisislondon.co.uk*, April 12, 2007.

25. *Knowledge Matters: Skills and Learning for Canadians* (Ottawa: Human Resources Development Canada, 2002), 7.

26. Ibid., 4.

27. *Achieving Excellence: Investing in People, Knowledge and Opportunity* (Ottawa: Government of Canada, 2001), 84.

28. Robert Atkinson, "Deep Competitiveness," *Issues in Science and Technology* (online) 23, no. 2 (Winter 2007).

29. Fishman, *China Inc.*, 12.

30. *Competitiveness Index*, 61–62.

31. Thomas L. Friedman, *The World Is Flat: A Brief History of the Twenty-first Century* (New York: Farrar, Straus and Giroux, 2005), 226.

32. Florida, *Flight of the Creative Class*, 16.

33. David Barboza, "Intel to Build Advanced Chip-Making Plant in China," *The New York Times*, March 27, 2007.

34. Jena McGregor et. al., "The World's Most Innovative Companies," *BusinessWeek*, April 24, 2006.

35. *Competitiveness Index*, 21–22.

36. Erkko Autio, "Global Entrepreneurship Monitor 2005 Report on High-Expectation Entrepreneurship," *Global Entrepreneurship Monitor*, October 25, 2005.

Issue #2: Educating and Recruiting Twenty-first-Century Workers

1. Fareed Zakaria, "How Long Will America Lead the World?," *Newsweek*, June 12, 2006, 42.

2. *Competitiveness Index*, 85.

3. Reich, *Work of Nations*, 60.

4. Bill Bradley, *The New American Story* (New York: Random House, 2007), 157.

5. Claudia Wallis and Sonja Steptoe, "How to Bring Our Schools Out of the 20th Century," *Time*, December 18, 2006.

6. Friedman, *The World Is Flat*, 317.

7. Suzanne Mettler, *Soldiers to Citizens: The G.I. Bill and the Making of the Greatest Generation* (New York: Oxford University Press, 2005), 170.

8. *Competitiveness Index*, 91.

9. Atkinson, *Past and Future of America's Economy*, 116.

10. *Competitiveness Index*, 90.

11. Mettler, *Soldiers to Citizens*, 16–17, 20.

12. Ibid., 6, 42.

13. Ibid., 68.

14. Ibid., 92.

15. Ibid., 173.

16. *Competitiveness Index*, 34.

17. Salil Tripathi, "India's High Tech Bounty," *The Wall Street Journal*, April 16, 2003.

18. Manjeet Kripalani, "India's Whiz Kids," *BusinessWeek* (international edition), December 7, 1998.

19. Tripathi, "India's High Tech Bounty."

20. Somini Sengupta, "India Attracts Universities from the U.S.," *The New York Times*, March 26, 2007.

21. Stuart Anderson, "The Multiplier Effect," *International Educator* (Summer 2004): 15.

22. Florida, *Flight of the Creative Class*, 99.

23. Ibid., 5.

24. Ibid., 8.

25. Richard L. Florida, *The Rise of the Creative Class: And How It's Transforming Work, Leisure, Community and Everyday Life* (New York: Basic Books, 2002), 355.

26. Florida, *Flight of the Creative Class*, 219.

Issue #3: Caring for Twenty-first-Century Workers

1. Bradley, *New American Story*, 173.

2. Gordon, *An Empire of Wealth*, 360.

3. U.S. Census Bureau, *Health Insurance Coverage Status and Type of Coverage by State All People: 1987 to 2005*.

4. David U. Himmelstein et al., "Illness and Injury as Contributors to Bankruptcy," *Health Affairs* (online), February 2, 2005.

5. Theda Skocpol, *Boomerang: Clinton's Health Security Effort and the Turn Against Government in U.S. Politics* (New York: W. W. Norton, 1996), 21.

6. Ibid., 23.

7. Ibid., 27.

8. Ibid., 44.

9. Ibid., 55.

10. William Jefferson Clinton, "Health Security for All Americans," speech before a joint session of Congress, September 22, 1993.

11. Michael Duffy, "Picture of Health," *Time*, October 4, 1993.

12. Skocpol, *Boomerang*, 5.

13. Ibid., 139.

14. Ibid., 98. A "plan that would guarantee a standard private health benefits package to all Americans, try to promote competition in the medical industry, include some government regulation to keep prices under control and require employers to buy insurance for their workers with

the promise of government subsidies to help the smallest companies."

15. Matt Miller, "The Senator from Starbucks," *Fortune*, July 26, 2006.

16. William L. Watts, "Seeking a Cure for Health-care Burden," *Market-Watch*, February 7, 2007.

17. David A. Fahrenthold, "Mass. Bill Requires Health Coverage," *The Washington Post*, April 5, 2006.

18. Mitt Romney, "Health Care for Everyone?" *OpinionJournal* (online), April 11, 2006.

19. Marilyn Werber Serafini, "The States Step Up," *National Journal*, March 17, 2007.

20. Bradley, *New American Story*, 140.

21. E. McGlynn et al. "The Quality of Health Care Delivered to Adults in the United States," *The New England Journal of Medicine* 348 (June 26, 2003): 2, 635.

22. Malcolm Gladwell, "Million-Dollar Murray," *The New Yorker*, February 13, 2006.

23. Lisa Margonelli, *Oil on the Brain: Adventures from the Pump to the Pipeline* (New York: Doubleday, 2007), 60.

Issue #4: Powering a Twenty-first-Century Economy

1. Tom Toles, cartoon, *The Washington Post*, August 27, 2006.

2. Jim Snyder, "Lobbyist Kept Slide Show Safe," *The Hill*, March 23, 2007.

3. Ryan Grim, "Gore Wonks Out, Lets It Sort of Rip," *The Politico*, March 22, 2007.

4. Al Gore, *The Daily Show with Jon Stewart*, June 28, 2006.

5. Al Gore, *Earth in the Balance: Ecology and the Human Spirit* (Boston: Houghton Mifflin, 1992), 271.

6. Margonelli, *Oil on the Brain*, 8.

7. Kurt M. Campbell, *Hard Power: The New Politics of National Security* (New York: Basic Books, 2006), 175.

8. Margonelli, *Oil on the Brain*, 265.

9. Daniel Yergin, "Ensuring Energy Security," *Foreign Policy*, March/April 2006.

10. Margonelli, *Oil on the Brain*, 197, 265.

11. Tim F. Flannery, *The Weather Makers: How Man Is Changing the Climate and What It Means for Life on Earth* (New York: Atlantic Monthly, 2005), 28–29, 59.

12. Gore, *Earth in the Balance*, 93.

13. Margonelli, *Oil on the Brain*, 8, 44.

14. Flannery, *Weather Makers*, 167, 77.

15. Joseph Romm, *Hell and High Water: Global Warning—the Solution and the Politics—and What We Should Do* (New York: William Morrow, 2006), 52.

16. Flannery, *Weather Makers*, 94, 317.
17. Romm, *Hell and High Water*, 74.
18. Ibid., 87.
19. Ibid., 75, 89.
20. Ibid., 92.
21. Ibid., 123.
22. Flannery, *Weather Makers*, 247.
23. Chris Mooney, *The Republican War on Science* (New York: Basic Books, 2005), 34.
24. Ibid., 36.
25. Ibid., 40.
26. Ibid., 42.
27. Ibid., 113.
28. Ibid., 71.
29. Ron Suskind, *One Percent Doctrine: Deep Inside America's Pursuit of Its Enemies Since 9/11* (New York: Simon & Schuster, 2006).
30. Mooney, *The Republican War on Science*, 226.
31. Eric Cohen, "Inflated Promise, Distorted Facts," *National Review Online*, May 25, 2004.
32. Michael Specter, "Political Science," *The New Yorker*, March 13, 2006, 58.
33. Mooney, *Republican War on Science*, 55.
34. Tim Dickinson, "A Polluter's Feast," *Rolling Stone*, September 22, 2005.
35. Mooney, *Republican War on Science*, 79.
36. Romm, *Hell and High Water*, 137.
37. "Bush Visits Renewable Energy Lab: President Acknowledges 'Mixed Signals' Over Energy Lab Layoffs," *CBS News* (online), February 21, 2006.
38. Margonelli, *Oil on the Brain*, 105.
39. Ibid., 115.
40. Dan Oko, "The Doggie Bag Dilemma," *Mother Jones*, November/December 2006, 84.
41. Andreas Lorenz, "The Chinese Miracle Will End Soon: Spiegel Interview with China's Deputy Minister of the Environment," *Spiegel* (online), March 7, 2005.
42. Fishman, *China, Inc.*, 110–11, 113.
43. Margonelli, *Oil on the Brain*, 268.
44. Warren Brown, "Why You Can't Buy This Car," *The Washington Post*, March 7, 2007.
45. Margonelli, *Oil on the Brain*, 276.
46. Sholnn Freeman, "Politics of Fuel Economy Catch Up to Automakers," *The Washington Post*, March 21, 2007.
47. Jerry Adler, "Moment of Truth," *Newsweek*, April 16, 2007.

48. David Runk, "Toyota's March Sales Rise; GM, Ford Fall," *Breitbart.com*, April 3, 2007.
49. James Surowiecki, "Deal Sweeteners," *The New Yorker*, November 26, 2006, 92.
50. Anne Underwood, "Mayors Take the Lead," *Newsweek*, April 16, 2007.
51. Jerome Ringo, "16 Ideas for the Planet," *Newsweek*, April 16, 2007.
52. Moises Velasquez-Manoff, "Unions See Greenbacks in 'Green' Future," *Christian Science Monitor*, January 25, 2007.
53. Margonelli, *Oil on the Brain*, 280.
54. Flannery, *Weather Makers*, 221.
55. Ibid., 74.
56. Seth Godin, "Do You Have to Be Anti-Change to Be Pro-Business?" *Seth Godin's Blog*, April 12, 2007.
57. Flannery, *Weather Makers*, 6.
58. Margonelli, *Oil on the Brain*, 57.
59. Atkinson, *Past and Future of America's Economy*, 145.
60. Campbell, *Hard Power*, 151.
61. Flannery, *Weather Makers*, 7.
62. Fareed Zakaria, "The Case for a Global Carbon Tax," *Newsweek*, April 16, 2007.
63. Arnold Schwarzenegger, "Remarks to the Georgetown University Environmental Conference," Georgetown University, Washington, D.C., April 11, 2007.
64. Flannery, *Weather Makers*, 301.

Web 2.0 Meets Campaigning 3.0

1. Dan Gillmor, "Some Candidates Cope Better Than Others with New Campaign Reality of the Web," *Washington Examiner*, February 13, 2007.
2. Sarah Wheaton, "Clinton on Big Sister Video," *The New York Times* (online), March 20, 2007.
3. Douglas B. Sosnik, Matthew J. Dowd, Ron Fournier, *Applebee's America: How Successful Political, Business, and Religious Leaders Connect with the New American Community* (New York: Simon & Schuster, 2006), 183.
4. Jose Antonio Vargas, "Online, GOP Is Playing Catch-Up: Democrats Have Big Edge on Web," *The Washington Post*, May 21, 2007.
5. Chris Cillizza, "The YouTube Effect (Part XIII)," *The Washington Post* (online), March 19, 2007.
6. Sosnik, Dowd, Fournier, *Applebee's America*, 54, 187.
7. Steve Rubel, "Work Ethic: What Dirk Nowitzki and the Big Influencers Have in Common," *micropersuasion.com*, March 19, 2007.
8. C. Mark Brinkley, "Patriot Games," *Army Times*, May 24, 2006.
9. Steve Davis, Larry Elin, and Grant Reeher, *Click on Democracy: The*

Internet's Power to Change Political Apathy into Civic Action (Boulder, Col.: Westview Press, 2002), 8.

10. Ibid., 59.
11. Dan Gilgoff, "Dialing for Dollars: Forget New Hampshire. The Contest for Cash Is the First Real Primary," *U.S. News & World Report*, March 18, 2007.
12. Davis, Elin, Reeher, *Click on Democracy*, 49.

Conclusion: Our Collective Future

1. Jose Antonio Vargas, "Binary America: Split in Two by a Digital Divide," *The Washington Post*, July 23, 2007.

ACKNOWLEDGMENTS

I want to first thank all the people—some named in these pages, some unnamed by request—who gave generously of their time and thoughts for interviews, even as they knew they wouldn't necessarily agree with everything I argue here. Among them: Tom Friedman, whose book and thoughts were a huge inspiration; Pat Cleary and J. P. Fielder at the National Association of Manufacturers; Deborah Wince-Smith, Bill Booher, and Mike Meneer at the Council on Competitiveness; Gina Glantz and Andy Stern at SEIU; Bruce Mehlman, Patrick Wilson, Andrew Rasiej, and the many fellow journalists whom I bounced various ideas off of over the last year.

I appreciate all the candidates and their staff who freely gave me access, especially Ellen Qualls and Mark Warner, who invited me along on the trip that began this entire project and who tolerated many inquiries along the way. I owe a special thanks to Ivette Almeida and the executives of Satyam and Sify, who provided me with incredible access to see India's rise up close and personal. Of course I never would have finished this without Heather, Kat, and the rest of the crew at Tryst, who gave me space and time to write. Thanks, too, to Ginny, who tolerated my dirty dishes and odd hours.

Many thanks to the team who gave me my introduction to politics in 2003: Howard Dean, Joe Trippi, Bob Rogan, Kate O'Connor, Tom McMahon, Susan Allen, Stephanie Carter, Stephanie Schriock, Julie Norton, Nicco Mele, Joe Rospars, Kathy Lash, Courtney O'Donnell, Trish Enright, Jay Carson, Michael Silberman, and Andrew Koneschusky, as well as the other Deaniacs in Burlington and across the country.

I owe much gratitude to a long line of people who have taken a chance on me: Elizabeth Spiers, Jack Limpert and Ken Decell, Tim

Seldes, and Paul Elie. Jack generously gave me the time to write and has been a fantastic, inspiring, and supportive editor; I owe thanks to all my colleagues at *Washingtonian* who tolerated my distractions—not least of all Ben, Sarah, and Catherine. A special thanks, too, to Brooke Foster, who proved an able reader and sounding board for some early drafts, and to Caleb Hannan and others for research assistance. There's also a long list of people who have been critical to the development of who and where I am today. Among them: Bert McCord; Charlotte Stocek, Mary Creedon, Rome Aja, Ed Skea, Kerrin McCadden, and Charlie Phillips; Brian Delay, Peter J. Gomes, Stephen Shoemaker, Jennifer Axsom, and Sugi Ganeshananthan; Kit Seeyle, Pat Leahy, Rusty Grieff, and, not least of all, Cousin Connie, to whom I owe a debt that I strive to repay each day.

I want to thank all my friends who put up with my disappearances and with my blabbering about this project, especially Katherine, who listened more than anyone and never once complained about the boring mornings, afternoons, and evenings that it took me to write this. Your support meant a lot to me.

Also, I owe much of the polish of the finished product to Paul Elie, whose enthusiasm was infectious from our first phone call and whose vision for this project magically seemed to be right in line with mine, as well as to Cara, Tim, and Jesseca, who were always happy to hear from me. I hope that we can continue working together in the future.

INDEX